THE

REFERENCE

SHELF

CHINA AT THE CROSSROADS

Edited by DONALD ALTSCHILLER

THE REFERENCE SHELF

Volume 66 Number 3

THE H. W. WILSON COMPANY

New York   1994

THE REFERENCE SHELF

The books in this series contain reprints of articles, excerpts from books, and addresses on current issues and social trends in the United States and other countries. There are six separately bound numbers in each volume, all of which are generally published in the same calendar year. One number is a collection of recent speeches; each of the others is devoted to a single subject and gives background information and discussion from various points of view, concluding with a comprehensive bibliography that contains books and pamphlets and abstracts of additional articles on the subject. Books in the series may be purchased individually or on subscription.

Library of Congress Cataloging-in-Publication Data

China at the crossroads / edited by Donald Altschiller.
     p.   cm. — (Reference shelf v. 66, no. 3)
  ISBN 0-8242-0854-4
    1. China—History—1976– 2. China—Politics and government—1976– 3. China—Economic conditions—1976– 4. China—Foreign relations—1976– 5. Human rights—China. I. Altschiller, Donald.
II. Series.
DS779.2.C448   1994
951.05—dc20   94-9187
                                                       CIP

Cover: Wangfujing Street, a trendy shopping center, where until recently the government had discouraged personal consumption.

Photo: AP/Wide World Photos

Printed in the United States of America

CONTENTS

PREFACE

> Nothing and no one can destroy the Chinese people. They are relentless survivors. They are the oldest civilized people on earth. Their civilization passes through phases but its basic characteristics remain the same. They yield, they bend to the wind, but they never break.
> —Pearl Buck
> *China, Past and Present* (1972)

China is a country of impressive numbers. The most populous nation on earth—1.2 billion people—it grows by the population of Texas every year. Indeed, one out of every five persons on earth is Chinese. A burgeoning economic power, the People's Republic of China (PRC) currently has a trade surplus with the U.S. of almost $20 billion. In 1991, China extended one billion Swiss francs in commercial credits to Russia. By February 1992 its foreign exchange reserves totaled almost $43 billion.

Besides its huge population and expanding economy, China is a major military power. Since 1989, China has increased its military spending by approximately 50 percent, and is vigorously trying to upgrade the technology of its armed forces. China's increasing military strength has caused worldwide concern, especially from Japan, Vietnam, and Taiwan, since China had made claims on islands in the South China Seas. Furthermore, as a permanent member of the United Nations Security Council, China possesses a crucial veto on vital world issues.

Although China's relations with the United States have improved since diplomatic relations were first established in 1979, American policymakers have not disregarded Beijing's human rights abuses, its lucrative worldwide arms sales, and the use of slave labor. Citing the 1989 massacre at Tiananmen Square, and the subsequent repression of students and intellectuals, human rights activists have urged both Presidents Bush and Clinton to veto a Most Favored Nation (MFN) status until China upholds basic human and political rights. Most of the business community, however, claims such pressure would be counterproductive to U.S. interest.

The oldest civilization in the world is now an awakened giant. This anthology will focus on China in the 1990s. In the first section, scholars and veteran China-watchers survey the country's history and analyze its present trends and future prospects.

China's economy, demography and environment are the subjects of the second section. How does China's growing economy affect the lives of rural peasants, the majority of the people, as well as urban dwellers? How has rapid technological development affected China's overburdened environment?

The third section analyzes U.S. relations with China. Several authors offer conflicting views about using American trade as leverage to liberalize Chinese policies toward political dissidents. Next, the fourth section examines human rights in China, including how religious minorities, intellectuals, and Tibetans under occupation are treated.

In the final section of articles, various experts on Chinese journalism, television and the arts examine current cultural trends. The alarming rise in drug trafficking is also considered.

The editor wishes to thank the H. W. Wilson General Publications staff for its assistance, his wife Ellen Birnbaum for her superb editing, and the authors and publishers who have granted permission to reprint their material in this compilation.

DONALD ALTSCHILLER

March 1994

I. HISTORICAL OVERVIEW AND PRESENT CONCERNS

EDITOR'S INTRODUCTION

Historians pose a perennial question: Is the past a prologue? Does a nation's history define—indeed limit—its future? This section examines how China's long and turbulent history may influence the country in the coming decade. In the first essay, reprinted from *Daedalus,* Princeton professor Perry Link discusses how Confucianism—China's cultural "core"—has shaped the nation's variegated past and may mold its future. In the next article, published in *Foreign Affairs,* Barber B. Conable, Jr. and David M. Lampton discuss the remarkable transformation of post-Maoist China to a market economy, and the political and economic ramifications of this change for the United States and the world.

China-watching has been a preoccupation of many Western intellectuals for more than a century. Charles Horner points out in *Commentary,* however, that sinologists have egregiously erred in their benign analyses of Chinese communism. Some observers, though, defend the 1949 revolution. Writing in the *Monthly Review,* William Hinton maintains that China may in fact be headed for a "neocolonial future." Ross Munro, a former correspondent in Beijing, disagrees. In the final article in this section, reprinted from *Policy Review,* he asserts that Chinese "Leninist policies" still threaten all of Asia, and possibly the United States.

CHINA'S "CORE" PROBLEM[1]

China has been experiencing an economic boom in recent years. During most of the 1980s, as markets advanced and central

[1]Article by Perry Link, professor of East Asian Studies, Princeton University. From *Daedalus* 122/2:189–205 Spring '93. Copyright © 1993 by Journal of the American Academy of Arts and Sciences. Reprinted with permission.

planning retreated, the gross national product grew 9 to 10 percent annually. It grew 12 percent in 1992. Foreign trade has grown even faster; by 1991, China's foreign exchange reserves equaled those of the United States. The economy's nonstate sector (including cooperatives, family and individual enterprises, and joint ventures with foreigners) has come to produce about half the country's industrial product, and it continues to grow rapidly.

Since 1989, when protest movements were violently suppressed, these economic trends have continued alongside a major political clampdown that has stifled overt dissent. But the repression today is very different from the repression during the Maoist period. Central authority then was strong enough to have its way in nearly every corner of the country; dissent, even in private, was extremely dangerous. Now, with the moral authority and political power of the center much diminished, local work units and governments are far more independent than before. Ideological pronouncements from the center are commonly accepted at a rhetorical level but ignored in practice. As the economy has moved increasingly into private markets, so, in fact, have any number of political arrangements. Burgeoning corruption accompanies the barter of power at every level. At the highest level, the grand bargain that Deng Xiaoping has temporarily forged between himself and the Chinese people can be seen as the ultimate example of power brokering. Deng's message is clear: economic reform, yes; political reform, no. So long as you make no move that could threaten the highest level of leadership, you are free to make money.

Some Western analysts, especially those who defend Western business interests and the policies of the former Bush administration, have argued that Deng's economic policies have put China on the right track, and in more than just the economic sense. They predict that wealth in China will lead, as in other societies, to the creation of a middle class, a modern "civil society," and hence to political liberalization as well. This prediction cannot be faulted so long as it is understood as pointing to certain effects that will weigh among many others. But to press the case more strongly than that reflects an optimism that is either ill-informed or—in the case of business interests—sometimes self-serving. The prospects for an early transition to a modern civil society in China are far from clear.

The same release of controls that has allowed the Chinese

economy to grow has also made space for a variety of serious problems: corruption is practically taken for granted; crime rates, including those for robbery and murder, have risen sharply; prostitution has returned and is flourishing again; in some areas a market has developed in kidnapped peasant women and children; and fraudulent products and services have appeared in the marketplace. School dropout rates have risen as state investment in education has continued to decline. Young people have become *liumang* (hoodlums) in increasing numbers. A "floating population" of people from the countryside who have flocked to major cities in search of work now number about fifty to seventy million nationwide. Unplanned and unchecked development in some areas is rapidly pushing China's already strained natural environment toward the brink of disaster. Reflecting on all this, Liu Binyan, China's famous investigative journalist, uses the Chinese word *xie* (bedeviled, irregular) to characterize much of Chinese life today.

Many of these mushrooming problems can be understood as the filling of a vacuum left by the retreat of Communist power. At its Maoist height, that power reached everywhere in Chinese society, structuring all public values, meting out severe punishment to those who did not conform, and destroying many of the values and nearly all the institutions that had formerly filled the space between the state and the individual. People conformed under a pervasive pressure that emanated from the top. The longer this great pressure lasted, the less necessary were family, clan, and religious values in shaping social behavior. Consequently, those values and institutions withered. Eventually, even personal integrity suffered. Now, as state power retreats and people leap toward "freedom," the distinction between freedom and license is sometimes lost. In celebrating their escape from authoritarian controls, people sometimes assume that whatever they do beyond those controls must be all right. This is not only a Chinese problem. The same kind of morality-vacuum is visible in Eastern Europe and in the former Soviet Union where the collapse of Communist authority has been even more abrupt than in China. Thus Václav Havel, looking at the Czechoslovak society emerging from decades of oppression, speaks of "an enormous and dazzling explosion of every imaginable human vice." And, in Russia, *The New York Times* reporter Craig Whitney finds that " . . . values, as well as buildings, fall into decay. A year after the end of the Soviet Union, anything goes in Moscow."

A fundamental question for China today is: What values and institutions can help to restructure a civil society within the current vacuum? A revival of family, clan, and religious practices as they existed in the early twentieth century? More modern associations, perhaps based on specific occupation? Certainly a modern legal system could help, but neither China's current legal system nor the level of understanding of modern civil law among the populace is anywhere near sufficient for law by itself to answer the tremendous need.

The most "Chinese" answer—originally a Confucian one, but after centuries of custom now so deeply rooted in Chinese culture that it tends to appear almost reflexively—would be to pursue some kind of moral education. People should be taught to behave properly and be subject to moral criticism if they do not. In imperial China, when the system worked properly, state officials were chosen for their learning and had a special obligation to behave correctly. Although China developed a considerable history of corruption among officials, this history was paralleled by an equally long history of popular moral condemnation of corruption. The eighteenth-century novel *Rulin waishi* (*Unofficial History of the Scholars*) spiritedly satirizes the corruption and hypocrisy that began to appear in the officialdom of the Qing dynasty at its height. In the early twentieth century, when the Qing was tottering, the novels *Guanchang xianxingji* (*Panorama of officialdom*) and *Ershi nian mudu zhi guai xianzhuang* (*Strange scenes witnessed over twenty years*) were even more cutting in their indictment of official corruption. There were other such novels in the Republican period. Post-Mao "scar" literature in the early 1980s was in many ways a similar outpouring of criticism of officials who betrayed their duty to act morally. At Tiananmen in 1989, official corruption was the most broad-based issue. No slogan was more popular than "Sell the Benzes to Pay the National Debt."

In the money-first ethos that has prevailed recently in China, the underlying cultural values of education and proper behavior have seemed to recede. But it would be naïve to suppose that such a long tradition has suddenly disappeared. Moreover, the continuing satire on official corruption, which remains lively and common in China's oral network of gossip called *xiaodao xiaoxi* (alleyway news), confirms the persistence of popular moral indignation. But indignation, of course, must rest on positive values. In order to judge certain behavior to be improper, one needs at least a hazy concept of what proper behavior is. The problem in China today is that there is no publicly accepted set of moral values to define proper behavior. Intellectuals speak today of a *sixiang weiji* (crisis of ideology) and even a *jingshen weiji* (spiritual crisis). The gap is especially discomfiting because of the traditional role that moral ideology enjoyed in China.

The Tradition of an Ethical-Ideological Core

During most of China's imperial history of the last thousand years, explicit Confucian guidelines were available. Set down in writing and widely accepted, they were assumed to be valid all the way from the personal level to affairs of the empire. *The Great Learning*, a seminal Confucian classic used in civil service examinations beginning in Song times (960–1279), explained how a person's moral power, rooted in learning, could benefit the rest of society. The success of ancient rulers, according to this classic work, originated in their "investigation of things," which led, in orderly sequence, to "thoroughness of understanding," "sincerity of will," and "personal cultivation." Cultivation, once it had taken root in character, led to a power that could, in turn, "regulate the family," "properly govern the state," and finally "bring peace under all of heaven." This theory—understood as true not only of ancient rulers but of all civilized human beings—found institutional expression in the civil service examination system, where scholars were tested for their mastery of classic texts and literary skills as a measure of whether their cultivation warranted appointment to public office. Scholars began their study of the classics by internalizing them in the most blunt manner—rote memorization. Their highest aspiration was to reach the level of giving advice to the emperor.

Tersely put, the basic tenets of this outlook were that morality was inscribed in publicly venerated texts, could be absorbed by individuals through study, and could then take root in personal character and radiate outward—to family and community— eventually to reach "all under heaven" via service to the Son of Heaven, the highest ruling authority. When working properly, the system defined what it meant to be Chinese, and justified the individual's pride in being so. These several notions comprised a seamless continuum, without the "disciplinary" boundaries taken for granted in the modern West. Were modern scholars of literature, ethics, sociology, and political science to travel to the China of four hundred years ago, they would be viewed as quaintly narrow specialists working on different aspects of the same thing.

The Confucian notion of proper behavior is, moreover, essen-

phrase *ni shuo de hen hao* can mean either "what you said is good" or "you said it well." (Chinese people have no trouble distinguishing these two meanings when they want to, but in common use the phrase means both, without the question of a distinction ever arising.) To correct a false statement, ordinary Chinese allows *bushi neme shuo de* (that is not the way you say it). The word *xue*, often translated as "study" or "learn," originally means "imitate" or "emulate," and is still often used in that sense; to learn something, at least at the beginning stages, is to train oneself to conform to a proper pattern. Communist jargon has drawn heavily upon the moral-performative underpinnings of ordinary Chinese language, for example in the use of *biaoxian* (performance, literally surface-showing) in measuring the political correctness of a person's overt speech and behavior.

In short, habits of language, memories of history, and other cultural tendencies continue to ask that a publicly-accepted moral ideology play a role in Chinese life. But what is that ideology today? Confucianism was explicitly repudiated in the early twentieth century. By the 1990s, Marxism-Maoism has fallen even lower than Confucianism in popular acceptance. Yet, while ideologies have slipped out of daily life, the space they have left remains and begs to be filled. Here and there one can observe signs of continued Chinese yearning for a distinctive moral-social-political core.

Shadows of a Core Today

In recent years there has been very little direct address of the "core" problem in Chinese political or intellectual life. It can be embarrassing, even painful, to admit that the problem exists. But if one listens for the assumptions that undergird discussion of more discussible topics, it is fairly easy to see that this large question animates a wide variety of other concerns, and is at work among a broad spectrum of men and women in Chinese society. Both the highly educated and the barely educated—both the regime and its critics—show clear signs of worry about it. I offer below six examples, chosen to illustrate the wide variety of contexts in which the core problem arises indirectly.

An Old Method. In early 1989, a distinguished Chinese historian in Beijing told a story about how his parents had fled the Japanese during World War II. In the fall of 1944, the fighting had approached to within two days of Chongqing, their temporary home.

I asked my parents what they would do if the Japanese really arrived. My father just looked out the window at the Yangzi River and said, "We Chinese have an old method." I panicked when I realized what he meant. "But what about *me?*," I asked. I was in high school then. My father answered, "If such a day really comes, can we still care for you?"

Although the historian went back forty-five years into the past for his anecdote, his point was to illustrate the timeless and exalted nature of Chinese patriotism and to signal his own loyalty to it. He felt that, with the dramatic decline in the moral prestige of the Communist movement, the younger generation of Chinese was in danger of not properly grasping this important cultural value.

Four Little Dragons. Shortly after China opened to the world in the late 1970s, many Chinese—especially along the southeastern coast and in the major cities, but elsewhere as well—became strongly attracted by the economic and technological development they saw outside. They felt that China had fallen terribly behind, and their admiration of foreign places was tinged with envy. On the fringes of China they observed the rise of the so-called "Four Little Dragons" of South Korea, Taiwan, Hong Kong, and Singapore. These three words ("four," "little," and "dragons"), while at one level comprising a mere catchphrase, have deeper connotations.

"Dragon" implies China. The populations of Taiwan, Hong Kong, and Singapore are predominantly Han Chinese; South Korea, although not Han, clearly falls within the China-centered, originally Confucian, culture of East Asia. "Dragon" further suggests not only China but august China, spiritually worthy China. Even the young rebels at Tiananmen in 1989 called themselves (after the lyrics of a Hou Dejian song) "children of the dragon."

But the four dragons are "little"—or, as the word *xiao* can also mean, "young." However advanced South Korea, Taiwan, Hong Kong, and Singapore may be in certain ways—however able to help China in such matters as technology, expertise, and capital—none of them is, or ever could be, a replacement for China proper. However decrepit and problem-ridden by comparison, China proper is still the principal dragon. Its superiority is not only in size but, ultimately, in nature—even if the only ground for this claim is an abiding confidence that this *ought* to be the case. In the end, there is something absurd about even comparing a place like Singapore with China. The two exist on different levels.

The word "four," besides counting the little dragons, also has a certain effect of pigeonholing them within a China-centered constellation of language. Especially in the Communist period, numbers have often been used to put things, good and bad, in their proper places: The Gang of Four, The Four Modernizations, and so on.

Four Basic Principles. Since the late 1970s, the Deng Xiaoping regime has found it necessary to anchor itself with "Four Basic Principles": 1) the socialist road, 2) dictatorship of the proletariat, 3) leadership of the Communist party, and 4) Marxism-Leninism-Mao Zedong Thought. To a Westerner this list of four looks redundant. For an ordinary Chinese, the same redundancy, added to the basic irrelevance of the principles to most of daily life, makes it unlikely that a given person on a given day will be able to recite all four. Even among hard-liners in high positions in the Chinese government, the four principles are not analytically distinct and have little daily-life relevance. Their role is to loom hazily overhead as spiritual capital, to invoke, as necessary, in support of conservative crackdowns (such as the massacre of June 4, 1989). What is noteworthy, for our present inquiry, is that the leadership feels it necessary to set down such principles and even to write them into the preambles of the country's post-Mao constitutions. After all, conservatism and brute force are available whether or not such an act of inscription is performed. But without a well-situated text, the claim of a moral basis for action would seem less secure.

People of Strong Will. In the United States in 1990, a group of dissident Chinese organized a "Center for the Research of Contemporary China." Their founding manifesto called for "people of strong will" to "offer themselves to the great mission" and "resolutely struggle for Chinese democracy." If a few of the document's key words were replaced with words drawn from the Four Basic Principles, there would be little to distinguish its style from a Communist Party text—or indeed, from a manifesto of the Republican Revolution of 1911. The lofty call to dedication and sacrifice for the sake of a greater China resonates especially with language used by the Communist Party and the Guomindang when they were young. Others among China's contemporary dissidents, both at home and overseas, have worried about the problem of escaping the mind-set of official language. Why, they ask, do we use the guerrilla-war metaphor *xiaomie* (annihilate) when encouraging friends to finish what is left of a few dishes on a dinner table? (Chinese from Taiwan and overseas do not use the term.) Why do we still overuse words that were favorites of Mao, such as *ji* (extreme) and *zuizui* (most, most)? Have decades of accepting Maospeak as China's official, publicly acknowledged, and morally proper language instilled habits that we cannot shed even when we want to do so?

Qigong. As Marxism-Leninism-Maoism declined through the 1970s and 1980s as a seat for Chinese identity and pride, a variety of things, many of them popular and originally pre-Communist, appeared as partial alternatives. Rural China has seen a resurgence of *yiguandao,* a moral-religious sect that arose in the early twentieth century and was repressed after the Communist revolution in 1949. In the cities, there was a dramatic rise through the 1980s of the practice of the physical-spiritual art called *qigong* (breath exercise, but also implying skill with *qi*—a mysterious, and distinctively Chinese, substance and/or force). Stories have arisen about *qigong* masters who can see through walls, make tables levitate, cure disease, and the like. *Qigong*'s appeal extends beyond the popular level, to government officials and even elite intellectuals. A distinguished literary critic in Beijing told me in early 1989 that he was skeptical of *qigong* until, one night on a lawn at a conference site outside Beijing, a *qigong* master emitted invisible rays that caused his head to lurch involuntarily to one side and the other. A young physicist, who doubted this story, commented that "*qigong* answers . . . the need for a fortress around our Chinese self-respect, a place that will always be safely Chinese, whatever else happens."

Backed by a Strong China. A Chinese scholar who came to the United States in the 1940s, and who had a full academic career in this country, is now living in retirement in New York. Despite his many attachments to his adopted country, he has never felt entirely American or 100 percent accepted as such. He has always had a wish for a "strong China" to be his backing. For many years, McCarthyism and the Cold War prevented him from openly expressing this need. But, instead of killing the need, the Cold War pressures only drove it to a more intensely personal level. In the fall of 1989, in discussing the Tiananmen massacre, he commented that "at least [the party leaders] could make the army obey. That's better than the Chinese government could do in the 1940s." I have no doubt that this statement was sincere and deep-

ly felt. But I am also confident that his siblings and cousins in
Beijing, some of whom I know personally, would find such a
statement utterly repugnant. For several days in May of 1989,
they and most other citizens of Beijing were hoping precisely for
the opposite—that the troops on the outskirts of the city would
refuse to obey orders to open fire. (I present this example in
order to demonstrate that the same China-centered values can
sometimes produce extremely different views on current issues. I
do not mean to suggest that the professor's view represents the
mainstream of overseas Chinese opinion on the massacre, which
clearly is not the case.)

The six preceding examples, because they are so disparate,
may seem a poor basis for generalization. But their very diversity
can also suggest that whatever commonalities do emerge are likely to be fairly deep-seated ones. In such a brief essay, I choose this
as a shortcut for making a broader point. My contention is that
the historian in Beijing and the professor in New York, for all the
differences of their situations, share a deep reverence for China,
a concept of its uniqueness, and a wish to be proud of it. Their
ideas are rooted in the 1940s, but the 1990s talk of the "Four
Little Dragons" implicitly reflects very similar assumptions
among the many people in the cities and coastal provinces who
use that phrase. The tiny group of senior leaders in Beijing who
care about the "Four Basic Principles" also proceed from such
assumptions, and add to them China's ancient notion that principles of social morality should be written down in authoritative
texts. The political opponents of those senior leaders, while in
one sense differing adamantly, embrace the same notions of
China-uniqueness, morality, self-sacrifice, and texts. When state-
sponsored definitions of Chinese identity fail, popular alternatives such as *yiguandao* and *qigong* arise to fill some of the space
where an identifying core should be.

The Inner Void

A new or revived identifying core for China, if it can emerge,
will probably need to resemble earlier ones. It will need to define
what is right in social relations, be accorded widespread assent, be
considered universally applicable, and perhaps be inscribed in
texts. These are all public features that the Chinese have traditionally wanted in their ideologies. But the public side is only half

the picture. For individuals, a sense of emptiness within can be as much of a problem as the lack of external symbols. In the early 1990s, Chinese intellectuals have been discussing the current "thought vacuum." A young Chinese historian, speaking in Beijing in early 1989, said, "I feel a need for something to hold on to, a *zhichidian* (point of purchase); I think many of us feel this way; it may be the special weakness of Chinese intellectuals, but we need this." This young man was unusually articulate; yet, he is undoubtedly correct to guess that his problem is not unique to him. Broadly conceived, it is not unique to intellectuals either. Many kinds of Chinese feel the need for the "point of purchase" he refers to.

The ideological crisis today can be viewed as an exacerbation of a problem that began when the impact of the West began to upset the Chinese world a century and a half ago. A leading Chinese sociologist, also speaking in 1989, put it this way:

Why do you think China's direction zigs and zags so much? Why are there so many policy reversals? Yes, of course, it is partly because the Communist leadership is continuously torn among factions. But fundamentally the phenomenon is much larger. The whole country is frantically searching for a way out, and has been for many decades, even before the Communists. We're like a big fish that has been pulled from the water and is flopping wildly to find its way back in. In such a condition the fish never asks where the next flip or flop will bring it. It senses only that its present position is intolerable and that *something* else must be tried. We intellectuals complain a lot about the influence of Soviet-style dictatorship in China. But originally, the "Soviet path" was also just one of the flops of the fish, an effort to find a way to save China.

The metaphor of a "path" or "road" (the socialist path, the capitalist road, and so on) has often been used in the Communist period to label alternative policies for development. The problem in the early 1990s is that, other than "make money," no road is clear. Many people, whether looking outside or peering within, come up empty. The Four Basic Principles? Repugnant to many, these seem at best to be a sickly shadow of what an official ideology should be. Democracy? For some the word generates genuine hope, but the concept remains poorly defined, ill-understood, and, because it is an import, raises questions about "Chineseness." *Qigong?* The Chineseness is solid, and the pride of ownership effective, but can something so narrow (and possibly superstitious) take the place of a proper Chinese ideology? A revival of Confucianism? There are advantages here, as the Four Little Dragons seem to demonstrate. But can there be a full return to

be the result of a full ideological breakdown—is deep in the modern Chinese mind. And there remains the issue of Chinese pride. Is the twentieth century to mark the end of China's history as a unique and exemplary place? (China has absorbed major outside influences before, such as Buddhism and the Mongol invasion, without dislodging the notion of a core of Chineseness.) If modern international culture does indeed become the first force in history to dissolve China's notion of its moral uniqueness, that process will, at a minimum, take decades or centuries to finish. Before then, the core problem will remain.

CHINA: THE COMING POWER[2]

A Troubled Relationship

One of the first tests of the Clinton administration's ability to develop a forward-looking foreign policy will be the troubled U.S.-China relationship. The successful conclusion of market-access negotiations with Beijing in October, and the decisions of the recently concluded 14th Party Congress to promote younger technocratic leaders and widen economic reform in China, provide an opportunity for progress.

Within the United States there has been little consensus on an appropriate China policy. Since the June 1989 Tiananmen tragedy Congress has tried to use sanctions to prod China to better observe human rights. Although President Bush imposed some sanctions in the aftermath of the crackdown, he consistently opposed legislation that would eliminate or impose conditions on Most Favored Nation [MFN] treatment for China. In September he vetoed legislation to place conditions on renewal of China's MFN trade status, saying it would hurt Chinese citizens and American companies that sell goods there. For his part President-elect Clinton has stated that he would be firmer, by linking con-

[2]Article by Barber B. Conable, Jr., chairman of the National Committee on United States–China Relations and David M. Lampton, president of the National Committee. From *Foreign Affairs* 71:133–149 Winter '92/'93. Copyright © 1992 by Council on Foreign Relations, Inc. Reprinted with permission.

tinued MFN status for China to improvements in human rights practices. Beijing categorically rejects such a linkage and promises retaliation.

China's political repression, its nuclear technology and weapons sales to Iran and other volatile regions of the world, along with some illegal trade practices and a mounting trade surplus with the United States, have only added to the tensions in a relationship already strained by the unnecessary and tragic violence of June 1989 and subsequent repression. China's strategic value is inaccurately perceived as having greatly diminished following the collapse of the Soviet Union. If the current strains in America's relations with China deteriorate into a U.S. policy of benign neglect or outright hostility, the damage could be widespread to the United States' economic future, its relations with other countries and its hopes for cooperation on global problems.

China is important to America's interests—the Clinton administration's policy should be premised on that fact. An economic boom is well underway on China's mainland, Taiwan and Hong Kong; yet the United States is in danger of isolating itself from its benefits. Not only does this regional growth offer great potential for American investment, trade and the jobs for Americans that both can bring, it also promises a more stable East Asia and will gradually create the conditions for a more pluralistic and humanely governed society on China's mainland. How can the new administration seize these opportunities, be true to core American values, and help avoid a dangerous worsening of U.S.-China relations?

Harmful Myths

The first task in reexamining U.S. policy toward China is to rid American thinking of three inaccurate and harmful assertions: China's system is performing dismally and therefore its stability is tenuous; China, since the Tiananmen crackdown, has pursued a course opposed to the free market, and current developments are antithetical to political liberalization; and China is of only secondary importance to American global interests. None of these assumptions stand up to careful examination.

The durability of China's leadership has confounded widespread Western expectations of its imminent collapse after the suppression of demonstrations in Tiananmen Square. The most important cause of stability has been the relatively good performance of China's economic system compared to that of eastern Europe and the U.S.S.R., which collapsed principally because they failed to meet basic economic and human needs. Second, the Chinese have yet to discern a successful road map in other countries' efforts to exit planned economies. In Poland, Czechoslovakia, Yugoslavia and the former Soviet Union, the Chinese see economic drift, political instability, ethnic fragmentation and violence, with more frightening outbursts possible in the foreseeable future. Finally, Deng Xiaoping and other survivors of the founding revolutionary generation are still in control. These elders, though increasingly frail, remain tremendously influential and, until their passing, are a factor for stability in its narrowest sense.

Despite a worsening budget deficit and enormous shortcomings and inefficiencies (about one-third of state enterprises lose money, even by Beijing's generous accounting standards), the Chinese economic system is not a basket case. Rather it is a system that in 1991 extended one billion Swiss francs in commercial credits to the Soviet Union, generated a worldwide trade surplus of about $8 billion, and by February 1992 had foreign exchange reserves totaling almost $43 billion. Recently it has extended food credits to the former Soviet Union. China's economic system also has performed well by the standards of its Asian neighbors. From 1984–90 the P.R.C.'s [People's Republic of China's] economic growth rate was nine percent—more than four times that of the Philippines, nearly twice that of Indonesia and a percentage point higher than Thailand's. Among the major economies of Asia, China's growth rate was exceeded only by South Korea's. In broader measures of performance, infant mortality in China in 1991 was 33 deaths per thousand live births, compared to 109 in Pakistan, 91 in India, 73 in Indonesia, 54 in the Philippines, 37 in Thailand, and 6 in Hong Kong.

Defense spending, so wildly out of balance with development expenditures throughout the Third World, is more proportional in China, though there are concerns. Since the mid-1980s China has reduced the number of people bearing arms by 25 percent, with indications of further manpower cuts to come. According to World Bank statistics, when China began its reform program in 1978, Beijing reportedly spent 4.7 percent of GNP [Gross National Product] on defense and 3.1 percent on culture, education and public health. In 1988 defense had fallen to 1.6 percent and culture, education and public health had risen marginally to 3.5 percent.

Despite this general trend, however, China has witnessed double-digit defense spending increases in the last three years. The CIA put these facts somewhat differently: "When adjusted for inflation, budgeted defense spending—which may account for only half of the country's military spending—fell 21 percent from 1984 to 1988 . . . but had risen 22 percent since 1988." These recent defense spending increases can be understood as efforts to mollify the military and to convert it to a force leaner in personnel and richer in sophisticated technology. Nonetheless trends in spending, procurement and strategy call for careful monitoring, given recent and contemplated Chinese weapons purchases, such as new-generation aircraft obtained from Russia.

China's system has done rather well in sustaining high rates of growth, meeting basic human and material needs and getting its development priorities in some sort of balance. Education and health are still in desperate need of more money, and underlying population growth and environmental stresses will become mounting problems in the years ahead. Moreover China remains an agricultural society whose almost 1.2 billion people collectively hover at a low per-capita GNP level. The economy is fragile, and suppressed inflationary pressures could explode rapidly. Nonetheless this is not a system that has entirely failed.

Demands for political change stem not so much from economic failure as from moderate economic success, the resulting rising expectations and the magnetic appeal of the neighboring Chinese free-market communities of Taiwan, Hong Kong and Singapore. Drawing lessons from the Soviet Union's demise, China's leaders have concluded that the regime's survival rests on genuine and rapid economic reform. Indeed it was precisely such an acceleration that was approved in mid-October at the 14th Party Congress in Beijing.

Economic Reform Continues

The 1989 political crisis, epitomized by the Tiananmen tragedy, did not create a new policy of economic retrenchment so much as it deepened the resolve of Chinese leaders to enforce a previously agreed upon recentralization of financial authority that was considered essential to building up China's foreign exchange reserves and to lowering inflation. (Inflation was running at an annual rate of 10–15 percent in early 1988 and had jumped to an annual rate of 26 percent by December of that year.) In late

1988 foreign observers were saying that something had to be done to increase China's foreign exchange holdings of $17.5 billion so that it could continue importing at a significant level while simultaneously repaying international obligations that were to come due in the early 1990s. Everyone inside and outside of China recognized the politically explosive character of inflation.

In the aftermath of Tiananmen, Western suspension of bilateral and multilateral loan and aid programs made it even more essential that China's leaders quickly halt the unnecessary expenditure of foreign exchange, increase exports to build foreign exchange reserves and immediately restore a stable domestic economic order by halting inflation. This policy, in part, accounts for the 22 percent fall in U.S. exports to China and the simultaneous 27 percent rise in Chinese exports to the United States that so angered Americans.

Beyond successful performance in foreign trade Beijing made remarkable headway against inflation, bringing it down to about one percent by the first quarter of 1990 and to an annual rate of 4.4 percent in 1991. Despite renewed concern about inflationary pressures this year (such as 19 percent industrial growth in the first six months), the CIA indicated in August that three consecutive bumper grain harvests and China's large foreign exchange holdings should moderate inflation, at least for a while.

In short, economic reform never was halted, but, instead, took a temporary back seat to dealing with the more pressing problems of maintaining a stable currency, assuring adequate hard currency reserves and boosting grain production. It was the backdrop of political repression and the elite argument over the direction of policy that created a widespread impression abroad that economic reform had been reversed or jettisoned.

During 1990–92 economic reform initiatives were apparent in several important areas. First, China's currency, the *renminbi* (RMB), was devalued on several occasions, bringing the exchange rate by early 1992 to a level that most observers believed was near to what its internationally market-determined value would be were it freely floated. Though in late 1992 the gap between the official and free-market rates for the RMB had widened somewhat, the regime seemingly remains committed to freely floating its currency and to doing away with the dual currency system of local currency and "foreign exchange certificates." Assuming these reforms are implemented, the P.R.C. will be integrated into the world economy to a high degree and will be even more subject to the external influence that such integration implies.

A second important area of economic reform saw China adjust upward such politically sensitive prices as those for grain and air and railway fares. Policymakers also continued to broaden the scope of market-determined prices in other areas. During the 1989–92 period there was a continual expansion of the numbers of goods for which prices were set in the market place. Indeed the fact that there were so many market-determined prices coexisting and overlapping with state-set prices has exacerbated corruption. State and party officials with access to goods at comparatively low, state-set prices use their power to acquire those goods and transfer them to the free market, where generally higher prices prevail. This and other corrupt practices by officials, along with inflation, may well be the largest immediate threats to social stability.

In other reforms during 1990–92 China modestly raised the cost of housing to more accurately reflect capital, operating and maintenance expenses, and began the long and arduous task of creating a housing ownership system. The package is intended to give people a personal stake in maintaining real property and to generate badly needed housing capital.

In the financial area stock markets opened in Shanghai and Shenzhen, albeit with restricted numbers of listings and trading, with some "B share" stock available for purchase by foreigners. By the third quarter of 1992 thirty Chinese cities had established short-term fund markets.

By early 1992 China was pushing efforts to introduce market mechanisms in the 40-year-old state-controlled materials distribution system, allowing market-driven trading in basic industrial inputs. If this reform expands, the prices of coal, rubber, farm machinery, building materials and chemicals will become market responsive, reverberating throughout the entire industrial structure.

In 1990 China adopted a copyright law that, while not adequately protecting foreign intellectual property, recognized ideas and technology as investments that need to be rewarded and protected. This recognition was given more currency in January 1992 when China and the United States reached agreement on the protection of intellectual property in the pharmaceutical, literary, artistic and software areas—protection that exceeds minimum international standards in several respects. Implementation, however, remains to be seen.

Building on this achievement, in early 1992 Beijing again began to push vigorously for entry into the General Agreement on

large number of younger, economic reform-minded people to the
Central Committee, Politburo and its Standing Committee, abolished the Central Advisory Commission that provided an organi-
zational base for China's conservatives, and called for an expansion of economic reforms in China. Nonetheless strong elements
of the central leadership are not fully reconciled to these policies.

As the 14th Party Congress showed, however, political reform
in China is not yet a serious priority. Deng Xiaoping remains
committed to accelerating economic reform while maintaining
the political status quo—the "neo-authoritarian" approach. What
is not open to question, however, is that the post-Tiananmen
economic reforms and the current acceleration of economic
change will soon put serious political reform back on the agenda.
The only issue is whether the elite gets out ahead of these demands or it is forced to respond. In the latter case ongoing economic reform (and the possible inflation it will bring) will be
setting the stage for further conflict and repression, regime failure or both. The convergence of such social, economic and political crises with the leadership succession in Beijing could spell
turmoil for China's Communist Party and its people. The solution
is to build legitimate channels by which dissatisfaction can be
expressed and moderated.

Phenomena of "Greater China"

Many now argue that American interests in China are secondary in the wake of the Cold War's end. Although the Soviet threat
has largely disappeared (but not the dangers arising from its
implosion), the intrinsic importance of the U.S.-China relationship is growing along several other dimensions. American interests can be put into global, regional and bilateral categories.

Globally an increasing role will be played by multilateral organizations, with the United Nations most prominent among them.
Given China's veto power as a permanent member of the Security
Council, Beijing must be part of a consensus for the United Nations to be effective. Therefore U.S. policy must seek common
ground where possible with China's leadership, while simultaneously criticizing its behavior in human rights, weapons proliferation and certain trade practices. The United States would not
have forged an internationally sanctioned coalition during the
Gulf War had China sought to obstruct the Security Council's
actions in early 1991, nor would subsequent U.N. actions concerning Libya, the Balkans, Iraq or Cambodia have been feasible.

Environmental protection also requires global cooperation. Today China depends on coal for 70 percent of its industrial fuel and power generation and 90 percent of its household energy needs. Most of this coal has a very high sulphur content and is inefficiently burned in the open atmosphere, which leads to tremendous pollution problems. There is little prospect of these percentages being significantly reduced in the next 25 years. With an expected real economic growth rate of about five percent over the next three decades, China's cooperation will be essential to limit global warming and acid rain in Asia.

In the world today refugees also are a major concern. The dislocations created by refugees from Cambodia, Vietnam and eastern Europe are small compared to the havoc a major exodus from China would produce. Each one percent of China's population totals almost 12 million persons—about a quarter of France's population, twice the size of Hong Kong's and more than half that of Taiwan's. It is in the world's interest, not to mention that of the P.R.C.'s immediate neighbors, that a Chinese exodus not be created by political failure (of which severe political repression is one form), natural disasters or widespread economic/agricultural collapse.

Finally, China is a major seller of affordable and serviceable weaponry to developing nations, and an actual or alleged source of nuclear and/or missile technology to Pakistan, North Korea, Iran, Syria and Saudi Arabia. The United States and other nations must continue to encourage China to cooperate on limiting proliferation of arms and technology for weapons of mass destruction, as well as better policing Western companies engaged in illicit and unwise technological transfers. China's recent accession to the Nuclear Nonproliferation Treaty—and its promise to adhere to the guidelines and parameters of the Missile Technology Control Regime—are testament to the importance of continued engagement and pressure by the United States, Europe and Japan.

Regionally American interests are both numerous and important. The two most protracted, economically distracting and politically explosive American military commitments in the post-World War II era were Korea and Vietnam. In both cases China figured prominently. The lesson is that regional stability requires workable U.S.-China relations. Competition between Beijing and Washington takes the form of exploiting indigenous regional conflicts by both powers, resulting in local problems that expand to suck both countries into a self-defeating vortex.

The most serious threats to American security and economic interests in Asia include armed conflict with nuclear potential between the two Koreas and between India and Pakistan; a deterioration of relations between Beijing and Taipei that could lead to economic or military conflict; a re-ignition of the Cambodian conflict; and a botched transition to Beijing's sovereignty in Hong Kong in 1997. None of these problems can be handled effectively without substantial Sino-American cooperation. Constructive relations with Beijing will not assure P.R.C. cooperation in all cases; needlessly bad relations will nearly ensure conflict. The Republic of Korea's formal diplomatic recognition of Beijing last August, at the expense of Taipei, is just one indication of the increasing importance the region attaches to building positive ties to the P.R.C.

In Cambodia . . . progress to date could not have occurred without China's cooperation. Further, Beijing's somewhat improved relationship with Hanoi has made progress in Cambodia more likely. It has further reduced the level of conflict in the region to the point where in 1991 Washington was able to contemplate eventual normalization of relations with Hanoi.

To China's southwest, Beijing is seeking to improve relations with New Delhi while maintaining its traditionally warm ties to Islamabad. China's apparent nuclear cooperation with Pakistan and recurring reports of pending and/or actual missile technology sales to Islamabad are contrary to U.S. interests and are regionally destabilizing. Nonetheless closer Sino-Indian relations are a trend very much in the U.S. interest.

In the Taiwan Strait relations between Taipei and Beijing have their own dynamic and are not under Washington's control. Indeed Beijing-Taipei relations easily could become one of the most serious problems in Sino-American relations. Recent Chinese protest over Washington's decision to sell F-16 fighter aircraft to Taiwan is just one indication of the conflict, contradictions and policy dilemmas that lie just below the surface. The P.R.C.'s incentive to continue a policy of moderation toward Taiwan would be greatly lessened by a deterioration of its relations with the United States.

Worsening China-Taiwan relations would also adversely affect U.S. interests. First, many of Taiwan's firms—with $3 billion plus investments in the mainland—are exporting to the United States. If the American market dries up for Chinese exports some of Taiwan's investment in the P.R.C. will also vanish. Second, the

1979 Taiwan Relations Act charges the U.S. president with assuring that America helps maintain Taiwan's capacity to defend itself. If U.S.-P.R.C. relations deteriorate one can expect more mainland hostility toward Taiwan, which will exacerbate the dilemmas facing Washington.

Hong Kong is America's thirteenth largest trading partner. U.S. investment exceeds $7 billion there, and nearly 22,000 Americans live in the territory. Moreover, about two-thirds of China's exports to the United States pass through the colony. Hong Kong's greatest insurance policy for its post-1997 future under communist sovereignty is its economic utility to China—that means trade. If the United States adopts policies that reduce trade with China, either by design or through a general deterioration in relations with Beijing, it will correspondingly reduce the incentives for restraint in Beijing toward both Taiwan and Hong Kong.

Bilaterally the United States has a stake not only in pursuing the interests specified above, but also in creating a niche in the world's most rapidly growing major economy today—"Greater China" (the P.R.C., Taiwan and Hong Kong). Exports have been the engine keeping the American economy going during the recent recession and exports will play an increasingly prominent role in America's future. If this emerging Chinese economic conglomerate were considered a single trading entity it already would have been America's third largest trading partner in 1989, following Canada and Japan (with Mexico ranking fourth). There is insufficient recognition among Americans that the increasing economic interdependence among Hong Kong, Taiwan and the Chinese mainland is creating new economic opportunities, policy problems and dependencies that hold the promise of creating greater regional security.

While there is increasing attention focused on the P.R.C.'s growing trade surplus with the United States ($2.8 billion in 1987, $10.4 billion in 1990, $12.7 billion in 1991 and an estimated $15 billion or more in 1992), America's trade deficit with Greater China actually declined very slightly during 1987–91. This occurred because Taiwan and Hong Kong moved much of their manufacturing and assembly operations aimed at the U.S. market to the mainland in order to take advantage of lower labor and land costs. Moreover Taiwan and Hong Kong enterprises exported to the mainland many of the components that were assembled into products, thereby shifting this value to the P.R.C.'s accounts, in the process reducing Taipei's and Hong Kong's surplus with the United States while simultaneously increasing Beijing's. Taiwan and Hong Kong, in effect, exported their political and economic conflicts with the United States to the mainland.

The gainers in this process were American consumers, who were able to purchase low-cost, high-quality goods; the P.R.C., which gained jobs; and Taiwan and Hong Kong, which were able to shift their own production efforts to higher value-added output and reduce trade frictions with Washington. As for American workers they were not going to get these low-paying jobs in any case. The only remaining questions are to which Third World country those jobs are going to move, and how can the United States rapidly raise the capacity of the American work force to add value in new product areas. High-quality education and job training, not protectionism, are the long-term answers to America's economic problems.

Not only is this emerging Chinese conglomerate becoming more economically integrated, each area is hedging its bets by placing substantial amounts of human and material resources in the United States. Students, resident businessmen and financial investments from the P.R.C., Taiwan and Hong Kong are growing in number in the United States. Students and scholars from Greater China, whether they stay in the United States or return to their native lands, constitute a human bridge between the Chinese economic conglomerate and America. They give Americans a huge advantage in dealing with this part of the world. Further, the Asian share of U.S. legal immigration soared from five percent in 1931–60 to nearly 50 percent in the 1980s, exceeding legal immigrants from Latin America. After Filipinos, ethnic Chinese are the second largest Asian group in the United States. The United States not only has an incentive to augment economic ties to China, it has a unique capacity to do so.

In sum the challenges facing American policy are twofold: to encourage and participate in economic developments that promote security, prosperity, and social and political change, as has occurred in other areas of high-speed Asian growth, most notably South Korea and Taiwan; and to remain flexible and diversified in dealings with China, given that the unexpected has been the norm in the P.R.C.

Challenges Ahead

Today the United States runs the very real danger of pursuing a self-defeating policy of benign neglect or overt hostility that is rationalized by moral outrage over the character of political rule in China. Moreover the United States is doing so at a time when no other country in the world is pursuing such a course. America may be in more peril of being isolated than China, if the trends of the recent past continue.

A policy of benign neglect or outright hostility will not only forego opportunities to build links to the most dynamic regional economy in the world and to gain the benefits to be derived from cooperation on global problems, it also will retard the ongoing processes that over the long run will produce the kinds of social change more compatible with basic American values. The United States needs a policy of active involvement in Greater China that consists of the following elements: vigorous engagement, diversification, multilateralization and recognition of interdependence.

Vigorous engagement means involving Chinese leaders and organizations at the highest levels in a dialogue about the problems and opportunities that America and China face together. These problems include proliferation, trade, human rights, the global environment and the development of multilateral institutions. In the course of these dialogues, such as recent and successful negotiations over intellectual property and market access, the United States may have to exert considerable pressure to assure a fair outcome. Nonetheless this pressure should be applied to achieve clearly defined objectives. To apply broad sanctions in the absence of dialogue, in order to achieve ill-defined purposes, is a formula for ineffective and counterproductive policy.

Diversification of relations has two principal dimensions. At the same time that Washington remains actively engaged with Beijing's leaders at the national level, it needs to develop relations with local leaders throughout China. A new generation of capable, younger, economically oriented leaders is moving up through the system. These individuals not only have growing influence because of the decentralization that has occurred over the last 15 years, they also increasingly have the skills and motivation to make cooperation with Americans more productive. America should not deceive itself, however, that the rise of younger, more technologically oriented leaders in China will dispel disputes. On the contrary the seriousness of their commitment to economic development may increase conflict, particularly in the trade and environmental domains. But one can expect that Americans and Chinese will speak the same language to an ever larger extent.

Diversification also has another dimension. With the tremendous economic, political and social change that has occurred in Taiwan, and Hong Kong's attempts to reach out in anticipation of the 1997 transition to Beijing's sovereignty, the United States needs to further develop its cultural and economic ties with these two exceedingly important areas.

There is a tendency in U.S. foreign policy thinking to bilateralize issues that could more productively be addressed multilaterally. The result is that China frequently shifts the issue from the subject at hand to one of big power pressure on Third World nations—this strikes a resonant chord in much of the world. Moreover American attempts to pressure nations are undermined by the actions of other countries that either do not share U.S. objectives or disapprove of U.S. methods. And finally, by bilateralizing issues the United States tends to throw too many issues into the cauldron of super-heated domestic politics. Rather, America increasingly must build a consensus supportive of its policies internationally and seek remedies through international organizations and cooperation.

The rise of the Chinese economic conglomerate is important not only because of the economic opportunity it presents to the United States and because it will be another force for moderation in Beijing, but also because of what it implies for the use of American leverage. To the degree that Hong Kong and Taiwan use China as a platform for the production of export products to the United States, Washington's use of economic sanctions (such as ending or placing conditions on China's MFN status) that seek to deny "P.R.C. exports" access to the American market will inadvertently create unintended victims in Taiwan and Hong Kong. The United States must not make economic cluster bombs that hit friends and opponents equally.

Whether the P.R.C. succeeds or fails it will present America with enormous challenges. System collapse would impose large-scale misery on the Chinese people, lead to a destabilizing foreign policy and produce a China with no authoritative center with which to deal and create migratory flows of enormous magnitude. Economic success in the P.R.C. will have negative global ecological effects, increase Chinese competition in some economic sectors (as well as provide a large market for many American industries), and enable China to project power and influence in ways the United States will not necessarily like. A China that has made rapid progress and becomes stronger will not be a pliable

China. However, it is far better that America face the problems of success in China than those of failure.

SINOLOGY IN CRISIS[3]

Fang Lizhi is an astrophysicist who is the closest thing there is to a Chinese Sakharov. After the Chinese government's murderous suppression of the democracy movement in July 1989, Fang spent about a year inside the American embassy until he was allowed to leave for Britain. Before his departure, he wrote an essay in which he discusses the "technique of forgetting history." It is, he says, a Chinese Communist device "to force the whole country to forget its history . . . to coerce all of society into a continuing forgetfulness." His immediate concern is that the details of the Tiananmen massacre will fade, but his point is larger:

If inside China, the whole of society has been coerced into forgetfulness by the authorities, in the West the act of forgetting can be observed in the work of a number of influential writers who have consciously ignored history and have willingly complied with the "standardized public opinion" of the Communists' censorial system.

What gives Fang's point all the more weight is that throughout China's modern history, Westerners have had a special custodial responsibility for that country's cultural and historical memories. For upheaval, followed by chaos, followed by totalitarianism made the traditional homegrown scholarly pursuits difficult, if not impossible. Yet in the past forty years, the Western Sinological community, convinced on the whole that the Communist takeover in 1949 ushered in a better regime than the one it successfully overthrew, has been more than passively complicit in the process Fang describes.

To be sure, a new attitude toward the Beijing regime has been created by the events of June 1989, not only among American Sinologists but among American intellectuals generally. A measure of this change is that a generation ago, one mark of a truly enlightened American was his insistence that his government

[3]Article by Charles Horner, executive vice-president of the Madison Center in Washington, D.C. From *Commentary* 91:45–48 F '91. Copyright © 1991 by the American Jewish Committee. Reprinted with permission.

"stop pretending that China doesn't exist." Now, as likely as not, he is apt to complain that the present Republican President is just too soft on Chinese Communism. But it remains to be seen whether this sudden new propensity to tell something of the truth about post-1949 China will persist and whether it will issue in some serious revaluation of the Sinologists' past illusions and mistakes.

How bad was it, then, in pre-Tiananmen days? As always, where Western attitudes toward Communist regimes are concerned, one is grateful to Paul Hollander's book *Political Pilgrims* for collecting the assessments of the typical visitor. Thus David Rockefeller once praised China for producing "dedicated administration, . . . high morale, . . . community of purpose." Simone de Beauvoir called life in China "exceptionally pleasant." Felix Greene thought "there was no jockeying for power or personal rivalry" in Beijing as there was in the Kremlin.

But these, after all, were laymen who were not necessarily supposed to know any better. What about a group from whom one would expect more—people steeped in the history and the language of China, and supported in their studies by great universities, rich foundations, and the federal treasury? Of these, probably the single most representative figure was Professor Emeritus John K. Fairbank of Harvard, who was also the most influential figure in the development of China studies in America. Back in 1972, after President Nixon established conspicuous political relations with China, Fairbank was asked by *Foreign Affairs* to provide the long view, which he did in an article whose conclusion was that "the Maoist revolution is on the whole the best thing that has happened to the Chinese people in centuries."

It is noteworthy that by the time Fairbank pronounced this confident judgment, the worst excesses of the Maoist regime were already on the record and, considering China's self-enforced isolation, reasonably well-documented. For example, there was the careful interviewing of Chinese refugees by Miriam and Ivan London, whose work in the aggregate produced a picture radically at variance with the conventional Sinophilia of the time. Moreover, in 1971, the Senate Judiciary Committee had published a minor, though unheralded, classic, 28 pages long, entitled "The Human Cost of Communism in China" and written by Richard Walker, then a professor at the University of South Carolina. Walker's estimates of "casualties to Communism in China" ranged between 34 and 64 *million*. In the years since, as more facts have been made known—many through casual admission by the Chinese government itself—Walker's work has held up very well. Even "mainstream" Sinologists will now quietly acknowledge it, although its implications for the profession's intellectual and *moral* standards these past decades have yet to be squarely faced.

Indeed, it was not the academic experts but a number of journalists (themselves exceptional within the media world) who first challenged the kind of attitude expressed in Fairbank's *Foreign Affairs* article of 1972. In the late 1970's Fox Butterfield of the New York *Times* and John Fraser of the Toronto *Globe and Mail* pioneered in reporting on Chinese dissidence. In 1982, Butterfield in particular published *China: Alive in the Bitter Sea,* which marked a revolution in foreign commentary about China. Since he had been Beijing bureau chief for the *Times,* as well as a student of Chinese history, and since he had proper credentials and background, his forthright account of what he had learned from individual Chinese about the real character of life in the People's Republic could not easily be dismissed. The book has recently been reissued and serves as a useful backdrop to a group of new volumes which carry the imprint of the 1989 Beijing [Tiananmen Square] massacres and the subsequent repressions.

Steven W. Mosher's *China Misperceived: From American Illusions to Chinese Reality* is a good starting point in the examination of these new books, for his dissection of "ideological flights of fancy" among scholars, academics, and others has a *prima-facie* plausibility that would have been unappreciated even eighteen months ago.

Mosher himself, now the director of the Asian Studies Center at the Claremont Institute in California, once seemed destined for conventional Sinology. He left the Navy in 1973 to take up the study of China in Hong Kong and Taiwan, and later went on to work on a dissertation at Stanford. When in 1979 he departed for field research in China, he was, he says, "favorably disposed toward the Communist revolution," which, he then believed, "had created a society that was egalitarian, just, unselfish, and liberated." But his observations of the harsh realities of China's village life changed his mind. In the end his relationship with Stanford was also poisoned; in something of an academic *cause célèbre,* the university severed its ties with him, preferring instead to maintain relations with a Chinese regime bent on punishing Mosher for his criticisms of its social practices.

Mosher's subject was China's birth-control programs and their coercive aspects, especially forced abortions, and the controversy proved prophetic, since his criticisms seem finally to have been accepted by mainstream demographers. In *Slaughter of the Innocents,* John Aird, formerly a senior China specialist at the U.S. Census Bureau and a contributor to the Congressional Joint Economic Committee's periodic reports on China, has produced a history of China's birth-control programs which confirms Mosher's earlier assessment. Aird's provocative title is justified by his highly detailed review of the available evidence, and his dispassionate methodology—some 70 pages of footnotes to about 110 pages of text—makes his indictment doubly devastating.

Thus Mosher was ahead of his time, even as his colleagues are now trying to catch up. Happily, his new book, which assembles many embarrassing pronouncements about China, is right up to date. Indeed, it now seems likely that many in the Sinological profession who previously did nothing but condescend to tough criticisms of Chinese Communism will merely coopt some of his outlook, implying that they, too, shared his skepticism about the Chinese regime all along.

But leaning on a "heretic" like Mosher is not necessary, since it is now possible to come to an emphasis on China's political deficiencies through a much safer and more acceptable academic route. A case in point is Andrew Nathan, a professor of political science at Columbia, whose earlier interest in China concerned warlords in the 1920's and factionalism within the Communist party in later decades. (His wife, Roxane Witke, wrote a biography of Jiang Qing, Mao Zedong's widow and the most famous member of the "Gang of Four.") Now, in a collection of his essays called *China's Crisis: Dilemmas of Reform and Prospects for Democracy,* Nathan offers an analysis essentially derived from Tocqueville's famous aphorism about the dangers faced by an incompetent dictatorship when it attempts to reform itself. As he sees it, the political dissidence of the 1980's originated in Deng Xiaoping's economic reforms. There was at the same time, in Nathan's view, a growing American interest in Chinese human-rights abuses made possible by the openness of the American political system to Chinese students in the United States (Deng's reforms having allowed thousands of Chinese to study here). A gradual deterioration of relations thus took place between the students here and the regime there, and then a subsequent deterioration in relations between the regime and intellectuals at home.

The "democracy movement" in China was also convoluted.

According to Nathan, many of the activists had a quite limited agenda, and were not interested in challenging the basic validity of "socialism." Others wanted a more modern regime, better suited to managing the rapid economic growth initiated by Deng's "four modernizations" of 1979. Inside the government itself, many of the reformers wanted a transition from totalitarianism, but only to a "new authoritarianism." They cited South Korea, Singapore, and Taiwan as the kind of polity best suited to China's condition as a developing country. But at the same time, Taiwan, and to a lesser extent some of the others, were undergoing democratic revolutions of their own.

In assessing future prospects, Nathan seems to think that nothing much can happen until the American Political Science Association agrees upon the proper analytical model. There is no doubt, as Nathan writes, "that the large number of democratic transitions in recent years have required political scientists to develop new perspectives on the problem." It reminds one of the old saw about the bumblebee, whose ability to fly seemingly contradicts the laws of aerodynamics. The bee, of course, is ignorant of such paradigms, and flies on anyway. So, too, the benighted peoples of the world who, having had no seminars in comparative politics at any of our great universities, press ahead in their "Eurocentrism" and in their struggle for capitalism and democracy, even as professors assure them that such are impossible, even unworthy, aspirations.

Until recently, Chinese themselves have been conspicuously absent from the discussion of these matters. Over the years, we had come to know the dissidents of the Soviet Union and Eastern Europe. Some of them had become world figures in either literature or politics. But we had never been able to personalize China's situation in this way, and we had effectively no knowledge of any local heroes. No doubt this is a comment on both Chinese society and our own, but it is slowly starting to change; though we are far from having a comfortable Chinese perspective, there are at least things to read.

Liu Binyan, for example, is a sixty-five-year-old Chinese journalist who is now writer-in-residence at Trinity College in Hartford, Connecticut. One way or another, he has been a victim of every major Chinese political "campaign" since 1957, but he was allowed to come to this country in 1988. *China's Crisis, China's Hope* is based on five lectures he gave last year at Harvard.

Trends of political thought within the Chinese intelligentsia

are not easy to categorize. The difficulty arises, in part, because
the intellectuals sometimes think themselves the heirs of the
scholar-mandarins who were the ruling group in imperial times by
dint of greater learning and superior virtue, while at other times
they think themselves heir to the reformist and revolutionary
thinkers and activists of this century, who brought down the old
order and struggled over what should replace it. But in all events,
they are accustomed to a role as the nation's conscience, and are
certainly used to a high standing and a degree of deference that
their Western counterparts do not enjoy. It is quite clear that Mao
and the party did not like them; as Liu stresses, the intellectuals
were singled out for special brutalities and humiliations, not
merely liquidation. But he also thinks that intellectuals often responded by even greater efforts to demonstrate their loyalty; at
the least, China's intellectuals "were far more compliant" in their
dealings with the Communist party than were their counterparts
in the Soviet Union and Eastern Europe. And for quite a while,
the Communist party retained its prestige among them.

For Liu, the problem is the alienation of the party from its
own ideals, its various abuses which Liu and his cohort coura-
geously exposed. Yet he seems not to have given up the hope "that
the false can be turned into the genuine," that is, that the nomi-
nally democratic mechanisms of the state might someday become
real. Liu is obviously a brave man who embodies more of a sensi-
bility than he does a political program. He foresees a slow dissolution of the apparatus, but the changes he envisions are more of
degree than of a fundamental kind.

It is therefore interesting to contrast the constrained hopes of
this older survivor with the experiences of a man but a third his
age. Shen Tong, now a biology student at Brandeis, was at age
twenty-one one of the principal leaders of the Tiananmen demonstrations. In *Almost a Revolution* (written with Marianne Yen) he
has produced what seems to be the first book-length memoir by
one of the important participants. Naturally talented
academically—Shen survived the brutal national competition for
a coveted spot at Beijing University—he is also politically preco-
cious. He tells us that two of his grandparents committed suicide
during the Cultural Revolution in 1966 rather than be "paraded
in the village square wearing dunce caps and humiliating
placards." Shen's father worked as a translator for China's Foreign Ministry. Born in 1968, with no direct experience of the
worst of Mao's excesses, Shen is of the generation that takes the
outer world rather than the condition of "preliberation" China as

a standard. If, for the elders, China's circumstances are wonderously improved over those of a generation ago, younger Chinese know enough about Taiwan, Singapore, Hong Kong, or South Korea to turn these into relevant examples. Thus, by the time young Shen and his equally gifted colleagues showed up on the nation's finest, most prestigious, campus, their obviously brilliant though highly eclectic and undisciplined intellectualism seemed destined to be turned on the regime. The regime, of course, regarded them as ignorant ingrates.

Shen offers us a day-by-day account of the crisis as it developed from April 15, 1989—the day of the death of the highly regarded reformist premier Hu Yaobang—to the massacres of June 3–4, until his own escape from the country. In the students' efforts to assimilate almost every strand of Western thought no matter how contradictory the parts, in their intense debates among themselves, in the noble futility of their outburst, they called to mind Peking University in the 1920's, and the efforts then to work a comparable political miracle. But however historians measure this latest event, it is already part of world culture. Now that he is a free man, Shen tells us that he has met Lech Walesa, the Dalai Lama, Vaclav Havel, and even served as a grand marshal of the Martin Luther King Day parade in Atlanta. His compatriot, and the best known of the students, Wuer Kaixi, has also been to the Kennedy compound in Hyannis.

It is, then, likely that many thousands of young Chinese will settle in for the long haul here in the United States and that they will, in fact, have to achieve a proper balance between future political activity and the other ordinary business of living. They are apt to develop a complicated outlook as they attempt to keep their relationship to two widely separated countries in common focus. It is in this connection that Bette Bao Lord's *Legacies: A Chinese Mosaic* has a particular interest, even beyond its obvious elegance and evocative power.

Mrs. Lord, Chinese by birth, is married to President Reagan's ambassador to China, Winston Lord, a man whose involvement in Chinese-American relations goes back to his work in 1971 as an aide to Henry Kissinger during the latter's now-fabled secret mission to China. Mrs. Lord, it will be remembered, is the author of the best-selling novel of a few years ago, *Spring Moon*, and former Ambassador Lord was conspicuous among the "new China lobby" for his outspoken criticism of President Bush's low-key response to the Tiananmen massacre.

Mrs. Lord had an interesting life even before all of this. In some respects, it foreshadowed the experiences that a newer generation of Chinese-Americans, and Chinese in America, seem destined to have. She was born in 1938 in Shanghai. Her family fled to the Chinese interior ahead of advancing Japanese armies. She left the country in 1946, accompanying her father, a Nationalist Chinese diplomat, to New York. The family did not return after the Communist takeover in 1949, and Mrs. Lord herself did not visit China until she was thirty-five; later, of course, she returned as the wife of the American ambassador.

Like so many of the extraordinary Chinese our country has come to know, she has a grasp of both cultural traditions at their highest. In particular, she has a great gift for marrying the English language to sensibilities it was not designed to depict. Her book is a collection both of brilliantly-done vignettes—renderings of personal tales she has been told—and, at the same time, a complex reflection on the meaning of these personal tragedies in the context of her own life in both her countries. This is thus a political book, in that it is designed to keep attention on the brutalities in China, but it is also a deeper rumination.

It may be that the latter part will be of greater interest over the longer run. For example, some have likened the arrival and the now seemingly indefinite stay of thousands of Chinese in our country to the flight of European intellectuals to America in the face of the Nazis, or even to the emigration of Jews from the Soviet Union. Whatever the differences in circumstances or scale, it is clear that the U.S. is now the home, and will remain the home, of some truly formidable people who will inevitably attain to positions of high standing. They will, of course, be Americans—indeed, exemplary Americans—and yet like other immigrants before them, they will retain a special interest in their ancestral homeland. How they will act on China, and how in turn that will influence that nation as a whole, remains to be seen. But we are aided in our understanding of how this might work itself out by Mrs. Lord, who reminds us that the methods will be intelligent and subtle.

As for professional students, analysts, and historians of China here in America, there is a ripple effect in the making. Just as the worldwide clamor for Western-style democratic capitalism has dissolved the conventional paradigms, the old enthusiasm of Sinologists for the New China may well have to bow to the testimony of those who have actually experienced it. And when recent events conspire to destroy the received interpretations of China's history, but before anything has yet appeared to replace them, the result can be striking.

For example, Professor Jonathan Spence of Yale is probably the man best suited to write the one-volume retrospective history of modern China. His past work has been unusually creative, insightful, even arresting, not at all in thrall to the reigning jargon. He has written about emperors, missionaries, foreign advisers, literary figures, dispossessed peasants. *The Search for Modern China* would almost certainly have been the most significant synthesis yet written, and yet the reader—and maybe even the author, too—must now be unsatisfied by it.

A decade ago, in *The Gate of Heavenly Peace* (1981), all of Spence's skills were present in an account of China's last century as seen through lives of three representative intellectuals. The book had the style and the assurance of a man who knew where things were going and was pleased enough with the direction. But now a story once thought exciting turns out to be depressing even for Spence himself. It shows in the writing. In searching for modern China, Spence seems to find merely the same old violence, upheavals, natural disasters, famines, and wars, but not the ability to impose much redeeming social importance on them. Most of all there is the plain fact that today's China is no longer in the vanguard of anything. China was the great failure in the historic year 1989: no velvet revolution, no bamboo curtain demolished once-and-for-all, not even very much *glasnost*. It is almost as big a disappointment as Vietnam.

All this has had a sobering effect of the Sinologists, but the profession still is not ready for real revisionism, revisionism that would cast a new glance at Western imperialism, at the Chinese civil wars, at "Marxism-Leninism Mao Zedong Thought," at the global vitality of Western liberal values. Of course no such revisionist interpretation will be possible until the profession comes to terms with its own less than honorable past; on the evidence of at least some among this recent crop of books, Sinologists are still too far from engaging in that kind of—shall we call it?—"self-criticism."

CAN THE CHINESE DRAGON MATCH
PEARLS WITH THE DRAGON GOD
OF THE SEA?[4]

Is China headed for a neocolonial future?

That all depends on how, with what awareness, attitudes, and policies this most populous nation enters the world market and relates, over the long haul, to an international economy that is "highly interdependent and fiercely competitive," that is "dominated and defined by a relatively small number of large firms," and where "priorities and directions of development in all parts of the globe get determined by the buying power of those who sit at the top of the heap."

No one is arguing that China should seal herself off. Her former isolation was, after all, not self-imposed. It was inflicted on her after 1949 by a hostile America intent on strangling the new revolutionary baby in its cradle. This American policy, not too resolutely supported by other powers, was only relaxed after it failed utterly, China refused to collapse, and America chose to cultivate China as a counterforce to a Soviet hegemony that both countries perceived as threatening.

At the same time no one should forget that to enter the world market at this stage in history on the basis of financial and commercial rules imposed by the world's dominant producers, financiers, and traders, is equivalent to "matching pearls with the dragon god of the sea." The multinational corporations, backed by powerful and experienced imperialist governments, hold most of the "pearls"—massive reserves of material, technical, financial, and cultural resources which they most certainly will use to penetrate and dominate any economy open to their intervention and manipulation. They are bound to win out in the end against any weak player who tries to go head-to-head with them. To preserve and extend their power they are busy bulldozing out the bumps on the "playing field" of world trade. That accomplished, they will "bar both rich and poor alike from sleeping under bridges,"

[4]Article by William Hinton, author, from *Monthly Review* 45:87–104 Jl/Ag '93. Copyright © 1993 by Monthly Review, Inc. Reprinted by permission of Monthly Review Foundation.

that is to say, from seeking any protection from market manipulations masquerading as forces of nature.

Yet it is common knowledge that:

All of the so-called developed countries achieved their development with heavy government regulation of foreign trade and in some cases of foreign investment. . . . Among the economically advanced countries, the latecomers have relied most heavily on government control of international commerce. . . . There are plenty of real world experiences that provide successful growth alternatives to free trade—and virtually no experiences demonstrating that free trade is the path to economic growth and development.

Professor Tang takes Deng's early rhetoric about self-reliance at face value and assures us that the current push to open wide is precisely to realize self-reliance and certainly not to subject China to foreign penetration and exploitation. But there are many disturbing trends in China's domestic economy and international economic relations which cast doubt, first, on the regime's commitment to any such policy, and, second, on it's ability to carry out such a policy should the commitment be made.

Without strong central direction, firm self-discipline, and a clear set of priorities that include self-reliance as the foundation stone of development, a China wheeling and dealing on the world stage can easily end up a passive victim of economic pressures beyond her power to avoid or control. Yet it is precisely in regard to direction, discipline, and priorities, including self-reliance, that China is currently demonstrating ambivalence and weakness. So far "opening wide" has meant "anything goes." Furthermore, at a price, it seems, there is nothing that is not for sale.

Any Third World nation striving for development with some measure of social justice—and what good is development without it?—must at least remain in firm control of certain key components of national life and foreign economic relations. The list, as I see it, not necessarily in order of importance, includes the following nine points.

1. National Borders

Almost all observers agree that China's Southern and Southeastern borders are now porous. Smuggling is big business from Hainan Island in the Southern China Sea to Xiamen on the Taiwan Strait. A large portion of the big spenders found in these regions are smugglers whose activities make a mockery of China's import controls, tariff regulations, and rhetoric of self-reliance.

Many of the smugglers deal in hard goods: from automobiles to refrigerators, from air conditioners to tape players, from personal computers to complete computerized work stations. The warehouses of Shenzen are stacked high with such goods all destined for a China market that suddenly has blossomed as one of the liveliest in the world.

One can assume that some smuggling profits are reinvested and contribute to the industrial boom in the delta counties of Southern Guangdong, but this does not lessen the threat posed by massive unplanned and illicit imports to the sound development of the economy of China.

2. Consumption Goods Imports

If illegal imports threaten sound development, so do the vast numbers of legally imported consumer commodities that compete with and pre-empt domestic production.

Since the age of capitalism began there is no record of any national economy developing without government protection for the home market. This applies to England at the time of the industrial revolution, to post-independence America, to the capitalist powers of the European continent, to Japan (both pre- and post-war) and to South Korea and Taiwan today. Yet China is openly handing over big chunks of her consumer market to foreign firms with world-wide sales networks—food and drink companies first of all: McDonalds, Kentucky Fried Chicken, Pizza Hut, Heinz Baby Food, Coca Cola, Pepsi Cola, Pabst Blue Ribbon; cosmetics, apparel, and footwear companies come next—Lux soap, Lever Brothers soap and detergents, Avon cosmetics (18,000 saleswomen already on hand), Elizabeth Arden (lotions at $100 a bottle), Pierre Cardin fashions, Giordano Clothes (five stores open, ten more planned), Nike shoes (Nike's retail outlet in Shanghai grossed $5,000 on opening day).

Famous names in hard goods such as cars, TVs, and computers do not lag behind. Chrysler, Volkswagen, Ford, Peugeot, and several Japanese companies are all assembling or will soon assemble cars on the mainland for the Chinese market, primarily from foreign manufactured kits. This is in addition to massive sales of complete cars. Toyota and Nissan currently lead the pack but the imports include a good number of Mercedes Benzes, Lincolns, Cadillacs, Audis, Lexuses, and similar expensive competitors. Japanese TVs and other electronic equipment from Sony, Hitachi, and other brand-name rivals flood the market along with computers, refrigerators, washing machines, cameras, and video recorders. The list goes on and on. American Standard already has a good share of the quality plumbing fixtures market—this in the country that invented porcelain!

Another huge sphere opening to consumer-oriented imports is culture. Opening wide has meant, not least of all, embracing Western capitalist culture, importing films, television programs, music, dance, and theater arts on a massive scale and at considerable expense. Once the world capital of pirated culture, China is now impelled to join the international network of rules, regulations, and conventions governing all aspects of intellectual property. Henceforth, China must pay not only for using Western technology, which is an inevitable expense linked to industrial modernization, but also for publishing Western books, showing Western films, staging Western plays, and playing Western music for which the market is apparently limitless.

Soon America will be pressing Beijing, as it already is pressing Taipei, over pirated software from American computer companies and copyright violations regarding compact discs, video games, video tapes, and laser discs, plus the illegal use of trademarks and drug patents. The bill is sure to be enormous.

I have no figures on how much wealth already flows out of China annually to sustain cultural and intellectual property imports, but it must loom large in the negative column of the balance of trade. Certainly the outflow is by no means balanced by any comparable flow of payments for Chinese intellectual property going Westward even though China has enjoyed some modest successes on this front. Wider, freer cultural exchange is positive and desirable. The issue here is not openness but domination through inundation. In their hurry to fill out air time at bargain rates, Chinese media moguls are importing reams of trash.

Foreign competition has already seriously harmed or even ruined a number of Chinese domestic consumer goods industries. The Ministry of Electronics and Heavy Industries originally planned to produce TV picture tubes, but on the eve of success, after years of effort and heavy expenditures, the State Council forced it to abandon the effort in favor of importing the tubes. The Ministry then dispersed the team of experts it had assembled, thus effectively turning over to foreign monopolists the future of TV and related industries in China, a country with by far the largest TV audience and market in the world.

Free milk powder and butterfat unloaded on China by the EEC [European Economic Community], ostensibly to help China build a dairy industry, has undermined the local milk market. Three quarters of the dairy products now sold in China are imported, forcing local dairies into bankruptcy. Municipal dairies in Beijing are selling off cows by the tens of thousands while small private milk producers are slaughtering dairy cows for meat.

Foreign competition has also hit dairy equipment manufacturing hard. Imports of bulk milk tanks and milking machines at cut-rate prices bid fair to crush the first successful sprouts of industry in this field before they can take root and grow.

True, China can play at the dumping game, as witness the current protest over the bicycle market in Europe (*Herald Tribune*, March 12, 1993) where Chinese bicycles have been selling at prices almost 35 percent below the prices charged for the same goods in China. However, considering the total range of products exchanged, when it comes to dumping China is not likely to win in the long run.

3. Capital Flight

In any underdeveloped country investment capital is most precious. Strict regulations against the export of capital, capital repatriation, and capital withdrawal are usually deemed essential if development is to proceed. But in the field of capital export, China has virtually lost control as private individuals and government units, both local and central, rush to invest abroad.

There are provincial capitalists from remote interior towns who periodically travel to Switzerland and deposit their profits in numbered bank accounts. There are provincial bureaus responsible for foreign trade that are buying up millions of dollars worth of land and assets in the United States. Their purpose: speculation. A central unit recently sent six persons to New York with tens of millions of dollars to be multiplied on the New York Stock Exchange. After suffering huge losses they invested their last six million in various savings accounts and now live high on the hog in New York City on interest alone. They do not intend to return to China.

Other government units and Chinese corporations—pseudo-, semi-, and genuinely autonomous—have bought forest land in Tennessee, a steel mill in Peru, farmland, apartments, and houses in California. Meanwhile China National Petroleum is negotiating to buy two oil fields in Canada, two oil wells in Peru, development rights in Venezuela, and options in Indonesia, India, Papua New Guinea, and Russia. The Shanghai Knitting Company (one of 260 Shanghai enterprises with overseas investments) has a mill in Mauritius with four branches, one of them in Australia. While there may be valid reasons for China to make certain investments abroad, the current scale and scope of capital flight is a questionable development strategy.

Countering the outflow is an unusual concealed tide of capital reverse flow—mainland money, laundered through Hongkong, for the sole purpose of reinvesting it in China as foreign and thus taking advantage of all the perks and privileges accorded joint venture funds of overseas origin.

Making due allowance for this aberrant counter-current, the total capital exported from China annually, both legally and illegally, must run into billions. And this from a country starved for the capital urgently needed for infrastructure, for the modernization of old plant, for the development of new industries, and for the development and diversification of agriculture; a country, furthermore, with its hand out to every international agency, every bilateral donor, and every non-governmental relief and development organization operating on the world scene.

4. Internal Investment

A large part of the surplus generated by the economy of any underdeveloped country ought to be invested in the reproduction of capital, in the expansion of the productive forces of society, including the infrastructure to facilitate and back up that expansion.

But it seems, from personal observation, that the emphasis in China in recent years has been more on consumption than production. The greatest single growth sector, both urban and rural, has been housing. In the main cities a huge drive to construct high-rise apartments, office buildings, and world-class hotels is ongoing. In the countryside an equally huge drive to construct peasant dwellings continues unabated. These dwellings are often two or three stories high, with the upper floors unoccupied. Plenty of cropland, walled-in and paved-over, provides courtyard elbow room. While housing is a vital necessity, the unplanned proliferation of housing should not be allowed to divert disproportionate amounts of cement, steel, bricks, and timber from other priority uses, nor should housing be allowed to cut so deeply into scarce cropland.

China's all-out building boom of the last decade-and-a-half appears to have warped the growth of the whole economy toward consumerism. Now conspicuous consumption of luxury goods, hard and soft, many of them imported, appears to have added a new twist to that warp. Expensive imports—cars, clothes, furniture, appliances, cosmetics, sound and video equipment, plus the tapes to activate them—are tying up and diverting money which could and should be invested in economic growth. Hard work, simple living, and saving to build up the country have given way to flash, dash, and extravagance unlimited.

It appears that most of the officials and virtually the entire educated elite have revolted against the restraints of country-building imposed on them by China's real position in the world. Dumping the erstwhile sober socialist response to underdevelopment, they have opted instead for a buying orgy targeted at such commodities and luxuries as the Indian bourgeoisie and other Third-World elites have long enjoyed in the midst of the mass squalor and deprivation that surround them. It's a response generated by a deep gut feeling. China's privileged strata sense that their homeland, with its vast size, huge population, and strong work ethic, can support, in world-class style, one hundred million or more entrepreneurs, coupon clippers, and a matching set of professional retainers. So why not go for it?

Given the power of the established economics China hopes to penetrate and challenge, the dream could well degenerate into a manipulated, boom-bust nightmare, but it seems to have seized hold of the imagination of everyone that matters. Anyone who doesn't buy in is looked upon with astonishment, pity, even ill-disguised contempt.

5. *"Comprador" Tendencies*

"Comprador" means buyer or agent in Portuguese. In Asia a comprador was:

the name given to the principal native servant employed in European establishments, and especially in houses of business, both as head of the staff of native employees and as intermediary between the house and its native customers. (*Oxford English Dictionary*)

The Chinese word is *maiban*, or purveyor. In modern times the concept has been greatly expanded to include certain aggregations of native capital linked to and serving foreign interests—comprador capital; also to holders of that capital—comprador bourgeoisie; and to national governments protecting the latter's interests and those of the foreigners standing behind them—comprador rulers.

What imperialist powers were always looking for in China was a comprador head of state strong enough to hold China but not strong enough to challenge their dominance. This, as it turned out, proved impossible. As Owen Lattimore pointed out, anyone strong enough to control China was strong enough to challenge imperialism. The candidates picked by imperialists—Yuan Shih-kai, Chiang Kai-shek, Wang Ching-wei, and the regional lords of the warlord era—could never bring the country or any major part of it under control for long.

Under Mao's leadership China stood up. The new people's state uprooted comprador economies and politics. But in the last decade new comprador tendencies have burgeoned. Impatience for world-class life styles is a powerful solvent of national will and national pride. Selling out to the dragon king of the sea pays off on a personal level and the current scene produces no shortage of candidates.

Most shocking are the number of leading revolutionaries' sons and daughters who have taken positions with the biggest American and European banks and multinational corporations and now represent them in China. The list reads like a "Who's Who" of new China. Some of them may, in spite of all temptation, still serve China's best interests, but the majority will serve the interests of those who hire them, and, unless one is naive enough to believe that there is no conflict of interest here, "comprador" is the word that describes them.

Other signs of a comprador spirit show up in the gradual relaxation of the terms for foreign investment, which, having started out reserving majority control for Chinese capital, now end up welcoming enterprises that are wholly foreign-owned on almost any terms almost anywhere they want to settle. The same goes for land use rights. China is insisting on the return of Hongkong after ninety-nine years of British rule, codified, at least for Kowloon, by a leasing agreement, but at the same time is leasing large chunks of Hainan Island and other economic zones to Japanese and other companies on terms that rival the Hongkong lease being closed out with such fanfare. Thus China re-creates certain facets of extra-territoriality without even so much as a blush of shame.

The terms imposed by the World Bank and the IMF [International Monetary Fund] for Third World loans—the privatization of production, wage cuts, reduced social services, drastically reduced imports except those needed to manufacture exports that can generate trade balances sufficient to pay back loans—these are colonial terms aimed at placing whole economies in dependency, at putting whole nations under comprador-type restraint.

Is China submitting to such pressure? There is evidence that suggests so. Take the "grain base" plan to consolidate land and mechanize production. World Bank opposition helped torpedo it because it required collective organization on the part of peasants (albeit of a new type) and consequently conflicted with the free-market ideology currently in ascendance. Never mind that the "grain base" concept is probably the best way for Chinese agriculture to climb into the modern world, it must be opposed as a socialist throwback. It has not been heard of since Deng went to Shenzhen in January, 1992.

One final point on the comprador question. The votes cast by China in the United Nations in recent years are redolent with the scent of comprador collaboration, especially the votes cast on the Gulf War, but also the votes on the Balkan crisis, Cambodia, and the Middle East. When the United States calls the tune, China, for the most part, will dance to it.

6. Trade Balances, Payment Balances, and Foreign Debts

In the 1950s and 1960s, the Japanese government protected the country's fledgling auto firms, first with a highly restrictive quota and then with prohibitively high tariffs. Foreign investment in Japan was virtually proscribed—it was allowed only insofar as it contributed to domestic industry. The Japanese also succeeded in protecting their computer industry. In the early 1970s, as the industry was developing, a foreign machine could be purchased only if a suitable Japanese model was not available.

South Korea and Taiwan followed similar strategies but China is reversing the priorities. China eagerly solicits foreign investment, relaxes erstwhile stiff conditions, and constantly sweetens the deals—sole ownership, full repatriation of profits, long-term leases on land, substantial tax concessions. The excuse is that foreign investment brings new technology to China and expands domestic production with Chinese materials and labor. For example, Colonel Sanders sells chicken raised in China on Chinese corn. Coca Cola sweetens its domestically-bottled product with

Chinese sugar, Jeep incorporates an increasing proportion of China-made parts, Lux purchases Chinese vegetable oils, etc.

Nevertheless, big fees are paid out for the use of big names that add little if anything to the utility of the product and surely have negative impact on the total balance of payments. In the year 1990 all the countries of the Third World (excluding the four Asian tigers and the big oil exporters) had a favorable balance of trade in commodities that amounted to $9 billion. But when repatriated profits, interest on loans and fees for services, licenses, etc. were figured in (total outlay: U.S. $50 billion), they had a net loss of $40 billion.

What the balance of payments figure is for China alone I do not know. I understand that many foreign companies are not repatriating profits currently but are reinvesting them. In the long run, however, if the welcome now being extended to foreign capital continues and full repatriation rights are honored the deficit could grow very large.

Tang is confident that on the question of balances and foreign debt China has everything under control. But on this front, as on others, there are danger signs. The year 1992 saw increases in both exports and imports but the imports went up much faster, cutting the favorable balance for the year to about U.S. $5 billion. Many analysts are predicting that in 1993 imports will surpass exports, creating a whole new situation at a time when ever-larger payments on foreign debt are due. It seems likely that the true balance may already be unfavorable, since the figures don't include the value of the goods smuggled in.

Foreign debt, already at $60 billion by 1990, is also growing at a fairly fast rate, up $10 billion from 1990 to 1991 and another $10 billion or more in 1992. On this question it is not so much the current size of the debt that is crucial but the trend. How long will the debt keep growing at such rates? Where will debt escalation end?

7. Culture

On the cultural front China has surrendered to the Western monopoly bourgeoisie all the way down the line. "Worship America Thought," against which the Communist Party struggled with marked success for so many years, has won the day. It is here, in the sphere of ideology, that the comprador warp of the current regime shows up most clearly. There is no longer any sign of struggle over world outlook, class consciousness, or even national integrity. Once the party accepted Deng's aphorism "It doesn't matter whether a cat is black or white as long as it can catch mice" and put "enrich yourselves" forward as the key slogan, a huge wave of naive and avaricious Babbitry flooded China, submerging everything in its path. Just as a large segment of officialdom and a large slice of the intelligentsia felt themselves affronted and frustrated by the frugality of socialist development and rushed to wallow in commodities and luxuries as soon as the bars were down, so they have longed for and now welcome with open arms Western bourgeois culture, including all its most Philistine and venal forms. They view as simple-minded and deserving of pity anyone who doesn't share their enthusiasm.

Free-market economics, rampant Friedmanism, dominates economic thinking. Soap operas, sitcoms, quiz programs, dancing girls, and fashion shows dominate primetime television along with, of course, a goodly dose of competitive sports. Cops-and-robbers crime films, featuring heroic, incorruptible law enforcement officers, and boy-meets-girl romances of upwardly mobile entrepreneurial types account for a goodly share of new films. Rock-and-roll, disco dancing, and karaoke sing-alongs dominate the music scene. Pornographic videos and erotic magazines pass from hand to eager hand, all the more in demand for being banned.

The neocolonial implications of such massive cultural inundation should alarm anyone concerned with the health and autonomy of China's values, mores, and national ethos. The minds of young successor generations are being warped, seduced, and possessed by the market-oriented mass culture of the monopoly bourgeoisie of America, Europe, and Japan.

8. Centrifugal Tendencies

Any country entering the world market must develop strong central leadership and maintain strong central control. Multinational corporations, backed up and subsidized by predatory imperialist states, have grown rich, large, and powerful enough to outspend, outmaneuver, outlast, and overwhelm political units as big as large American states and even much larger sovereign countries. Driven by the categorical imperative of capitalism—expand or die—these corporations constantly strive to carve out new spheres of influence, monopolize raw material resources, expand market share, and make less-developed lands safe for investment capital. A country the size of China, with a strong national government and a coherent development strategy can, if it maintains its integrity, withstand the onslaught of such states and corporations and find its own way forward on its own time schedule. But only if it is willing to carry on a protracted struggle for political, economic, and cultural autonomy, and only if it patiently pursues its goals and does not try for short cuts and quick fixes.

It is in respect to such matters that China is displaying troubling signs of weakness. As China's market economy expands her central authority weakens. Layer by layer, sphere by sphere, Beijing is losing control over her Southern and Southeastern coastal provinces, and over her borders, customs revenues, currencies in circulation, tax collections, investment strategies, land-use allocations, environmental protection standards, and even basic law and order. No one doubts there is a boom in progress. Some areas are becoming very prosperous. But the richer they grow the more independence they show and the less they listen to national ministries, party organs, or leaders in Beijing. This is a situation made to order for multinational penetration and manipulation. A united China may be big enough and strong enough to withstand the onslaught, preserve discipline, and pursue a self-reliant strategy, but provinces, regions, and municipalities taken one by one can be easily overwhelmed.

One big question is: how far will this centrifugal disintegration go? The question is especially acute since China is in the midst of a serious succession crisis. Without consensus on who will fill Deng's shoes a protracted struggle could well ensue after he is gone. China could break up. That has happened before. If it happens again the multinationals, fronting for various rival powers, would find it comparatively easy to carve out new spheres of influence, dividing the investment opportunities, the market, and the spoils between them—all in the name of a new "open door."

9. Corruption

Last but not least we come to the issue of corruption.

Corruption influences, and in the final analysis may determine, the outcome of the struggle to resolve all the other problems raised here.

Tang is long on the rhetoric of the Deng regime—rules regarding bank accounts to pay back foreign debt, rules regarding import substitution, rules regarding foreign exchange controls—but how seriously can any of it be taken, given the corruption that starts right at the top and spreads downward to every nook and cranny?

In China, when some particularly brazen scandal does surface, disrupting the harmony of ever more corrupt relationships, all sides unite to smooth things over, as they did two years ago when Hainan Island, exercising rights as a special economic zone, imported thousands of duty-free vans from Japan, then sold them at enormous profit throughout the mainland and beyond. Some of the vans even found a market in Soviet Kazakhstan. One zealous party secretary of a land-locked inland province impounded scores of these illegal imports pending some word from the central authorities as to how to proceed against the profiteers. He was called to Beijing, severely criticized, and summarily removed from his post. He had unwittingly interfered with business arrangements tied in to Rong Yiren, the mainland's foremost capitalist, head of CITIC (China International Trust and Investment Corporation) and now Vice-President of the People's Republic of China. Furthermore, this particular deal involved Deng Pufang (Deng Xiaoping's crippled son, head of the Foundation for the Disabled) who had parlayed charitable activities into one of China's largest private fortunes. The governor of Hainan got a slap on the wrist. Ron Yiren's minions found an outlet for the left-over vans, unloading them on a mandatory quota basis to central government units. Thus the scandal quietly disappeared from public view.

Today almost every purchase made through official channels, including purchases tied to international relief and development projects, is made at an inflated price that allows for a kickback to the official or officials negotiating the deal. Thus China is cheated at every turn, paying more than the market price for goods and services that are already overpriced on markets dominated by the most "wealthy and powerful individuals and firms and the governments that represent them."

A large percentage of existing joint ventures are fronts set up for speculative purposes, shelters rigged to free entrepreneurs from currency controls. They have nothing to do with production but have a whole lot to do with wheeling and dealing in money and commodities. They give foreigners an opening to wheel and deal in like manner.

As for import substitution programs effectively constricting the inflow of consumer goods and expanding China's export capacity, large-scale smuggling has made a mockery of them. Smuggling, in turn, can only reach such levels when coupled with endemic corruption. Border guards and customs officials look the other way, then share in the loot.

Under present circumstances, with corruption so deep and widespread, almost everyone has their price for selling out China's interests. At the same time the powers that be are willing to pay whatever it takes to open up avenues of penetration, market share, and financial control. Sad to say, often it doesn't take much. An expensive car will suffice for some, a generous kickback for others. A scholarship at a prestigious foreign university for the son or daughter of a high official will put the latter in debt to whoever can arrange the favor and smooth the way for return favors to come. Thus the rot spreads.

Conclusion

Given the depth and breadth of corruption in China today, the decadent moral atmosphere, the get-rich-quick fever, the scramble to sell influence for a price, the porosity of the borders, the burgeoning tide of imports, the flight of capital, the warped investment strategy, the comprador ideology, the tenuous trade balance, the cultural surrender, the centrifugal spin, who can possibly guarantee that on entering the world market China will be able to maintain autonomy, independence, economic initiative, and self-reliance in the main?

One is reminded of a cogent passage in Li Husheng's *Imperialism and Chinese Politics*. It is about an earlier "reformer" who had delusions of grandeur, the Ching dynasty viceroy, Li Hungzhang:

Regarding the final outcome of Li Hungzhang's days of glory the English diplomat, J. O. P. Bland, wrote the following: "Li's last triennial inspection of the coast naval defenses (1893) partook of the nature of triumphant progress. There was his life's work for all men to see and admire; his forts and schools, railways and dockyards, ships and guns, all bright with paint and polish. The guns boomed salutes, myriads of Dragon flags greeted his coming and going. . . . This was the heyday of the viceroy's fame; but already the clouds were gathering fast on the horizon that would obscure forever the sunshine of his prosperity. In the mind's eye, as one sees him returning from that highly successful exposition of his handiwork amidst the chorus of praise and thanksgiving, one cannot but wonder how far the old man was himself deceived, how far acquiescent in his magnificent framework of illusion. For all around him, on the decks of his ships, in the very office of his Yamen, were sleek rogues of his own appointing who were selling the safety of the state in their haste to put money in their pockets. . . "

As is well known, in the Sino-Japanese War that followed only three years later (1895), the modern army and navy Li Hung-zhang had built up with such painstaking effort completely disintegrated. The defeat postponed China's dream of independence and modernization until the middle of the twentieth century.

Will the full realization of that dream again be postponed?

AWAKENING DRAGON[5]

Since Napoleon, Westerners have been predicting that once the Chinese dragon awoke, the world would shake. Finally, after almost a century of false starts, China seems firmly embarked on a course of explosive economic growth and military assertiveness that will indeed reverberate throughout Asia and the world. The implications for the economic and security interests of the United States are enormous. China is the only major country in the world whose military now is expanding rapidly. And it is the first example of a Communist political system on its way to meeting the economic aspirations of its people.

China today is a dynamic, bubbling stew of a country in which the Tiananmen massacre of 1989 has been mostly forgotten. The people of China seem much more concerned about getting their share of the biggest economic take-off in world history. This year, China's only major disturbances have occurred when ordinary Chinese felt cheated out of a chance to buy shares in new, private companies, as did hundreds of thousands of would-be share-holders in Shenzhen in August. With a mixed bag of mercantilist and free-market economic policies, China has resumed its red-hot, 1980s' pace of 10-percent annual growth. Foreign and over-seas Chinese companies are rushing to invest ever-larger stakes in China's booming economy. Meanwhile, China's exports to world markets are soaring. The foundation for all this is a grand com-promise, fashioned by China's paramount leader Deng Xiaoping,

    [5]Article by Ross H. Munro, coordinator of the Asia Program, Foreign Policy Research Institute, Philadelphia. From *Policy Review* 62:10–16 Fall '92. Copyright © 1992 by *Policy Review*. Reprinted with permission.

and now evidently accepted by a broad cross-section of the Communist Party, that combines sweeping economic freedoms with rigid political controls. While such a combination has never worked in the long run elsewhere, Leninist capitalism could provide the formula for many years to come for the expansion of China's wealth and power.

Recently, Chinese military power has been growing rapidly in both relative and absolute terms. With the collapse of the Soviet Union and the prevailing pacifist mood in Japan, China faces no serious regional threat for the first time in centuries. Indeed, no other East Asian country alone could conceivably confront China today. Nevertheless, Beijing has increased military spending by more than 50 percent since 1989. Much of the new money is being spent to give China's armed forces the capability to fight and win major conflicts outside Chinese borders.

Sixty New Taiwans

All this affects the United States. The U.S. trade deficit with China, negligible in the late 1980s, was $13 billion last year; this year it's approaching $20 billion, second only to our deficit with Japan. The growth of the Chinese market is of course a spectacular opportunity for U.S. exporters. But American policy-makers don't have a clue about how to cope with the world's first economically successful Communist country. Our trade negotiators treat China as just another rapidly developing Asian tiger, whose trade surplus with the United States can be substantially reduced by resorting to traditional market-opening measures. Little thought is being devoted to the staggering implications that China's development holds for the United States, let alone for world trade: China could soon become an Asian economy as dynamic as Taiwan's, yet 60 times larger. President Bush's sale of F-16s to Taiwan is a first response to this emerging danger.

Nor is Washington coming to grips with the implications of China's growing military strength. The sudden spurt in China's relative and absolute military power inevitably affects security relations with our best friends in Asia. Japan, Taiwan, and capitalist Southeast Asia are all unnerved by China's new assertiveness in the region, now that Beijing no longer has the Soviet Union to worry about. All of them are anxiously looking to the United States to maintain its military presence in the region and, somehow, to protect them from China.

Our long-term problem in Asia is China—not stable, democratic, and still quasi-pacifist Japan. Despite all the speculation that Japan is destined to become our primary adversary in the world, our common interests and growing interdependence make that highly unlikely. This does not mean that China will replace the former Soviet Union as "the new enemy." But in both the economic and strategic spheres, China will pose a growing threat to our vital interests. Precious little binds the United States and China together now that our mutual concern about Soviet expansionism, the essential glue of our relationship in the 1970s and most of the 1980s, has dissolved. For the United States, the challenge will be to prevent an inevitably conflict-ridden relationship from deteriorating into full-blown hostility.

Sinologists Wrong

The militarily assertive, economically vigorous China that the United States faces today is not the one that U.S. China watchers had expected to emerge after Tiananmen. As recently as this spring, many of our best Sinologists were still insisting that the Communist regime had been so discredited internally by the Tiananmen massacre that it wouldn't long outlive Deng Xiaoping and the other gerontocrats who ordered tanks onto the square. This judgment was understandable given that, until recently, the Chinese leadership itself had been reeling, not only from the Tiananmen crisis, but even more so from the collapse of Communism in the Soviet bloc. Traumatized by the Soviet crackup, China's leaders had been asking what lessons were to be learned—or, in crasser terms, how they could avoid the fate of Soviet bloc leaders. For China's leaders, the Tiananmen affair demonstrated, first and foremost, the urgency of coming up with the right answers.

The one issue on which all of China's post-Tiananmen leaders agreed they couldn't compromise was the inviolability of one-party, Communist rule. They agreed that if they allowed a non-Communist opposition to exist, the Chinese Communist party would start down the same slippery slope to oblivion as their Soviet counterparts. This conviction fueled the post-Tiananmen purge of media, academic, and cultural circles whose independence had been growing during the 1980s.

In the economic sphere, China's Stalinists initially appeared to prevail with their argument that only a tightly controlled, centrally planned economy could guarantee continued Communist Party rule. In effect, the Stalinists agreed with Western observers who argue that totalitarian or authoritarian rule will inevitably be undermined by an economy with a large private or foreign market sector that resists state directives. The hard-liners in 1989 announced new controls that worsened the economic slowdown until well into 1990.

By 1991, however, it was clear that the Stalinists had failed to reimpose tight, central controls on most of China's economy. Local and provincial authorities, quietly determined to keep their economies growing, had never stopped encouraging local entrepreneurs and overseas Chinese investors from Hong Kong and Taiwan. Today, the private sector—including family, cooperative and foreign enterprises—accounts for about two-thirds of China's economic output. Even in the industrial sector, the traditional core of the Communist economy, state enterprises now account for only half of production. Nowhere is the dominance of the entrepreneurial sector more pronounced than in China's southern coastal regions. By 1991 in Guangdong Province an estimated three million workers were employed by more than 25,000 Hong Kong-owned and -operated enterprises.

Local Chinese officials haven't chosen market economics because of an ideological conversion. Their reasons are practical, even somewhat cynical. A growing local economy, particularly with the inflow of investment and the creation of new factory jobs, shores up their local political power. Economic growth also provides the authorities with many unofficial benefits: jobs for family members, secret shares in new enterprises, and cash payoffs to finance high living. Today, corruption is standard business practice in China. The pattern extends from municipal officials in rural southern China to cabinet ministers in Beijing. Even Communist-Party Politburo members have children who have climbed on the capitalist gravy train.

Leninist Politics, Capitalist Economics

Meanwhile, Deng and his supporters saw an economic element in the collapse of Communism in the Soviet Union and Eastern Europe. The Soviet-bloc leaders had invited their downfall not just by diluting the principle of one-party rule, but also by failing to provide their people with a decent and improving standard of living. The lesson here, Deng insisted, was that China must achieve economic growth at almost any cost.

This January, in what will probably prove to be his last hurrah, the 87-year-old Deng launched his campaign to make market economics official policy. In a carefully orchestrated tour of southern China's special economic zones—where Hong Kong-style capitalism is at its rawest and most successful—Deng extolled "borrowing freely from capitalism." Since then, his pronouncements in favor of market economics, foreign investment, and export-led growth have been endlessly recycled in the official media. A nationwide propaganda campaign insists that China can somehow remain socialist and yet have free markets, private business, stock exchanges, and even large income inequalities.

At the same time, Deng remained as hard-line as ever on the key issue of Leninism, the Communist Party's exclusive right to rule. Deng had crafted the grand compromise: Leninist capitalism. By mid-year, the Communist Party Politburo had adopted Deng's line, endorsing the goal of continuous, rapid growth and adherence to market economics for the next century. As even reputed leftists get in line, the consensus should easily prevail at the 14th Party Congress, scheduled for late this year, which will set policy guidelines for many years to come.

In short, China's Communists have concluded that the only way to preserve Communist rule and keep themselves in power is to junk Communist economics and convert to capitalism. In fact, the key document that came out of Deng's campaign made it clear that the main issue was the party elite's survival. "If we . . . do not develop the economy, and do not try to improve the people's livelihood, then there will only be the road to ruin."

China's new Leninist-capitalist consensus has convinced Hong Kong and Taiwan businessmen (who make the most prescient China watchers, since both their cultural antennae and their money are in play) that Communist economics is dead in China. Their optimism is largely responsible for soaring foreign investment in China in the first half of this year—$14.7 billion in new commitments, or more than 20 times what would-be capitalist India could garner. Investors are looking beyond the first stage of the Chinese boom, when they were interested largely in the cheap land and unskilled labor that south coastal China could offer. Now the boom is rippling northward and into the interior. On the horizon are massive investments in major industrial projects, such as a Taiwan-financed computer industry complex near Shanghai, and infrastructure development, such as a new transportation and distribution center in interior Wuhan, linked to Hong Kong by a new railroad and super highway.

Mercantilist Trade Policy

A central element of China's Leninist capitalism is a trade policy rooted in mercantilism, that ancient but still-fashionable practice of concertedly subsidizing exports and limiting imports. The Chinese authorities, for instance, are effectively subsidizing exporters' labor costs. Hong Kong businessmen operating in Guangdong boast that their total labor costs are only $30 a month, because officials have waived company obligations to cover such costs as pensions, health care, and other benefits. Small wonder that Guangdong's exports, most of them U.S.-bound, are running 35 percent ahead of last year.

On the import side, the Chinese government still can limit imports almost at will. It was official Chinese policy, for example, that was primarily responsible for transforming a modest U.S. trade surplus with China in the late 1980s into a large and growing deficit. This year, the U.S. trade deficit with China is projected to be almost $20 billion, 50 percent higher than last year.

Assuming that China's exports continue to soar, neither the United States nor the world economy will long be able to cope with Chinese mercantilism. In the 1950s and 1960s, the United States tolerated the mercantilism of its cold war allies Japan, South Korea and Taiwan, which kept their markets closed while pumping exports into the relatively open U.S. market. But today the United States has neither the strategic incentive nor the economic capacity to accept a huge trade deficit with a mercantilist and non-allied nation that is 60 times Taiwan's size.

Internal Contradictions

The domestic implications of Leninist capitalism for China are also immense. Rising income disparities between regions—one study indicates that per capita income in southern, coastal China is already 16 times that of the interior northwest—will get worse. So will class differences. Those becoming rich will usually be members of the Communist Party elite, their relatives and cronies, or entrepreneurs who pay off the Communists. In the short term, at least, it's unlikely that the disparities and the corruption will prompt a political struggle between the haves and the have-nots. More likely is a huge, public order problem, with millions of poor peasants' sons trekking coastward to seek their fortunes.

Already, even official estimates of China's population of unregistered workers and vagabonds range as high as 50 million. Since

Tiananmen, China's leaders have advertised their determination to suppress disturbances and demonstrations, whether they are economically or politically rooted. In the name of Leninist stability, they are pouring resources into the 600,000-strong People's Armed Police Force, which has the task of rapidly and ruthlessly quelling organized protests.

In the long term, these contradictions and problems will probably become intolerable to a growing middle class; then the Leninist-capitalist consensus will crumble. But this could take decades, particularly if the economy continues to grow rapidly. With economic growth, the political elite will probably have sufficient funds at its disposal to placate the military and to co-opt the potentially restive intelligentsia with well-paying jobs.

In the short run, China may soon witness a nasty leadership succession struggle, fueled by personal and factional antipathies. But it would be a mistake to equate elite turmoil for a change in political course. When the smoke clears, it is highly likely that the Leninist-capitalist consensus will still be in place, no matter who is in charge. Likewise, conflict between the Beijing regime and the provincial governments is bound to grow as capitalist development creates increasingly distinct economic interests. But such conflict, intense and tumultuous as it may be, won't inevitably undermine the Leninist-capitalist consensus prevailing nationwide, particularly with a Chinese military committed to maintaining China's unity.

The most far-fetched scenario is that China will become democratic in the near future. There is no organized democratic movement in China today. Even within the relatively small but important exile community, the commitment to democracy seems largely confined to a small community of liberal intellectuals. But talk with a Chinese graduate student who refused to return to China after Tiananmen, and you will usually find someone who wants little more than a reversion to the mid-1980s, when the Chinese educated class enjoyed status, a modicum of intellectual freedom, and a relatively decent standard of living. This was even true of most demonstrators at Tiananmen, who were calling for reform of the existing system, not a democratic upheaval.

New Drive for Military Power

Having hollowed out the leftist rationale for one-party rule, China's Communist elite is increasingly flirting with nationalist, expansionist, and anti-Western themes. These themes strike a resonant chord among many Chinese, who want their nation to be a military power that commands the world's respect. For them, expansionism would expunge the humiliation of the 19th and early 20th centuries, when Western nations and Japan carved China into spheres of influence. But China's new drive for military power may prove to be an even greater problem for the United States than its mercantilist trade policies.

For decades, Sinologists of all political stripes argued persuasively that Communist China, no matter how radical its domestic policies, was a status quo power on the international stage, dispatching troops beyond its borders rarely, reluctantly, and then only defensively. But in the wake of the Soviet Union's collapse, China is rapidly demonstrating in word and deed that it now views its East Asian neighborhood in expansionist terms. With its armed forces no longer tied down by a Soviet military threat to the north, China's military power relative to its neighbors has suddenly increased. Yet China has increased its officially acknowledged military spending by 52 percent since 1989. Some of that money is being spent on making the military better able to suppress domestic uprisings, particularly in border areas peopled by non-Han Chinese minorities. But much of the increase is committed to a military buildup aimed at giving China its first capability to project naval and air power well beyond its shores.

No group has been more enthusiastic about the recent, firesale prices at Russia's arms bazaar than Chinese generals. China is buying both advanced hardware and the modern technology needed to build it. It recently purchased 24 Su-27s, the most advanced warplanes China has ever deployed, and is reportedly negotiating for two additional squadrons. It is also negotiating the purchase of advanced missile guidance systems from the Soviets. China has also been modernizing its military-industrial complex by entering into joint ventures with foreign companies, including some in the United States, in order to acquire up-to-date technology in electronics and other fields. This spring, an increasingly assertive China conducted its largest ever nuclear test, breaking the informal international ban on large detonations. The armed forces are also proclaiming their growing offensive capabilities with well-publicized military exercises.

Simultaneously, China is adopting a strikingly assertive stance toward its neighbors. It is transforming Burma into a satellite, reestablishing its sphere of influence in Laos, and ensuring itself

veto power over events in Cambodia. While none of these developments directly affects vital U.S. interests, the same cannot be
said of China's actions elsewhere in East Asia. China claims U.S.-
ally Japan's Senkaku Islands south of Okinawa. It also reserves the
right to invade or, more realistically, to blockade Taiwan. The
United States is legally obligated under the Taiwan Relations Act
to defend Taiwan, an obligation that has deepened over the years
as Taiwan has become an increasingly open and democratic society.

Aggressiveness in South China Sea

Nowhere has China recently been more aggressive, or set off
more international alarm bells, than in the South China Sea. In
1974 and again in 1988, the Chinese military routed Vietnamese
forces from islands they occupied. Beijing claims almost the entire South China Sea as Chinese territory, including islands currently held by Vietnam, Malaysia, and the Philippines. Tensions
have grown since February, when the National People's Congress,
China's parliament, passed a law reaffirming those claims in un-
compromising language. In May, China humiliated Vietnam by
granting an offshore oil concession to Crestone Energy Corporation of Colorado for a tract hundreds of miles from the Chinese
mainland, but only 84 miles from Vietnam's coastal islands. Vietnam's subsequent protests counted for very little since, weak and
friendless, it could do nothing about China's de facto territory
grab. (Washington has taken a hands-off stance. If Vietnam were
rash enough to attack a Crestone platform, China would happily
seize the excuse to thrash Vietnamese forces.) In July, China further humiliated Vietnam by placing a marker on a partly sub-
merged reef claimed by Hanoi.

China is clearly rushing to establish an overwhelming military
presence in the South China Sea area that can't be challenged by
any combination of Southeast Asian military forces. It has built an
airbase on one island that could be used as a staging area for
military operations against the islands still occupied by rival
claimants. There are credible reports that a brigade-sized, rapid-
deployment force with amphibious capabilities—clearly meant
for operations in the South China Sea—has been deployed in
South China. China also has acquired inflight refueling technology so that it can keep its warplanes over the Sea's southernmost
islands for extended periods. And there are persistent reports

that indicate China will soon purchase an aircraft carrier recently built in Ukraine, primarily for use in the South China Sea area.

China's actions prompted a recent spate of articles suggesting that military conflict is imminent. Indeed, China will probably continue to harass, and possibly to attack, Vietnamese forces in the area. Otherwise, China will likely continue on its present course: establishing de facto control of the South China Sea while ignoring the Philippines' and Malaysia's largely symbolic military garrisons. Characteristically, Chinese authorities have combined their aggressive actions with conciliatory words, claiming they favor peaceful joint development of the Sea's islands and seabed resources. The Southeast Asians are wary, suspecting that China would manipulate any agreement on joint development to force them into acquiescing to its sovereignty claims.

Beijing's claim that the entire South China Sea is Chinese territory is legally and historically flimsy. But the realities of China's size and military power make Chinese domination of the South China Sea virtually certain. As the Sea becomes a Chinese lake and the nations of Southeast Asia adjust to a Chinese military presence that in some cases will be just offshore, the balance of power in Asia is going to shift. The United States can live with this historical shift if it succeeds in convincing China not to overplay its hand. Clearly there is little standing in the way of China's routing Vietnam from its island bases, even though this would cause alarm in the region. But if Chinese forces were to attack and wipe out a Malaysian or Philippine island garrison, for example, all of Southeast Asia would be compelled to treat China as a hostile power. Japan also would feel threatened and vulnerable, since Japan views Southeast Asia as a vital market and source of raw materials and has huge investments there. These U.S. friends wouldn't expect us to go to war to wrest back the islands, but they would ask us to forge closer military ties and to join them in diplomatic and economic actions aimed at punishing China. If we did any less, we would have little choice but to give up our military access agreements with countries like Singapore and limp back across the Pacific to Hawaii.

An even starker test of wills would occur if China ever demanded that foreign vessels obtain its permission before using what are now the Sea's international shipping lanes. This possibility isn't farfetched; China's new law explicitly asserts its right to use military force to prevent foreign ships from entering the South China Sea. Such an action would be an attack on the vital

interests of the United States, for which the South China Sea
serves as a link between the Pacific and Indian Oceans; on Japan,
for which the Sea is its petroleum lifeline; and certainly on Southeast Asia itself. In such a situation, the United States would have
to choose between defying China and retreating entirely from
Asia.

Washington at Sea

China today is deeply ambivalent about the important role
that the United States plays in Asia. Internal party documents
portray the United States as, on balance, a threat to Chinese
interests. Yet Chinese leaders consider the U.S. military presence
in Asia to be "useful" as long as we defend Japan, thereby discour-
aging it from full-fledged rearmament. Nevertheless, it is only the
U.S. military presence that prevents China from realizing its strategic goal of being the dominant and unchallenged military power throughout East Asia. China's current military buildup suggests that China is preparing for the day when the United States
will withdraw militarily from Asia. By then, China intends to be so
strong that Japan will be forced to come to terms with China's
domination of the entire region.

Clearly, this new Leninist, capitalist, mercantilist, expansionist
China now emerging poses a major challenge to the basic economic
and strategic interests of the United States. Inevitably, the U.S.–
China relationship is going to be difficult, complicated, and dangerous for the foreseeable future. Yet Congressional Democrats,
the Bush administration, and the media don't seem to have noticed. For Washington, the key issue in U.S.–China relations is how
best to promote Chinese democracy and human rights. Since Tiananmen, Congressional Democrats have in effect been trying to
punish China for its human rights violations by increasing tariffs
on Chinese imports. The Democrats don't put it that way, of
course. Specifically, what they're proposing is conditioning the
renewal of China's Most Favored Nation (MFN) trading status on
specific improvements in China's human rights policies that are
patently unacceptable to Beijing. (The Democrats' task is made
easier by widespread misunderstanding of what MFN means. Most
Favored Nation status indicates only that a country has a normal
trade relationship with the United States. Imports from a country
without MFN status are subject to prohibitively high tariffs.)

A characteristically reactive Bush administration has compounded the air of unreality by accepting the Democrats' terms of debate. Senior administration officials continue to insist (as recently as this summer) that the first priority of U.S. China policy is furthering human rights and democracy. The Bush administration defends MFN status for China with the argument that foreign trade and investment promote reform and liberalization in China. That argument is superficially correct but deeply flawed. The best that can be assumed is that U.S. trade and investment dollars will aid China's economic growth, which in turn will have some positive impact on Chinese politics in the future. It is hard to imagine a flimsier rationale for U.S. China policy.

Safeguarding U.S.–China Trade

The debate about how best to promote human rights and democracy in China is the latest manifestation of the old "We-can-change-China" myth that has warped U.S. thinking about China for a century. At best, any U.S. administration can bring about only a tiny, marginal improvement in Chinese political conditions. Conversely, U.S. China policy can have a huge impact for good or ill on America's economic and strategic interests. This will never be truer than in future years, when the United States comes to grips with China's growing economic and military power.

The most urgent issue is trade. The soaring U.S. trade deficit with China will not be significantly reduced by the market-opening measures that the Bush administration is currently pressuring China to accept. Even with those measures in place, the still powerful Communist state will use the many levers at its command to subsidize its exports and limit U.S. imports. With China indefinitely and instinctively continuing its mercantilist ways, not even the entire U.S. International Trade Administration could cope. The U.S. government should negotiate a U.S.–China trade agreement that would compel China to increase its imports from the United States or decrease its exports to the United States whenever the U.S. trade deficit with China approached a target zone. Few immediate prospects for the American economy are more appealing than growing and balanced two-way trade with China. Americans as disparate as wheat farmers and aircraft builders already rely on the booming China market for their livelihoods. Meanwhile, low- and middle-income Americans increasingly depend on inexpensive clothing, footwear and household goods imported from China.

To safeguard the potential of U.S.–China trade, the administration that takes office next January must act quickly. Already, the U.S. garment industry is donning human rights clothing to call for new trade barriers against Chinese imports. Unless measures are taken to reduce the ballooning U.S. trade deficit with China, an alliance of protectionists and human-rights advocates will seize control of U.S. trade policy toward China. The U.S.–China trade war that they would inevitably provoke would have only one set of winners—our trade competitors, primarily Japan and Europe, who would seize the opportunity to increase their exports to China at our expense.

Human Rights Challenge

Both the administration and the Congress must break from the post-Tiananmen era and stop treating trade primarily as a lever to promote human rights and democracy. Only after that is accomplished can the United States realistically fulfill its unique obligation to promote democracy and human rights in China without jeopardizing American interests. U.S. officials can and should continue to emphasize the need for political liberalization in China, without linking that stance to the threat of sanctions. We should continue to intervene on behalf of jailed and persecuted dissidents and, of course, maintain our import ban on products made by prisoners. We should step up exchanges and visits of all kinds in both directions, since they are subtly but profoundly subversive. Washington's information offensive, from the State Department's annual human rights report to the Voice of America's immensely popular broadcasts to China, should be strengthened.

At the same time, it must be recognized that much of the struggle for human rights and democracy is best waged outside government. Human rights organizations as well as private media must continue to expose and embarrass China's persecution of political dissidents. Religious organizations should continue their quiet, good, and subversive work. Washington should make better use of our special relationship with democratic and capitalist Taiwan. U.S. officials should remind officials of the Republic of China that they have a unique responsibility for promoting greater political and economic freedom on the mainland. Taiwan should have a plan for pumping not just its exports and investment dollars into the mainland, but information as well. Taiwan, not

America, has the unique resources to run successfully the proposed new radio service to the mainland.

Long-Term Danger: Chinese Expansionism

Ultimately, the biggest problem in U.S.–China relations will be neither human rights nor bilateral trade. It will be the fundamental conflict between the security interests of the two nations. Here we can learn little from our long struggle with Soviet imperialism. In sharp contrast to the Soviets, the Chinese have never viewed conflict with the United States as global, zero-sum, or primarily ideological. It will be basically an old-fashioned, bilateral contest over power and influence, focused on the Asian region.

While an expansionist China tries to assert itself as East Asia's dominant military power, Japan, Taiwan, and capitalist Southeast Asia will try to strengthen existing military ties with their old friend, the United States, as a balancer against China. India, too, might look to the United States as a balancer against the rival Asian colossus. Such a trend would mesh, although imperfectly, with the fundamental and long-term U.S. interest in an Asia not dominated by a single power. (Where a united Korea would stand is uncertain: Korea's deep-seated antipathy toward Japan might cause it to draw closer to China.)

But the United States must navigate this new Asia with great caution. We must do everything possible to avoid stepping across the line that separates the role of the balanced from that of the leader of a hostile, anti-China alliance. We must also avoid applying the containment model to China. It would be tragic if the United States found itself compelled to maintain a huge naval and air presence in the western Pacific specifically aimed at restraining China. Nor should we ever be drawn into a fight over the rocky atolls and coral reefs of the South China Sea. Our vital interests will not be threatened if China consolidates its hegemony over Burma, Laos, or even Vietnam. Up to a point, it is in our interest—and Southeast Asia's—to accommodate China's growing economic and military power.

In reassessing the American relationship with an awakening China, we can learn something from the Chinese leaders in Beijing. They view the United States as a threat, but they never forget that it is in China's national interest to continue working with us on several levels. The United States could do worse than adopt this approach toward China.

II. DOMESTIC POLICIES

EDITOR'S INTRODUCTION

Ralph Waldo Emerson once referred to China as a "booby nation" that did not match the greatness of other civilizations. "All she can say at the convocation of nations must be, 'I made the tea,'" Emerson condescendingly declared. The statement was as inaccurate in the 19th century as it is today.

China is an awakened giant. The most populous nation in the world has a Gross National Product increasing at a startling 13 percent per year. Nevertheless, its staggering population and economic growth rate place a huge strain on the environment. This section discusses China's demography and economy and also their environmental consequences. In the first article, reprinted from *Current History*, University of Manitoba geography professor Vaclav Smil asks, "How Rich Is China?"

"Large Is Not Beautiful" is the subtitle of the second article, by University of Minnesota geography professor Mei-Ling Hsu. She surveys the size of the population throughout China's history and concludes that it is important to curb population growth to improve the quality of life. "China's Environment: Issues and Implications," by Rutgers University professor Baruch Boxer, is a detailed analysis of economic and demographic trends and their impact upon China's environment and resources. In the final article, Miami University professor Stanley Toops analyzes what repercussions the June 4, 1989 massacre at Tiananmen Square has had on tourism, an important mainstay of the economy.

HOW RICH IS CHINA?[1]

The obviously important question of how rich China is has no easy answers. Although in many ways still a poor country, China is already an international economic power. But Western figures on it have misled more than they have informed, keeping alive an outdated view of the world.

The trail of misleading numbers begins with paramount leader Deng Xiaoping's economic revolution of the late 1970s, which set as its goals a quadrupling of the economy and China's rapid integration into the world market. When the State Statistical Bureau prepared the first account of Chinese gross national product in 1979, it put the GNP for the previous year at 358.81 billion renminbi, or Rmb 375 per capita. [Author's Note: GNP is the sum of gross domestic product (total value of a country's yearly output of goods and services) and income from abroad minus the income of nonresidents living in the country.] During the subsequent decade of rapid expansion, per capita GNP, according to the Chinese figures, rose more than fourfold, or a still very impressive 230 percent gain when adjusted for inflation.

But most foreigners do not consult State Statistical Bureau publications; they get their information on the Chinese economy from international data books. Of this group, the most widely distributed and quoted annual is the World Bank's *World Development Report,* which gave China's per capita GNP for 1978 as $230, and listed it at $310 in 1985 and $370 in 1990. This amounts to a yearly increase of less than 2 percent—and would actually mean a 10 percent decline in terms of constant 1978 dollars.

Even an unobservant visitor who had traveled in China in both periods would find nonsensical the notion that the country in the early 1990s was slightly poorer than in the late 1970s. And a connoisseur of international statistics would point out that the World Bank figure of $370 per capita GNP put China right between the 1990 per capita figures for Haiti and Benin. This is strange company for a country that provides an average daily food supply for its citizens close to the Japanese mean, and whose

[1]Article by Vaclav Smil, professor of geography, University of Manitoba. *Current History* 92:265–269 S '93. Copyright © Current History, Inc., 1993. Reprinted with permission.

total annual foreign trade turnover amounts to well over $100 billion.

A Blind Conversion Game

The reason for all these ludicrous dollar-denominated figures for China is simple: falling exchange rates.

In 1978 the official rate stood at 1.42 renminbi to the United States dollar; by 1985 it had weakened to around 3:1, and by 1990 the currency was devalued to 4.79 to the dollar. As the dollar is almost invariably used as the common denominator in international comparisons of GNP, the Chinese expansion of the 1980s disappears, and China ends up ranking behind Haiti.

The blind conversion into dollars also makes a mockery of Deng's goal of quadrupling the economy in 20 years. When the Chinese government was formulating long-term economic strategy at the end of the 1970s, it simply took the newly estimated per capita GNP for 1979 and divided it by the current official exchange rate to come up with a figure of just over $250 per capita. Quadrupling this would elevate China to the magic level of $1,000 per capita—but in 1990, halfway through the process, official GNP stood at less than $300 per capita (1980 dollars).

China has not been alone in this accounting predicament. The gross national products of nearly all poor, industrializing countries are substantially undervalued by conversion to dollars using official exchange rates. What is needed is some systematic adjustment of national accounts based on purchasing power parity (PPP), which measures the value of a country's GDP based on the domestic purchasing power of the country's own currency. This fundamental correction opens the way for meaningful comparisons between countries—one that, after several years of internal debate, the IMF in its 1993 *World Economic Outlook* embraced. Using purchasing power parity as the basis for its calculations, the IMF rankings catapulted China from tenth to third place among the world's economies; the World Bank has developed its own PPP-adjusted figures, but continues to measure economies by using exchange rate conversions.

A Better Approach

University of Pennsylvania economists Robert Summers and Allen Heston were the first, in 1984, to publish PPP-adjusted estimates for the per capita gross domestic product of countries. Expressed in constant 1975 dollars, their figures for China showed a rise from $300 in 1950 to $1,135 in 1980. An update in constant 1980 dollars put real per capita GDP at $1,619 in 1980 and $2,444 in 1985, and the team's most recent tabulations gave the figure for 1988 at $2,308. Thus China's closest economic "neighbor" in Asia is Thailand (at $2,879), while Haiti's per capita GDP according to this method is only $877.

If these adjustments come much closer to the actual wealth of China, where do they leave Deng's target? If China's real 1980 GDP was about $1,600 per capita (more than five times the exchange rate–biased level), can one reasonably expect a quadrupling by the year 2000—assuming a population of at least 1.25 billion—to $5,100. This would be an impossible goal, putting China on a par with the Ireland of 1985, and making it richer than the South Korea, Portugal, or Greece of 1990.

While exchange rate conversions considerably undervalue Chinese economic output, Summers and Heston's adjustments do just the opposite. Strong evidence of both biases can be demonstrated by calculating the average energy intensities of the world's largest economies. This is done by dividing total annual primary energy requirements by GDP. [*Author's note:* Energy intensity is an important marker of national economic performance. For details, see Vaclav Smil, *General Energetics* (New York: Wiley, 1991).] When using the World Bank's GDP calculation, China's 1990 energy intensity would be around 1,600 kilograms of oil equivalent (kgoe) per $1,000. In contrast Summers and Heston's adjustments would result, assuming a rounded GDP value of at least $2,500 per capita for 1990, in an energy intensity of less than 250 kgoe per $1,000. Both results are clearly wrong. In the first case China's energy intensity would be nearly 2.7 times higher than India's, which is roughly 600 kgoe per $1,000; in the other case it would be actually slightly better than Japanese performance!

Extensive conservation and modernization campaigns boosted the performance of Chinese industry during the 1980s, as did the massive shift toward light manufactures and export-oriented growth that made for one of the most rapidly expanding economies of the decade. In spite of this, China's industries, transportation system, and households still remain relatively inefficient users of energy—but not nearly three times worse than their Indian counterparts. For example, an International Energy Agency study shows that in 1985 China used about 1,360 tons of kgoe for every ton of crude steel produced, compared to about 880 kgoe per ton in India. This is a difference of about 50 percent, and given the notorious inefficiency of China's ferrous metallurgy, it is unlikely such a gap would be usual in other industrial sectors.

Conversely, it is ridiculous even to suggest that the still too rigidly controlled Chinese economy, operating with unrealistically low fuel and electricity prices and with much outdated equipment, could approach the Japanese performance in this area. It must be expected that China will lag behind—although the numbers indicate that the country's real energy intensity is not so grossly inferior. But in any case, if China were using the essential energy inputs into its economy with an efficiency comparable to that seen in Japan, and significantly higher than that in France or Germany, there would be no need for fundamental economic reforms! Clearly neither old-style exchange rate conversions nor the newer PPP-adjusted estimates come close to the elusive reality. The challenge is to reduce the broad range of GDP values produced by the two methods.

The Hamburger Standard

The easiest shortcut is the simplest of all PPP adjustments: the surprisingly effective hamburger standard pioneered by *The Economist* in 1986. Dividing the price of a Big Mac in the local currency by the price in the United States has consistently indicated an overvaluation of the deutsche mark or yen that is surprisingly close to elaborate PPP calculations. China last year saw the opening of its first McDonald's outlet, peddling Big Macs for Rmb 6.30 apiece. With the average price in the United States at $2.19, the implied PPP value was Rmb 2.88 to the dollar, compared with the official exchange rate of 5.44. The hamburger standard thus suggests China's 1992 real dollar-denominated GDP is 1.89 times higher than the exchange rate-converted value, or close to $800.

I believe the real purchasing power parity of the Chinese currency is higher still. This conviction is borne out if one assembles a minibasket of three essential foodstuffs—rice, pork, and cooking oil—and compares the average price in the United States and China for the amount of each item consumed annually by the average city dweller. For 1988 such a comparison implies a purchasing power parity of 0.81 renminbi to the dollar. A 20 percent markup is made to reflect the higher quality of American food.

(In this basket the difference could be minimal for rice, substantial for cooking oil, and enormous for pork—indeed, a typical piece of Chinese pork has no counterpart even among the inferior cuts in American stores. Similar differences often exist for fruits and vegetables.) This leaves the purchasing power of the renminbi inside China about equal to that of the dollar in the United States: one renminbi bought roughly as much food in Shanghai as one dollar did in Boston.

Consequently in 1988 the purchasing power parity of the renminbi was about 3.7 times greater than the official exchange rate with the dollar. This adjustment would put China's real 1988 GNP at $1,300 or, in constant 1980 dollars, at almost exactly $1,000. Encouragingly, this adjustment produces a much more credible energy intensity ratio than do either the World Bank's or Summers and Heston's values: the overall energy intensity of the Chinese economy works out as comparable to that in Poland or Russia, and about double the Japanese level. The $1,300 per capita figure also receives noteworthy confirmation by a Rand Corporation estimate based on a CIA study of purchasing power parities, which produces a per capita GNP of $1,200 for 1988 [*Author's note:* Charles Wolf et al., *Long-term Economic and Military Trends, 1950–2010* (Santa Monica, Calif.: Rand Corporation, 1989). This assessment also contained provocative predictions that China's aggregate real GNP will almost equal the former Soviet economic product by the end of the century, and that it will surpass it by some 20 percent a decade later, when it will rival even the Japanese total. An unidentified high-ranking Chinese official saw these estimates as "a friendly exaggeration" of China's economic strength; see "Bridging the Economic Gap," *Beijing Review*, vol. 32, no. 5 (1989).] And most important, applying plausible GDP growth rates to this adjusted base does not generate absurd future totals. Continuation of the long-term inflation-adjusted growth of 4.7 percent would raise per capita GDP to $1,600 in the year 2000, and a 6 percent rate would up it to $2,000 (in 1980 dollars). The second figure is the IMF's calculation published in the fund's 1993 *World Economic Outlook;* the IMF developed this estimate precisely in order to correct the unrealistically high published PPP values.

Living Well, and For How Long?

Although clearly giving a more realistic picture of China's wealth, these adjustments do not measure quality of life under the new affluence. Modernization's achievements cannot be subsumed under a single aggregate measure; an evaluation should encompass a broad range of quality-of-life variables, from food availability, health, and education to material possessions and housing.

Data on average per capita supplies of food energy, protein, dietary fats, and the principal minerals and vitamins in countries worldwide are readily available in United Nations Food and Agriculture Organization yearbooks. These values, and especially the means of per capita food energy and protein supply, are undoubtedly the most frequently reprinted and quoted indicators of national food availability, and the global coverage allows for revealing international comparisons. China's current standing in these lists, especially considering the combination of the country's physical limitations (less than one-fifteenth of the world's arable land) and population burden (more than one-fifth of all people), is definitely enviable.

With more than 2,600 kilocalories (kcal) of food energy available daily to its average citizen, China was just 8 percent behind the Japanese rate, well ahead of India (2,200 kcal per day), and above the Asian mean of just shy of 2,500 kcal per day; besides Japan, only Taiwan, Mongolia, and the Koreas enjoy a better food supply in East Asia. But these impressive quantitative achievements in China have been accompanied by only limited qualitative improvement, and by the persistence of a huge gap between average rural and urban consumption. Although the per capita availability of meat and eggs has more than doubled since the late 1970s, plant foods still provide all but about 5 percent of food energy. Moreover, by 1990 average yearly consumption in the countryside of the three principal animal foods (about 11 kilograms of pork and 2 kilograms of poultry, and less than 2.5 kilograms of eggs) remained far below the city means (18.5, 3.5, and 8 kilograms, respectively).

In China's poorest provinces the basic challenge of providing minimum rations is as acute as ever. The southwest and northwest must contend with a below-average supply of grain. Drought has been always a major factor limiting production in the arid northwest, but during the 1980s chronic grain shortages were also recurrently aggravated by drought in normally wet Guangxi province. During the spring and summer of 1989, when some 16 million people depended on state emergency relief, the region's grain deficit was close to the shortfall during the great famine of

1959–1961. And given the inadequate transportation between provinces, serious drought can still cause large-scale shortages of grain even in areas of normally adequate supply. For example, during the fall of 1989 10 million people in Shandong were short of grain.

There are no reliable figures for the number of chronically undernourished people in China. In 1984, a year of record harvest, Deng Xiaoping spoke in *Beijing Review* of "tens of millions of peasants in the countryside who do not yet have enough food." Liu Bang, in *Liaowang,* put the number at 11 percent of the rural population, or some 90 million people—equivalent to the entire population of Mexico. [*Author's note:* Deng Xiaoping, "Current Policies Will Continue," *Beijing Review,* vol. 28, no. 4, (1985), p. 5; Liu Bang, "Speaking of the Good Situation in Rural Areas," *Liaowang,* vol. 5 (1984), p. 6.] But given the dominance of staple grains in the Chinese diet, it is possible to come up with an approximate estimate for undernourished population from the mean grain production in each of the provinces.

In 1990, 230 million people lived in nine provinces where average grain harvests per capita were more than 20 percent below the national mean. The average daily food supply per person in these provinces would be around 2,200 kcal—thus, some 110 to 120 million people would be subsisting on less than this minimum caloric requirement. The limited food transfers between provinces and higher local reliance on aquatic or dairy products could reduce this number to about 100 million. These people do not necessarily starve, but their food intake does not provide for proper growth and demanding rural work. Simply put, they fall below the supply level guaranteeing enough food for a healthy and vigorous life.

In spite of persistent nutrition problems in parts of the interior, China has done very well in extending average life expectancy. The figure rose from just 40 years in the early 1950s to about 65 years by the late 1970s, with four more years added during the 1980s. A Chinese male born today can expect to live about 69 years, and a female about 71. This makes for some surprising comparisons. The life expectancy for males is more than a decade above the level in India, two to five years higher than in Argentina and Mexico, about three years ahead of the mean for the former Soviet Union, and just a year or two behind such Western nations as Austria or Ireland; although nearly fifteen years above India's level, the survival rates for Chinese females are relatively less impressive, equaling those in Mexico or Malaysia, and between three and five years behind the lower end of means in Europe.

These achievements would not be possible without very low infant and child mortality. Chinese rates during the late 1980s—just over 30 and in the mid-40s, respectively, per 1,000 live births—were only about one-third Indian levels, and substantially lower than those in Brazil or Mexico. China thus belongs to a small group of countries where life expectancy is much higher and infant and child mortality much lower than would be expected from the exchange rate–converted gross domestic product—and this disparity is yet another strong proof that actual GDP is considerably higher.

In contrast, China does not come off exceptionally well in international comparisons of education: its record is only average among other populous nations in primary education, and is decidedly inferior in postsecondary studies. The situation is best at the primary level: all but a few percent of children between the ages of 6 and 14 attend school. But many grade school pupils drop out in order to work. In some rural areas one-tenth or even one-fifth of all laborers are school-age children, with the percentage of girls disproportionately high.

The Chinese share of the world's illiterate adult population (over 15 years old) is not as large as Pakistan's or India's, but the rate of 20 percent remains unacceptably high, with the official total at 220 million people as of late 1988. [*Author's note:* Literacy rates are not easily comparable. In China literate workers should recognize at least 2,000 characters, peasants about 1,500; people reading fewer than 500 are considered illiterate.] Peasants account for 95 percent and women for 70 percent of this. The secondary school enrollment ratio in the late 1980s of just over 40 percent was unexceptional among populous poor countries, but the postsecondary share of just 1.7 percent was lower than in any large nation except Bangladesh.

The enormous shortage of university-educated people in China is perhaps the most persistent legacy of anti-intellectual Maoism, a price to be paid for decades and a loss that will not be remedied in a single generation. Naturally this weakness carries over into the availability of scientific and engineering manpower: in the late 1980s there were only 1,000 such experts per million people in China, compared to more than 3,000 in India and 10,000 in Brazil.

The "Four Big Items" and Other Consumer Dreams

Some measures of material affluence commonly employed in international comparisons of living standards make little sense in the Chinese (or Indian, or Nigerian) setting. To insist that car ownership rates chronicle a nation's advance toward modernity is untenable in Asia; indeed, a sound argument can be made that the opposite is true (based largely on the enormous negative environmental impact) even in the case of much less densely populated Western nations. But whether for good or ill, the Chinese have been both heavy importers of Japanese cars and resolute developers of a domestic car industry.

The number of telephones per 1,000 people, another popular measure of technical progress, is more acceptable. Environmental negatives are minor, while economic and social benefits are obvious. China's 10 phones per 1,000 people in 1990 was equivalent to the Pakistani average, marginally higher than the figure in India or Indonesia, and less than one-tenth typical Latin American rates. A tenfold expansion would seem to be the minimum required for good basic management and better personal communication.

Similar multipliers would apply to the ownership of washing machines (fewer than 10 per 100 Chinese in 1990) and refrigerators (a mere 3 per 100); rates for both in Japan during the 1980s were about 40 per 100 people. Purchases of television sets rose rapidly in China during the 1980s, and an ownership rate of 16 per 100 in 1990 compared to one of more than 60 per 100 in Japan. Indeed, color television sets became one of the principals badges of affluence during the 1980s, with fridges, washers, and tape recorders right up there.

The rapid advance of Chinese consumer aspirations can be seen from the changing list of most desirable wedding gifts. During the 1960s there were the "three rounds"—wristwatches, bicycles, and sewing machines. In the 1980s the "four big items" were color televisions, double-door refrigerators, twin-tub washing machines, and double-deck tape recorders, and supplementing these with the "three golds"—gold rings, bracelets, and necklaces—was often de rigueur.

But while tens of millions of Chinese are undoubtedly pleased at the variety of new household gadgets they have been able to afford since their purchasing power began rising in the early 1980s, they would be even more pleased if their food bills went down. And no material advance would be more important for the country's modernization than a substantial improvement in average housing conditions.

Although rationed staple grains are still heavily subsidized in China (rice costs nearly five times more on the free market), expenditures for food averaged nearly 55 percent of typical rural, and just over 50 percent of urban, disposable income in the late 1980s. This is a burden shared by the inhabitants of other poor, populous Asian nations (the figure in India is also 55 percent). In better-off poor countries people spend less than 40 percent of their disposable income on food, while in the most highly developed nations outlays range between 13 percent (United States) and 21 percent (Japan). In reality, the gap is even wider than indicated by these figures; smaller slices of income in rich countries buy more food containing higher amounts of nutrients in a greater variety of safer foodstuffs.

While the near future holds little hope for significantly lower food prices, the recent past has seen great improvement in housing. Rural reforms of the 1980s, and especially the incipient affluence in the suburban countryside of richer coastal provinces, led to a surge in new, and better, house construction in villages. Belatedly increased investment in urban apartment building brought some substantial gains in most major cities.

General conditions, however, remain unsatisfactory. The first representative survey of urban housing in China, carried out by the State Statistical Bureau in 1985 and 1986, found that average living space amounted to a mere 6.1 cubic meters per capita, with smaller cities (less than 200,000 people) averaging 6.65 and the largest ones (over 1 million) only 5.86 square meters per person. One-quarter of all urban inhabitants lived in less than 4 square meters—little more than a single bed with an equally narrow strip alongside. Merely bringing China's urban housing up to the standard of notoriously cramped Japanese homes would require a roughly 70 percent increase in average living space. By 1990 the average for China's 424 largest cities had risen marginally, and the goal for the year 2000 is to raise the mean to just over 8 square meters per person.

Villagers had more living space than their city cousins even before the reforms, and since the late 1970s their gains have been relatively large. Before 1978 no more than 100 million square meters of new housing was built in China's countryside each year, but the total for 1979–1988 rose to 6.8 billion square meters (including a record 1 billion square meters in 1986), and the quality of the buildings also improved substantially. Between 1980 and 1988 average rural living space rose from 9.4 to nearly 17 square meters per capita, ranging from just 9 square meters in Tibet to up to 30 square meters on Shanghai's outskirts. But the general quality of rural housing is still quite poor: late last decade a variety of adobe-and-thatch structures were still dominant, with only about 9 percent of all existing houses built of brick and wood (even in Shanghai's periurban area this share was no higher than 30 percent). Just over half of all rural houses had electricity, and less than one-seventh had running water.

Any realistic review of China's recent quest for greater personal wealth would be incomplete without noting the persistence of extensive rural poverty—and the growing income disparities since 1984. The 1980s saw the black marketeers of Hainan Island reaping fabulous profits by importing nearly 100,000 Japanese cars and 3 million television sets and reselling them to buyers from inland provinces. It saw suburban farm families in Jiangsu and Zhejiang get rich from a combination of mushroom growing, poultry raising, and local manufactures. But these are the peasants and others best able to take advantage of Deng's revolution, which gave them the power to make money. That power is easier to exercise in suburban Nanjing or in the Zhujiang River Delta than in the scrubby hills of Guizhou or the eroded, arid Loess Plateau. Millions of rural households in Guizhou, Gansu, and Shanxi provinces could not extricate themselves from dire poverty. Their incomes rose, but far from enough to secure them a better standard of living; they were left even further behind newly rich areas.

While the coefficient of variation expressing the gap between rich and poor provinces narrowed from 35 percent in 1978 to 26 percent by 1983, it rose to 37 percent in 1988. Taking rural per capita income of less than 200 renminbi in 1987 as an indicator of abject poverty, no fewer than 8.3 percent of peasant households, or more than 60 million people, were below that line, and it is unlikely the total dipped below 50 million by 1990. For these people a well-padded coat, a well-heated room, or a well-built chair are still beyond reach. Lifting these families—a population equivalent to a large European nation—at least to a level of bearable subsistence will not be accomplished easily.

The question "How rich is China?" thus raises the question: "Which China?" The one of burgeoning special manufacturing zones, property speculation, and ties to the global market, or that of remote interior counties where the isolation and degraded land, air, and water offer little hope for any appreciable material improvement in people's lives?

POPULATION OF CHINA: LARGE IS NOT BEAUTIFUL[2]

Population Size and Distribution

The People's Republic of China (PRC) is the most populous country in the world, a "distinction" it shared with the South Asian countries and the Roman Empire at the beginning of the Christian Era. Since 1200 China has held the "distinction" alone. In the year 2 A.D., the Chinese population was around 60 million; between 2 A.D. and the 17th century, the population fluctuated around this figure as it followed the rise and fall of successive dynasties. It briefly passed the 100 million mark three times: in the early years of the 12th and 13th centuries, and once more around 1570. The population escalated during the 18th century, the strongest and agriculturally richest period of the Qing Dynasty, reaching 300 million by the century's end. Before 1842, the year of the Opium War with the British, the figure topped the 400 million mark.

The first PRC census in 1953 reported a population of 582.6 million; in the 1990 census, the figure had risen to 1,133.6 million. The increase alone over this 37-year period equals twice the current total populations of Canada and the United States!

Such a large and ever-growing population has placed a heavy burden on China's economy. For example, between 1948–80, the PRC spent 30 percent of its total gross national income merely to raise the children born during the period. Meanwhile, the amount of land farmed per person dropped from 0.44 to 0.25 acre. The importance of this drop must be considered in relation to the facts that a large number of Chinese are farmers and the

[2]Article by Mei-Ling Hsu, professor of geography, University of Minnesota, Minneapolis. From Focus 42:13–16, Spring '92. Copyright © 1992 by the American Geographical Society. Reprinted with permission.

amount of cultivated land is limited by the physical geography of the country.

In 1935, geographer Hu Huanyong drew a northeast to southwest line, from today's Heihe in Heilongjiang Province to Tengchong in Yunnan, dividing China into two parts, one populous and the other sparse. Today, this line remains relevant: the eastern half occupies only 43 percent of China's total area but contains 94 percent of the total population. The average density was 236 people for each square kilometer in 1982. In contrast, the density in the western half—the sparse area—was only 10.6 people for each square kilometer. The areas of high density are the cities and agricultural basins and lowlands of east China. In short, the density pattern reflects China's varied physical environment, long settlement history, and recent contrasting socio-economic regional developments.

Population Growth and Control

Population growth is determined by birth, death and migration. The volume of international migration in and out of China is very small. Although the death rate surged during the Great Leap Forward, a period of economic and political turmoil lasting from 1958 to 1961, the death rate has declined overall since 1953 and is stabilized at between 6–7 per thousand. Therefore, the critical determinant in Chinese population growth is births. Each year the difference between the rates of birth and death delimits the rate of natural increase.

Both the birth rate and the rate of natural increase have declined since the 1960s, but only after the People's Republic had two periods of rapid population growth, one in the 1950s and the other in the 1960s. Consequently, the two large female cohorts born in those periods are now in their childbearing years, between the ages of 19 and 49. As these women go through their life cycle, a large number of children have been and will be born in China.

The decline in the birth rate was brought about largely through the government's campaigns on birth control. In the 1950s, when the government first confronted the rapid population growth, it relaxed abortion restrictions and ordered health agencies to assist people on contraceptive matters. Meanwhile, officials and several eminent scholars argued for birth control. The birth control efforts were suspended during the Great Leap Forward, and a "catch-up" rise in birth rates occurred afterwards.

Clearly, there was an urgent need to resume the birth control campaign, and the government did so. Unfortunately, the effort was again interrupted, this time by the Cultural Revolution in the late 1960s. However, the campaign has had an effect on the fertility decline.

In the early 1970s, China had gone through two periods of rapid population growth and was facing a stagnated economy; its government implemented the policy termed "wan xi shao," or "later, farther, fewer": marry later, have fewer children, and with longer spacing between. The policy was successful; the nation's total fertility rate (TFR) dropped from 4.8 to 2.4 between 1970–80. TFR is the average number of children a woman will have, assuming that current age-specific birth rates remain constant throughout her childbearing years.

Beginning in 1978, China boldly entered a decade of socioeconomic reforms in which birth planning was recognized as a basic national policy. In 1979, the government began to implement the one child per family policy. Its aim was to reduce the rate of natural increase to 5 per thousand by 1985 and to zero by the year 2000, at which time the total population would be around 1.2 billion.

The one-child policy denied the universal human desire for two children of different gender; and it was too restrictive for the Chinese families that desired at least one son. This policy was rigorously administered from 1979 to 1983, leaving a trail of mismanaged official actions and the resistance of unhappy people, particularly in rural areas. Those who suffered the most from the official and *family* mistreatment were women whose first-born was a girl. In the cities, however, the policy was fairly successful.

By 1984 it was apparent that the policy was at best only partially successful in reducing China's fertility and it had failed to gain public acceptance. Thus the central government issued a directive to allow modifications at the local level. Today, the one-child principle remains intact but the policy is more flexible, promoting late marriage, later and fewer but healthier children, and advocating the principle of "one couple, one child." In addition, in more "difficult rural circumstances," a second child is allowed, but following a longer spacing after the first; and in minority areas, regulations may be drafted to meet local conditions. In essence, the current Population policy is a hybrid of the "one or two-child" and "later-farther-fewer" policies.

During the 1980s, the one-child policy was implemented and

modified, but the birth rates changed little. For example, in the 1982 and 1990 censuses the birth rate was reported to be 20.9 per thousand. However, these reports must not be interpreted to suggest that "little happened" in fertility. In fact, studies have shown that during these years birth rates increased because a significant proportion of rural women married and gave birth at younger ages, and owing to the change in age structure, there were more women of childbearing age than before. On the other hand, in many provinces, the fertility rate actually declined. Thus, the "stable" birth rates in 1982 and 1990 are a balance between two positive and one negative effect on births that took place in the intervening years.

The original one-child policy was too restrictive to be successful, and there were also three concurrent government actions that contradicted the goals of the policy. First, the 1981 marriage law set the minimum marrying age younger than many previously set by local governments, and it "encouraged" many people to marry at younger ages.

Second, under the rural responsibility system, each household was assigned land for production based on its size and labor force. Farmers quickly realized that it was to their advantage to have a large family including several sons in order to get more land and to have more hands for the farming and sideline productions such as making handicrafts and planting flowers to sell in the city.

Third, the commune system was abolished and replaced by the xiang (township) government. Under the xiang administration and the reformed economy, rural China has become less restricted in family planning and economic activities. Consequently, it has been more difficult for the government to regulate rural births and marriages; not unrelated has been the shortage of funds and human power to administer the birth control work. Today, cadres are more interested in economic affairs than birth control. Every year a large number of births are above township quotas, and it is common at the local level to under-report births and falsify birth-control records. In short, the effectiveness of the nation's birth control policy has been seriously undermined. A renewed energy and discipline are required in the 1990s if the modified one-child policy is to be successful.

Socioeconomic Characteristics of the Population

The socialist government has prided itself on its social programs. This pride can be justified, particularly if we keep in mind that China's gross national product per inhabitant is $360 [U.S. dollars] annually. Generally, on all demographic indicators China ranks in the middle *between* the more and less developed countries in the world. The Chinese total fertility rate is one-half that of the less developed countries, while the percentage of Chinese women "using contraception" is as high as that of developed countries. Only in percentage of population living in urban areas is China lower than the two groupings. China's progress in education is less impressive. In both the 1982 and 1990 census data, respectively, 6.8 percent and 8.0 percent of Chinese had 12 years of schooling, and 35.2 percent and 37.0 percent had 6 years of schooling. These percentages are low as compared with some Southeast Asian countries; they are very low as compared with Taiwan and the Republic of Korea.

Female education, employment and social status are known to be critical to the decline of fertility in a nation. Since the 1950s, China has reduced the rate of illiteracy (including semi-illiteracy) from 33.6 percent in 1964 to 31.9 in 1982, and to 26.8 in 1987 (The 1990 census reports a questionably low figure: 15.9 percent). To date, however, around 70 percent of the illiterates are females; moreover, the pace of decline in female illiteracy has been slower than that of male illiteracy. In China's different regions, female illiteracy appears linked to several urban and economic factors.

The Chinese tradition of "patrilocal exogamous" marriage customs in which girls move into their husbands' households (sometimes away from the home village) has been preserved in socialist China. This custom limits young women's growth and independence. Parents are reluctant to invest in daughters' education which will be of more benefit to future husbands' families. Once in their husbands' households in a patriarchal village setting, young women are isolated and lack support. Usually, they have the obligation to bear sons but have no right to decide on the number of children to have. Their work mainly is farming, rural sideline productions, and household chores. Considering the importance of improving female education and status in order to obtain a decline in fertility, the government's effort in this area is wanting.

Population and Urbanization

Urban and rural living conditions have a big impact on fertility in China. Urbanites get better and more kinds of social services. The birth control campaign started at least one decade earlier in cities; consequently, the better educated urbanites have a lower average total fertility rate, a lower infant mortality rate, and a higher age at first marriage and first child bearing.

Migration from the countryside to the cities is restricted in China. Nevertheless since the 1980s, under the economic reforms a significant number of rural inhabitants have legally and illegally entered cities to work temporarily or for longer periods. Studies, including my own, have shown that in time the fertility of such immigrants tends to decline. This suggests that as China becomes more urban, people's values will change and fertility will decline as a result, slowing population growth.

I noted earlier that there have been two periods of rapid population growth in China's recent history. The two large cohorts born during those periods now are in the labor force, yet at the same time, the amount of land cultivated per inhabitant has declined: recent efforts to develop rural industries have yielded positive results but also created new problems. In short, there simply are not enough jobs for all able-bodied Chinese! Today, the surplus labor force in agriculture is conservatively estimated at 25–30 percent, or 60–80 million people. The solution is to transfer the excess population to nonfarming occupations in rural and urban areas—but this requires rapid growth of the urban economy to provide greatly increased job opportunities.

Population and Development Geography

Socioeconomic variables cannot directly affect fertility; however, they can help change people's views and behavior, such as marrying late and the use of contraception. Recent studies clearly show that socioeconomic development leads to fertility decline in China. People in more developed areas, in nonfarming occupations, and in higher income households are more attentive to the cost and benefit of having children. These people tend to spend more money on raising a child and to conclude that it is more rational to have fewer but healthier and better educated children.

Comparing provinces, it is clear that the total fertility rates differ, based on such factors as per capita gross national product and urban development. In reality, socioeconomic development and population control and planning are synergistic: from their interaction comes a new future for China. The more developed areas, such as the three largest cities (Beijing, Shanghai and Tianjin) and some coastal provinces, generally have lower total fertility rates.

The top-down government-sponsored birth control campaigns have, until now, played a dominant role in Chinese demography. Total fertility rates declined decisively in the last two decades but problems occurred with the policies and how to make them both doable and effective. Narrowly conceived control policies are not sufficient to maintain a low fertility rate. In fact, broadly based socioeconomic development is required to effectively curb population growth and genuinely to improve the quality of life for the nation's population.

CHINA'S ENVIRONMENT[3]

We know a good deal about the extent of China's environmental problems, but little about how to measure their economic impacts. Attempts in recent years to introduce innovative, market-based regulatory programs have resulted from increased foreign investment and the activities of multilateral development agencies. These activities, however, are focused on individual industries, enterprises, municipalities, and provinces. Prospects are reasonably good for development of innovative economic strategies to strengthen existing administrative enforcement measures in a few places, like Beijing and Shanghai, where a great deal of money is being invested, and foreign expertise is available. It is unlikely, however, that the central government in the early 1990s has the expertise or will to implement a national program that can respond satisfactorily to China's unique problems of size, physical diversity, resource imbalance, and population concentration. Despite early recognition of the inevitable environmental cost of pursuing the Stalinist development model, China's leaders made their choice, and still continue to live with the consequences.

I. Introduction: Categorization and Interpretation

Environmental problems in China seriously threaten 1990s economic modernization plans. Technological remedies and reg-

[3]Article by Baruch Boxer, professor at Rutgers University, from *China's Economic Dilemmas in the 1990s*, pp. 290–307. Joint Economic Committee, 102nd Congress, 1st Session, 1991.

ulatory controls at national and provincial levels are generally weak and ineffective despite a constitutional guarantee of environmental protection as a "national principle." Economic productivity suffers from pollution and resource degradation in industry, agriculture, fisheries, animal husbandry, forestry, energy, and other sectors. Problems include rural and urban air and water pollution; arable land encroachment, conversion, and reclamation; soil erosion and fertility loss; deforestation; and health effects of random disposal of municipal garbage and hazardous wastes. In some respects, factors contributing to China's poor environmental condition resemble those in other developing countries. Population pressure overwhelms natural systems' ability to remain productive in the face of pollution insults and physical degradation. Ecosystem processes which support food production, waste assimilation, watershed and aquifer recharge, and other functions essential to human welfare are undermined.

Having recognized this there are major difficulties in moving from description of problems to analysis of their significance. How should economic and other policy aspects of China's environmental situation be assessed? Against what standard? At what scale? Do China's domestic environmental problems have international or global dimensions? Understanding environmental change requires that local events and processes be interpreted in relation to wider economic and social impacts. This facilitates cross-national and regional comparison of problems and remedies.

Analyzing economic implications of environmental issues is made difficult by the tendency in recent years to dwell primarily on the extent and magnitude of China's problems. Many accounts tell of polluted water supplies, foul rivers, degraded natural habitats, choking urban air pollution, and other examples of environmental abuse. Problems frequently are put in the worst light by domestic and foreign observers who draw heavily upon dubious official aggregated data on pollution and resource degradation. This deters attempts to look realistically at economic factors in environmental policymaking. Benefits and costs of environmental protection can be considered at several scales, in various time frames, and in relation to a host of ecological and health considerations. Environmental concerns influence in investment decisions, trade patterns, industrial standards, pricing strategies, and management goals in many ways.

In each case, however, there is much uncertainty regarding economic risks and benefits of environmental regulation and investment, and the costs of neglect to people and the environment. Unresolved issues in the long-term debate over clean air legislation in the United States point up the extent of uncertainties even in countries with strong, long-standing commitment to finding economically equitable solutions to problems like air pollution. Formal analysis in China of economic factors to be considered in managing air pollution or any other environmental problem has barely begun.

Economically significant issues with environmental ramifications include toxic waste import and recycling, market factors in pollution control equipment import and export, the effects on industrial development of weakened central environmental and land use regulations in southeast coastal provinces and special economic zones, and factors affecting choice of industrial pollution control standards by line ministries and government agencies. Until now, foreign observers of China's environment have mainly described problems. Comprehensive analysis has focused primarily on the politics of agenda-setting, interpretation of laws and regulations, and problems of policy implementation.

Writers on China's environment, moreover, have only begun to explore the connections between domestic and international policy. Global concerns like climate change, biodiversity, soil loss, and deforestation that currently command the greatest international attention are slow to emerge and are unconstrained by national boundaries. They mainly reflect developed country perspectives. China has actively participated in multilateral negotiations on chlorofluorocarbon reduction to protect stratospheric ozone. Here, as in other multilateral discussions of global environmental issues, however, technical questions of appropriate standards, chemical substitutes, legal precedents, and financial risk-benefit delimit the scope of debate on remedial options.

International demands for domestic policy shifts to address global problems like climate change often are unrealistic in light of national conditions. For example, pressure on China to improve energy efficiency and reduce coal use underestimates difficulties of finding politically and economically acceptable alternatives. Problems include dependency on cheap coal and unwillingness or inability of technical and financial institutions in China to support alternative energy and conservation programs like centralized heating systems for cities. It is assumed by foreigners that information availability, technology and capital transfer, and management assistance are sufficient to bring China into line with international environmental norms. This is questionable. A range of potential climate change phenomena (e.g., sea level rise, temperature migration, spatial shifts in biological productivity, increased ultraviolet radiation) could affect domestic economic performance in unknown ways. There has been little study in China (or elsewhere) of relations between economic and environmental impacts of domestic climate change scenarios.

Another problem facing analysts is that oversimplified environmental quality measures are frequently used to compare China with other regions, countries, and to global norms. These indices are often expressed in per capita units. Per capita data are used in many areas including national resource accounting, pollutant discharge levels, water resources infrastructure and quality, energy utilization, land management, and resource endowment. Simple comparisons, however, tell us very little about how to interpret the economic or human significance of China's rapidly deteriorating environment, especially since information overload and self-serving report by competing bureaucracies often confuse the picture.

Problem characterization (e.g., "ecological environment," industrial pollution, hazardous waste, etc.) and reports on enforcement pursue well-trodden paths that are either strewn with superficial observations or prejudices of local and foreign critics, or glowingly hortatory and self-serving in the best tradition of Party obfuscation. Seldom are there attempts to frame problems in analytical terms conducive to estimation of the technical or financial feasibility of regulatory or technical management options.

How will environmental constraints affect China's economic modernization? This paper briefly reviews historical and institutional factors, surveys several key problem areas, and concludes with comments on economic implications of policy choices. My purpose is to point up some difficulties in understanding and applying economic factors in assessment of China's environmental experience.

II. Background and Context

Several factors influence how environment and resource issues have come to be seen, priorities determined, and technical and policy responses framed. Foremost among these are China's size, population, physical and climatic variability, unevenly distributed resource base, and the contributions of environmental science and administrative work through the 1980s. Since the founding of the PRC in 1949, environment and resource questions have been prominent in theoretical discussions of nature-society relations and in debates over how best to deal with the historical legacy of environmental deterioration. This was best exemplified in the 1950s by the prominence given water conservation. There was great urgency in seeking technical and institutional remedies for controlling physical and human impacts of flooding, soil loss, and drought.

Government and Party have since the late 1960s sought to enhance public awareness of pollution, conservation, and environmental health. This is no small achievement, given economic policy shifts, 1980s decentralization of economic decision-making, changing center-local relations, and the daunting challenge of governing a poor country of China's size and regional diversity. Before the 1960s, environment-related work was tied to public health and sanitation [huanjing weisheng]. These efforts, while an important early affirmation of government and party concern for public welfare, focused mainly on recycling of household garbage and other nontoxic urban and agricultural wastes, and with sanitary engineering and domestic water supply. Until the 1960s, few institutional or technical measures were taken to deal with burgeoning health and environmental impacts of industry, agriculture, urbanization, and energy development.

In the late 1960s and early 1970s, with the strong encouragement of Zhou Enlai, an institutional base for environmental protection was established, and monitoring and regulatory strategies specific to China's needs were formulated. China embarked on a two-fold environmental initiative. In a national program laid out at an August 1973 conference, problems, goals, and implementing strategies were specified. Initial government efforts were backed by ideological principles which promoted pollution control and resource conservation as economically beneficial. Raw materials were to be conserved, industrial processes improved through materials recycling and residuals recovery, and natural productivity sustained.

Social productive forces, presumably emerging from the synergism of nature and society, were to be maximized to assure the well-being of present and future generations. Theoretically, control over nature leads to more "rational" and efficient use of natural resources, and pollution and waste is reduced. In areas as diverse as desert management and fisheries genetics, impressive scientific efforts were made to probe physical and biological aspects of the interaction between people and nature. The aim was to sustain the productivity of natural systems, thereby minimizing harmful effects of economic development on people and the environment.

From the early 1970s through the 1980s, China promulgated wide-ranging environmental laws, regulations, and standards, supported extensive scientific and technical research and monitoring programs through government agencies, line ministries, and educational institutions, and mounted numerous educational and propaganda campaigns in support of environmental protection. Several principles underlie environmental protection in China: as national policy it should guide social and economic development, provide economic incentives and administrative oversight to prevent and reduce pollution, and combine enforcement of regulations with technology and infrastructure improvement for pollution control. Despite a continuous outpouring of laws and regulations since the late 1970s, however, enforcement is weak and uneven.

There are contradictions between local needs and national directives and standards. On the resource side, localities must feed more people in the face of shrinking land resources. Sichuan's population, for example, is over 100 million. Provincial land use regulations of the 1980s prohibit cultivation on mountain slopes steeper than 20 degrees, but land shortage and population pressure in hilly areas throughout the province make a mockery of these standards. Intensive planting on 40 degree or greater slopes is common, leading to soil erosion, landslides, and rapid reservoir sedimentation. National industrial pollutant discharge guidelines are similarly undermined in many situations where local production needs take precedence over national environmental goals. Chongqing University officials, for example, have for over a decade unsuccessfully appealed to municipal and national agencies to force several polluting industries located below the University along the Changjiang (Yangtze River) to reduce toxic emissions affecting the health of students and faculty. In rapidly developing coastal cities and provinces, moreover, pollution regulations are increasingly ignored.

The 1970s efforts were distinctive in several respects. They strengthened links between ideology and institution-building both in bureaucratic and scientific and technical realms. In the late 1960s and during the 1970s, pollution control was promoted as broadly supportive of conservation and resource recovery. Health and environmental benefits of point-source control were emphasized along with wider national benefits of resource conservation and nature protection. Mid-1970s appeals for improved "three-waste" (liquid, solid, gaseous) recovery were thus couched in terms of the macroeconomic benefits of integrating environmental protection and development. Much original research was done on regulatory and administrative strategies for maintaining environmental quality while pursuing development goals. A distinctively Chinese approach to environmental protection emerged. Efforts of national research and regulatory agencies were also coordinated with provincial and municipal agencies and activities.

Research and policy development was regionally focused with respect to specific problems. Academy of Sciences institutes and universities took the lead in making research findings available to regulatory agencies that carried out monitoring and enforcement. In Dalian, for example, the Institute of Chemical Physics coordinated industrial pollution monitoring and control studies with provincial and municipal line agencies in the northeast and the Beijing-Tianjin region; the Beijing Institute of Geography took the lead in sophisticated studies of relations between land source and marine pollution in Bo Hai Bay; the desert research institute in Lanzhou coordinated desert control studies and programs with provincial agencies in the northwest; and Academy of Sciences, provincial, and State Oceanic Administration fisheries research institutes in Guangdong and Fujian coordinated their work with researchers in Zhongshan and other universities to control effects of land source pollution on coastal marine fisheries.

China also participated in the 1972 Stockholm U.N. Conference on the Human Environment. She asserted herself as a major participant in emerging international discussions of global environmental issues, especially issues like "pollution export," which served to solidify China's identification with Third World interests in North-South debates on pollution causes and remedies. Poor countries blamed industrialized countries for causing pollution and resource destruction through their own development and exploitation of resources in developing countries. Poor countries equated pollution with poverty, and maintained that environmental problems could only be solved with technical and economic support from rich countries to assist their development.

China was an outspoken advocate of this position throughout the 1970s.

Yet in China it is especially difficult to establish criteria for weighing the costs of doing nothing or something about environmental problems. While problems are interconnected in China as elsewhere, the China case poses special challenges beyond those of size, physical constraints and population pressure on resources. For instance, there is no tradition, as in the West, of neoclassical cost-benefit analysis to test assumptions about how to value natural resources in relation to short or long-term human welfare goals. Nor is there sensitivity to the time value (discount rate) of investment in environmental infrastructure or nature conservation in weighing present versus future environmental and health benefits and costs. Capital investment decisions are the product of a complex system where rivalry among territorial units and bureaucracies and competition among high level agencies for investment funds determines project priority. Most important, cost-benefit concerns seldom enter into the planning process, and capital is not valued as a commodity.

China has for over 20 years forged its own perspectives on what its environmental problems are and how they should be thought about and managed. While it is easy for outsiders to criticize perceived shortcomings in policy development and enforcement, no other poor country has developed a more extensive institutional, research, and educational base for environmental programs. What should be expected of China, given the spotty record of Western countries, including the United States? Why should China be held to a higher standards?

III. Major Environmental Challenges

Impacts of environmental problems are made worse in China by economic policies that since 1949 give highest priority to industrial and agricultural production. Legal and regulatory directives in recent years to foster environmental sensitivity in the selection of project sites and in their operation have been only partially effective.

Construction of large water, industrial, agricultural, and energy projects like dams and storage reservoirs, irrigation schemes, thermal and nuclear power plants, mines, petrochemical complexes, and steel mills have devastating effects. They severely damage forest, grassland, mountain, freshwater, marine, and other ecosystems. Growth policies thus contradict and call into question the sincerity of official pronouncements on the need to balance economic growth and environmental conservation. These contradictions reflect the challenges and unique circumstances of various problem areas. Water pollution, energy/environment issues, and waste management are illustrative.

A. WATER

Water pollution is China's most pressing environmental problem because of its widespread, direct impact on human health and natural productivity. Water pollution results from interrelated natural and human causes. These include severe water shortages in the north and in some southern coastal areas. China's annual surface water runoff volume of 264 million [cubic meters] is the world's sixth largest, but uneven distribution of ground and surface water, as well as erratic precipitation patterns, results in regional shortages and difficulties in maintaining timely water availability for agriculture and industry. The Changjiang (Yangtze) Basin, and areas to the south and southwest, for example, have only 33 percent of China's total cultivated land, but nearly 70 percent of the country's water resources. Over the years, there have been many proposed schemes for transferring water from south to north. Ecological and health implications of these schemes have been studied, but debates have mainly centered on costs and engineering feasibility.

Excessive "mining" of groundwater and loss of surface water through poor construction and maintenance of storage facilities contributes to water shortages. Other causes include industrial waste discharge and modification and reclamation of lakes and fresh water and coastal wetlands for urban, industrial, and agricultural development. This leads to species loss, polluted drinking water, aquifer contamination from salt water intrusion, and estuarine siltation. Pressure on rural water supply and deteriorating water quality also results from high agricultural chemical use, poor drainage, and the recent explosive growth of rural industries, especially in southeast coastal areas. In 1987, there were approximately 15 million rural enterprises for building materials, food processing, textile and chemical manufacturing, and other light industry activities. They employ about 80 million people. Few enterprises can treat wastewater, and it is mostly discharged untreated into rural waterways.

Good water supply and management have been crucial to China's economic success since ancient times. Economic activity in China has centered on roughly 5000 river basins with watersheds greater than 100 [square kilometers]. River basins defined China spatially and socially, and focused defense, food supply, marketing, water conservancy, transport, and other key economic activities. These basins still are basic support systems of the national economy because rivers and streams provide surface water, restore groundwater, and collect and disperse wastes. They also serve as the physical base for construction of flood control, irrigation, storage, and power generating works. A major reason for current widespread water pollution is that natural functions have been undermined through failure to adapt traditional knowledge and practice to modern requirements, as has been done in France, the Netherlands, and other Western European countries.

Recent official views on water supply and pollution emphasize conservation and more effective water reutilization to compensate for inadequate natural supply. Other policy remedies have called for greater attention to demand (economic), rather than supply (engineering) approaches to water management. Price reforms to remove subsidies and foster conservation have not been introduced to any substantial degree, however, although there has been much talk of the need for reforms. Water is priced so low that there are few economic incentives to conserve or reuse water in industry and agriculture. Competition for capital investment funds for water projects among political jurisdictions has also hindered attempts to price water more realistically to foster conservation.

Reduction of industrial water pollution, which makes up 70–80 percent of China's total wastewater load, is a top government priority. There has been some success in combining waste reduction, biological treatment, and process modification in smaller installations, and many new factories are required to install pollution control devices. There is little consistency from province to province, however, in use of technical controls or enforcement of discharge standards. Nationally, industrial waste discharge remains the most serious sources of contamination of drinking water crops, and fish and shellfish resources.

Total wastewater discharge in China in 1988 was estimated at roughly 40 billion [cubic meters]. Aggregate supply and demand statistics, however, are not very useful for policy planning except as they can help to clarify specific problems and needs of agriculture, industry, and households. These estimates require confidence in data accuracy, and in assumptions underlying statistical analysis of supply and demand factors affecting water quality, price and the availability of water for various purposes. Data, unfortunately, are notoriously unreliable. There are frequent discrepancies between official sources in reporting wastewater discharge levels. Inconsistent and excessive data from several agencies with overlapping jurisdictions also reflect poor reporting and interpretation of monitoring results. The National Environmental Protection Agency (NEPA) is unable to coordinate policies and assessments on a national scale. This is not surprising, in that NEPA has limited authority and staff (about 300) to implement technical programs. Implementation and enforcement responsibilities mainly rest with bureaus in line ministries and with thinly-staffed provincial and lower-level environmental units.

Industrial discharge also contributes to the recent sharp decline of freshwater resources in China. Mid-1980s studies indicate that over a quarter of fresh water in lakes, rivers and aquifers is polluted, and water quality is declining rapidly. Already, nearly 25 percent of water flowing in 53,000 kilometers of rivers is unsuitable for irrigation or domestic use, and 86 percent of river water flowing through urban areas is too polluted for irrigation or aquaculture. Surveys of groundwater quality in 47 cities revealed that 43 of them were dependent on groundwater containing toxic contaminants at levels exceeding state water quality standards.

The ubiquity of water pollution challenges national, provincial, and local governments to control individual pollution sources and to coordinate efforts among sectors. On paper, environmental bureaucracies are vertically linked from national to local levels to facilitate research, but information exchange, monitoring, and enforcement for achieving significant reduction of water pollution and improvement control for the nation as a whole are poor.

A major problem is that officials responsible for water pollution in environmental protection, agriculture, urban construction, planning, and water development agencies seldom interact. Environmental agencies are marginalized by politically powerful line ministries, and find it increasingly difficult to enforce laws and regulations through administrative, legal, or economic means. Agency fragmentation and poor coordination hinders policy implementation. For example, a high-level workshop on pollution in China, sponsored by the State Science and Technology Commission and the United Nations Development Program, was held in

February, 1990. The workshop report noted that Ministry of Health experts on environmental health were not in attendance. This was seen as seriously weakening prospects for implementing workshop recommendations to improve institutional response to the health effects of water pollution.

B. Energy

China is amply endowed with coal (the world's second largest reserves), there is underutilized hydropower potential, and many thermal and nuclear electric generating plants, with associated power grids, are being built throughout the country. In aggregate terms, energy supply from various sources appears adequate for development needs in the 1990s, despite the current financial crisis in the petroleum industry which supplies about 18 percent of China's energy. By comparison, coal provides 76 percent of the country's industrial energy, hydropower 5 percent, and natural gas 2 percent. Problems in the oil industry stem from unrealistic underpricing (now about U.S. $2.00/barrel, compared with a 1980 price U.S. of $9.00), a problem shared with other state-subsidized energy sectors. State oil companies are also reticent to allow foreign oil companies to engage in onshore exploration and production, offshore production is not at anticipated levels despite heavy investment over the past decade, and there is a continuing need to export about 400,000 barrels of oil a day to earn scarce foreign exchange.

Energy and environmental issues are closely related, but it is difficult to define cost-effective strategies for remedying existing environmental problems and avoiding new ones. The problem is that national energy planning and policy development are not considering energy production impacts on health and the environment. China by necessity will increase its reliance on coal as primary energy source, thereby intensifying already serious air pollution. This will occur even if more flue gas desulphurizing devices ("scrubbers") can be installed in large industries, a doubtful prospect in the presently constrained fiscal climate.

A major reason for mounting energy-related environmental problems is wasteful use of coal to generate electricity that is carried over power grids to grossly inefficient heavy industries. Heavy industry consumes roughly 65 percent of power generated nationally. But China's steel industry uses more than twice as much energy to produce a ton of steel as producers in Western countries or Japan. Energy shortages occur because of both regional imbalance in availability of coal and other energy resources, and poor interregional transportation. The country relies too heavily on centrally distributed power linked to urban and industrial centers, with rural areas undersupplied. More efficient use of existing energy sources, especially hydropower, would better satisfy local needs with reduced environmental costs, and there would be less need for large generating plants.

Although China's coal is generally of good quality, with relatively low sulfur and ash content, high consumption levels and inefficient combustion in industry and households (cooking briquets) results in harmful levels of suspended particulates, sulphur dioxide (SO_2), and carbon monoxide (CO). Pollutant loadings in most urban areas exceed state standards and, especially in northern cities, contribute to high incidence of respiratory disease. Uncontrolled motor vehicle emissions, a growing, but unaddressed problem, aggravates air pollution in urban airsheds. Source breakdown of total suspended particulates and SO_2 from coal combustion is approximately: industry, 43 percent; domestic use, 23 percent; thermal power generation, 24 percent; coking plants, 8 percent; and locomotives, 3 percent.

Acid precipitation affects many areas of China including the Chongquing-Yibin area in Sichuan, Guiyang in Guizhou Province, the Liuzhao area of Guangxi Zhuang Autonomous Region, parts of Hunan, Guangzhou. There is superficial evidence of damage to crops, trees, and fresh water bodies, but there has been little careful research on actual sources and sinks and on the dynamics of inter-regional atmospheric transport of pollutants. Secondary sources estimate 1 billion yuan in annual damage to farm crops from acid rain.

A basic obstacle to reducing air pollution is the absence of comprehensive and reliable source emission data as well as enforceable control policies. Because mid-1980s emissions survey data have not been made available for national-level impact assessment, it has been impossible to develop effective monitoring and cost assessment procedures to plan and implement national control strategies for industry. These could include using limestone injection in conventional boiler systems, fluidized bed combustion, and other sulfur capture technologies.

Another frequently overlooked energy-related environmental issue is the acute shortage of household fuel in the countryside. Growing demand for household fuel contributes to land loss and deforestation, thereby affecting agricultural productivity. Trees are felled for firewood, and plant stalks (estimated 400 million tons annually) are burned for household fuel rather than plowed under to enhance soil structure and fertility. Risk of erosion and land loss through desert encroachment is also increased, especially in northern arid areas. In the south, biogas generation has partially ameliorated farm household energy shortage (mainly for domestic cooking and preparation of feed for pigs), although biogas generation is feasible only in hot areas with ample supply of organic waste materials. Rural electricity supply could be increased with minimum environmental damage through greater reliance on small-scale hydropower stations. Despite problems with local sedimentation and inappropriate design of facilities for some locations, about 70,000 installations are used in over three-quarters of China's 2,133 counties, with a third of the counties relying on these small facilities for most of their power.

Construction of hydroelectric and thermal power plants, water storage and flood control reservoirs, power lines, and other energy-related structures has wide and immediate social and ecological impact. Especially in the crowded eastern third of the country, construction displaces many people, destroys precious agricultural land and natural habitats, induces erosion from site preparation, pollutes water bodies, and increases deforestation. Offshore oil drilling and production platforms also contribute to marine pollution in biologically productive nearshore areas, although there has been better control in recent years, especially in Bo Hai Bay, an important oil and gas production area.

Environment impacts of energy development are felt at many levels. As with water pollution, however, impacts are difficult to manage comprehensively because of poor program coordination among national and provincial agencies. Separate bureaucracies are responsible for nuclear, hydropower, coal, and petroleum industries. In 1988, the State Council sought to streamline energy bureaucracies by removing the electric power element of the Ministry of Water Resources and Electric Power. The electric power bureaucracy was merged with other energy groups, although it is not clear if this has improved national policy planning and program implementation.

It is doubtful that administrative measures alone can significantly reduce pollution and ecological impacts of construction and operation of energy production, processing, and distribution facilities. Prospects for improved policy coordination among government agencies became weaker in the 1980s as bureaus, agencies, and research units spawned quasi-governmental corporations to facilitate cooperation with foreign investors and firms. In the early 1990s, in a period of fiscal austerity, it remains to be seen whether this openness will continue. Resistance to foreign contacts on the part of the oil industry has been mentioned, although wider state control in oil and other energy sectors does not necessarily imply that there will be more attention paid to environmental concerns in energy development and distribution. Limited environmentally benign solar, wind, and tidal energy production capability has been achieved, but soft energy contributions to easing environmental impacts remain insignificant.

C. WASTE MANAGEMENT

Despite this foundation, in the 1990s China is faced with overwhelming pollution prevention and cleanup tasks. This is not surprising. Many of today's challenges stem from the leadership's failure in the 1960s to heed those who warned that continued pursuit of Soviet-style development, based on profligate resource use in heavy industry for short-term production gain, would ultimately lead to environmental disaster. Failure to sustain a productive relationship between natural and human systems, the key to China's longevity, is bound to have harmful social and economic, as well as ecological effects.

The traditional system sought maximum efficiency in the exchange and conservation of energy, moisture, labor, and materials. This was expressed physically and culturally in the interplay of soil, water, animals, plants, and people, even in areas like North China with difficult growing conditions. For centuries, engineering and agronomic skills were combined in complex agroecosystems which supplied human needs in face of formidable natural constraints and population pressure. Food crops, aquatic products, and medicinal herbs, along with cash and industrial crops like tung oil, ramine, tea, and pig bristles, were produced interdependently. Forty years of rampant, capital-intensive development, however, has damaged the biological resilience of the productive base. Soil quality, watershed integrity, biodiversity, and clean air and water have suffered.

This decline is well-illustrated in problems of waste management. Traditionally, exchange of organic and nontoxic materials (human and animal waste, vegetables, household garbage, broken glass, etc.) between city and country supported sustained use of densely settled zones near urban centers for food supply. Favorable economies of waste recycling and agricultural production were achieved in spatially-delimited urban-rural exchange zones. The shape and extent of these zones depended upon access to transportation, efficiency of marketing systems, soil fertility, and food price dynamics which governed supply and demand. Labor was never a problem. Nutrients and energy (from food, fertilizer from human waste, and labor) were "cycled" back and forth from city to country, to use the prescient terminology of the American soil scientist, James Thorp, who clearly described the process in the Shanghai area in the late 1930s.

Similar processes were at work as recently as the early 1980s in Shanghai, where complex contractual ties listed between urban districts and municipal recycling and wastewater treatment bureaus to exchange vegetables and other foodstuffs for human waste, organic garbage, and materials like pottery shards and broken bricks. Urban to rural exports were used to fertilize, compost pile construction, and fowl and animal feed. These arrangements were being rapidly displaced by the mid-1980s, however, as increased market demand for vegetables and desire for quicker harvests and higher profits from private vegetable plots led to greatly increased use of chemical fertilizer, herbicides, and pesticides. Chemical runoff, along with industrial and housing development, has severely polluted soil and waterways in rural Shanghai counties. The sustainable, organic foundation is effectively destroyed.

Evidence of rapid decline in traditional waste recycling capability is clear from recently released statistics. Official sources now report that nationally, only a small portion of solid industrial wastes and urban garbage is being recycled. In 1988, only 26 percent of 560 million tons of solid industrial waste and slag materials from industries and mines were reprocessed, and cities are increasingly surrounded by piles of industrial and mining wastes and garbage for which authorities have no disposal options. Even more disturbing is the seriousness of the hazardous waste disposal problem.

Very few industrialized countries (e.g., Denmark, Sweden, and parts of Germany) have effective hazardous waste management programs. Successful efforts must combine economic incentives, reliable technologies, and administrative authority to assure that waste is either reduced at source or rendered harmless to people and the environment through pyrolysis or other treatment processes. Administrative, economic, and technical components of programs must be coordinated and effectively integrated. This involves source reduction, collection, recycling, and treatment of household, municipal, and industrial wastes. National programs should be supported by public policies that provide tax and other incentives that assure profitable returns at each level of operation and lead to maximum participation of waste generators. China today has no effective hazardous waste management program, and prospects for developing a program are remote.

Failure of the traditional organic recycling system in urban areas is compounded by the overwhelming burden of having to manage nontraditional wastes from industries, mines, and rural enterprises. A recent review of the problem identifies chromium wastes, wastes from electroplating, textile dyeing, and leather processing industries, and township and village enterprise wastes, as priority concerns. Suggested remedial measures for chromium wastes include waste minimization, slag pile stabilization, and landfill construction. Chromium wastes have already seriously contaminated drinking water wells in the vicinity of mines and processing works.

Electroplating shops, to take one example, are small, numerous, and scattered throughout large and small cities. There are over 300 in Shanghai and 200 in Beijing alone. This makes it difficult to apply effective controls in individual cases, and to introduce centralized waste collection and treatment operations. It is even more difficult to implement source reduction and recycling policies in the millions of small rural enterprises that have sprung up throughout the countryside in the past decade. The Chinese government has given lip service to controlling this growth as a long-term solution to the waste generation problem, but there is little evidence that this is being done. In fact, devolution of economic decision-making from center to local government levels in recent years mitigates against prospects for effective waste management in these enterprises.

IV. Economic Implications and Prospects

Economic policies directly influence environmental protection programs and outcomes. In principle, economic analysis of environmental issues in industrially advanced countries helps inform choice of regulatory options. Mutually satisfactory balance between technical and administrative solutions is seldom achieved, however, because conflicts among government regulators, polluters, and public interest groups often lead to lengthy litigation. As noted above, some disputes remain unsolved for long periods, as with clean air legislation in the United States. Agreement in the U.S. Congress on updating 1977 technical amendments to the Clean Air Act, for example, took over ten years to negotiate.

In China, there is no public participation in environmental law-drafting and management. Public protests over pollution insults to health, or damage to resources (e.g. in agriculture, aquatic products, animal husbandry, or forestry), may lead to improved local controls in isolated cases. Responsibility for policymaking in China, however, still lies with the government. Most important, economic aspects of environmental and resource problems in China still must be initially addressed from the narrow perspective of Party views on acceptable strategies and goals. This differs from many Western countries, the Soviet Union and Eastern Europe, developing nations like Brazil, India, and Mexico. Increasingly, citizen activists influence policymaking through litigation, lobbying of legislative bodies, government agencies, and professional groups, and by raising public awareness through rallies and protests.

Even in the late 1970s and early 1980s, a time of active (and often productive) searching for theoretical rationales to link environmental protection and economic policy, Chinese analysts were straightjacketed by the need to develop policy in response to vaguely defined theoretical assumptions based on Party dogma. The prevailing wisdom of the time viewed laws of nature and the economy as complementary dialectical poles. Central planners were expected to find ways of "rationally" balancing investment in development and conservation at local and national levels, to avoid pollution excesses while facilitating essential economic growth. The larger aim was to sustain productivity in keeping with "the laws of proportional development," a vague spatial planning concept never meaningfully applied at a national scale. Experiments aimed at adapting theory to local needs, however, were tried in some provinces.

During the 1980s, as China's command economy weakened, consideration of economic dimensions of environmental issues has shifted from broad theoretical approaches to a more specific focus on local and regional concerns. Emphasis has been on finding solutions to specific industrial siting and pollution control problems, nature and habitat protection, and strengthening of urban water supply and wastewater treatment infrastructure to reduce harmful effects of contaminated water.

China's main problem in formulating environmental policy has been inability at the national level to frame regulatory strategies that can be consistently and effectively applied throughout the country. There have been frequent shifts in emphasis among ideological, administrative, planning, legal, and economic approaches. This has made it difficult to set clear environmental goals, and to establish criteria for policies to achieve these goals. There has been much confusion over ends and means in environmental protection. One reason is that the uncertain progress of price and fiscal reforms has slowed emergence of market mechanisms that might improve efficiency in land and resource use and lead to improved resource conservation and materials recycling. Prospects for creative environmental policy development in the present period of economic retrenchment are uncertain.

Progress will depend to a large degree on the rate and level of investment in environmental protection. Several questions arise. Should domestic and foreign investment be directed at technical upgrading of pollution control capability in factories, mines, cities, and provinces, or should investment primarily support institution-building, technical training, education, and public awareness? What are the sources of investment funds? At present, Japan and The World Bank are the main sources of funding to support environmental improvement in China, although loan prospects are still uncertain because of international reaction to the June, 1989 Tiananmen incident. An environmental investment strategy and allocation plan for China are currently under development by the Bank.

Prospects for implementing an effective national environmental investment strategy are also clouded by the growing economic independence of Guangdon and Fujian. In recent years, this independence has weakened central ability to enforce regulatory programs in fast-growing coastal areas. Despite the slowdown in foreign investment in China since 1988, there has been a rapid increase in Taiwanese industrial investment in Fujian, especially around Xiamen. Through early 1990, about 500 Taiwan investors invested $1 billion in consumer goods factories that produce bicycles, appliances, clothing, and shoes. To facilitate investment, local authorities sell "land use rights" for up to 70 years to speculators who have little concern for environmental protection. For example, Wang Yung-ching, the powerful head of Taiwan's Formosa Plastics Group, has been discussing with Chinese authorities for several years the possibility of building a $7 billion petrochemical complex in Fujian. A major attraction of the proposed Fujian site is that it would not be subject to stringent environmental controls. Wang was deterred from building the project in Taiwan by intense pressure from environmentalists.

Finally, there are several ways in which regulators can employ tax and fiscal incentives to further pollution control objectives. These include buying and selling pollution rights to stimulate cost-effective pollution clean-up, introducing least-cost, long-term investment strategies at municipal or provincial levels to foster integrated technical and institutional response to pollution, and recycling effluent fees to factories to improve technical controls. None of these measures, however, are effective on a national scale. The Environmental Protection Law, passed by the Standing Committee of the National People's Congress in December 1989, establishes norms and codifies many existing regulations. It was intended also to improve the efficiency of an effluent fee and rebate system introduced in the 1980s, which has led to reduced pollution in some large industries. However, low fee structures, misleading assumptions in pollutant discharge assessment, and technical flaws in the rebate return system have weakened the effectiveness of this regulatory tool.

Clearly, China's leaders are well aware of the serious environmental problems the country faces. Nevertheless, as is the case in most developing countries, the quest for economic modernization has superceded concern over environmental pollution. Formal analysis of environmental policy issues has barely begun and given budgetary constraints, institutional inadequacies, and lack of recognition by the population of the seriousness of the pollution problem, China's environment is not likely to see much improvement during the decade of the 1990s.

TOURISM IN CHINA AND THE IMPACT OF
JUNE 4, 1989[4]

Tourism is the attraction of the other: other places, times, peoples, practices. Without that attraction of the other, tourism does not really exist. The other, the exotic, may have its roots in the cultural, historical, or natural landscapes of an area and its people. In China, foreign tourists come not to relax but to experience scenic beauty, historical treasures, and cultural activities.

Developing countries have seen international tourism as a relatively quick way to garner foreign capital. Tourism, as the smokeless, clean, and green industry, is said to make fewer demands on the resources of developing countries. The World Bank has made loans for tourism development, especially for roads, airports, water, sewage, and other infrastructural improvements. The tourism industry is attractive to the People's Republic of China as a way to increase foreign exchange.

Besides its cultural and economic dimension, tourism can also have a political dimension. A country uses tourism to present its positive qualities. For China, tourism has provided an opportunity to showcase its economic strengths and political wisdom, and to increase positive foreign perceptions. The crackdown on dissent in 1989, broadcast globally from Tiananmen Square in Beijing, has had an effect on China's tourism industry.

Geographies of Tourism

International tourists are defined by geographer Peter Murphy as visitors who make at least one overnight stop in a country other than that which is their usual place of residence, for any reason other than following an occupation remunerated from within the country visited.

There is not just one geography of tourism, but many. Start with the raw materials: places to go, sights to see. Then consider the world's tourism consumers: people from countless cultural backgrounds, with money, curiosity, or longing.

[4]Article by Stanley W. Toops, professor of international studies and geography, Miami University in Ohio. From *Focus* 42:3–6 Spring '92. Copyright © 1992 by the American Geographical Society. Reprinted with permission.

Intervening between the raw material and the consumer are the producers: corporations or governments, big or little. The producer uses or develops the local infrastructure so tourists can come to the sites and spend their money. International tourists visit in search of a particular tourist product, through the structure of the tourism industry. All of these contribute to the total touristic web of interaction, the attraction of the other.

Is tourism good for a place? Is it an appropriate way to bring new wealth to a community, region or country? As one author has asked, is tourism a "passport to development"? The answer depends on the consequences—economic benefits of tourism must be weighed against the sociocultural costs. For example, tourists travel by the busload to a remote community to admire a traditional way of life, and their money is very welcome; but the local community finds itself having to perform its sacred ceremonies six times a day for camera-carrying outsiders; and the money replaces tradition with convenience. Does tourism destroy the very object it desires?

Geographers studying tourism try to answer this question, examining efforts to create tourism-based development, the stages of development, and the sociocultural effects.

China's Approach to Tourism

In China the international tourist market has several distinct parts used by the Chinese government to provide tourism services. The foreigners are the most obvious of the international tourists, those who see China as genuinely exotic. Another group is the *huaqiao,* the overseas Chinese. China welcomes its cultural descendants from far-away lands, regardless of their citizenship or how long their family has been away from China. A third group is the *tongbao* or compatriots. These are the Chinese of Taiwan, Hong Kong, and Macao, who because of the vagaries of international capitalism (according to the perspective of the People's Republic), have been separated from the land of their ancestors.

The preparations for the welcoming of these groups are all different. The geographies of these tourists are all different. This is not unexpected because the demands of these tourists vary also.

The domestic market is also growing. As the Chinese domestic economy expands, people have more discretionary income and can spend money and time beyond basic necessities. China's domestic tourism industry will eventually increase in size and significance to approach that of international tourism. The impact of domestic tourists is already beginning to have an impact on the scenic places of China.

Tourism in China is performing its economic function while providing needed foreign currency. Tourist income is increasing as the tourist market matures, attracting travelers who spend more.

National Trends

In 1978, China adopted an open door policy allowing the rebirth of China's tourism industry. In 1980, nearly 6 million visitors spent $600 million [U.S. dollars]. By 1988, almost 32 million visitors spend $2.2 billion [U.S. dollars]. All through the 1980s, most of the arrivals to China were *tongbao*, mostly from Hong Kong. Foreign tourists accounted for a relatively small percentage of the total visitor arrivals, ranging from 5.8%–9.6% of the total. Through the 1980s China saw a steady increase in the numbers of visits until the events of June 4, 1989, after which there was a dramatic decrease. Early 1990s reports from the Chinese press indicate that the numbers of tourists are recovering, approaching the levels reached before the Tiananmen Incident.

The tourism receipts for China have a similar temporal pattern: a steady increase until the drop in 1989. For the whole of 1989, purchase of commodities accounted for 33.9% of total tourist receipts, accommodation 21.8%, long-distance transportation 33.6%, while local transportation and other travel services accounted for 10.7% of total tourist receipts. Tourism in 1989 amounted to 3.5% of the total value of China's exports; previously tourism had amounted to as much as 5% of the value of exports, in 1986.

Where do the visitors go? The top draws were Guangzhou, Shenzhen, Shanghai, Beijing, Guilin, and Xian. Most of the rest of the tourist spots are in the coastal provinces. Accessibility, ease in getting there, is a key feature in the spatial distribution of tourists. The only major attractions inland were in Xian and Guilin. The government has made efforts to broaden the tourist base, but there is still a spatial concentration of tourists in just a few places. Not unexpectedly some of the sites with major transportation bottlenecks in China are in Xian and Guilin.

In China, the raw materials—places to go, sights to see—do

not determine where tourists go; instead it is China's internal open/closed policy that controls tourism traffic. Those areas that foreigners can visit with valid visas are labeled "open". "Closed" areas can only be visited by those having an "Alien Travel Permit" issued by the Public Security Bureau. China has a variety of reasons for restricting the extent of tourist activity. Before an area can be opened, the government provides the appropriate infrastructure for tourism, such as a China International Travel Service (CITS) office, guides, chauffeurs, hotels, vehicles, and restaurants. Of course, administrative, military, and geopolitical factors are major considerations as well, in determining which areas are open, and which remain hidden to prying foreign eyes.

Regional Centers: The Cities

The Chinese tourism industry has produced several sites that rank at the top consistently. The basis for their success in attracting international visitors includes proximity to the market: Guangzhou and Shenzhen are just inland from Hong Kong, a major entry point for visitors; cultural and historical landscapes including those of Xian, Beijing, Shanghai, and Guangzhou; the political landscape of Beijing; and the natural landscape of Guilin.

Guangzhou, on the southeast coast, is a major business and commercial center. The first city on this site began during the initial advance of the Chinese into the south around 200 BC. The city was the major port of entry for foreigners during the 1800s and remains the first view that many tourists have of China. The parks, gardens, temples, markets, and busy street life are all part of the attractiveness of this quintessential Southern Chinese city. A focal point is Shamian Island with its row of hotels and teahouses.

Nearby is Shenzhen, a new boomtown, bordering on Hong Kong. Shenzhen is one of China's new Special Economic Zones and the city is a bustling center for entrepreneurs. Both Guangzhou and Shenzhen are favored sites for Hong Kong visitors. The same Chinese dialect, Cantonese, is spoken in Hong Kong, Guangzhou and Shenzhen.

On the east coast near the mouth of the Changjiang (the Yangzi River) is Shanghai, China's major industrial and commercial center. Before the development of Shanghai in the 1800s, it was a small town. The imprint of colonialism is visible in the city edifices with European stylings. Tourists stroll along the Bund, the waterfront embankment, or visit the gardens and parks. There is ample opportunity to rub elbows with the residents in Shanghai who also are watching the scene as it goes by. Shanghai provides a starting point for further excursions into China up the Changjiang.

Beijing, at the northern edge of the North China Plain, is the site of Tiananmen, the Gate of Heavenly Peace, the symbol of New China's restructuring of the Forbidden City. As the country's capital, it is the political and cultural center for China, representing the socialist heart as well as the imperial past. The Temple of Heaven, Mao's Mausoleum, and the side streets are all major attractions for domestic and foreign tourists. Another obligatory stop is the Great Wall, *Chang Cheng* (the Long Wall) outside of the city, with its restored portions.

Beijing's rectangular city plan was modeled on Xian, ancient capital of the Qin, Han, and Tang Dynasties. Xian, or Changan (Eternal Peace) as it was known then, was the cultural focus of East Asia; foreign dignitaries and traders came to partake of cosmopolitan China. The major tourist site today is the tomb of Emperor Qin Shihuang, with its famous terra cotta warriors. While Xian is the hearth of Chinese culture, it is also the jumping off point for points west into Tibet and Turkestan.

Guilin graces the southwest, offering its magnificent natural scenery. The karst topography with its eerie crags entices many tourists. The tourist scene itself is an amazing sight, because the city's economy is geared up for tourism in a major way. Guilin is more dependent on tourists for economic development than any of the other major tourist centers.

Beijing, Shanghai, Guangzhou, Xian, and Guilin are the top five sites for foreign visitors. For all tourists, including *tongbao*, however, Guangzhou, Shenzhen, Beijing, Shanghai, and Guilin are the top five destinations. Thus there is a distinct difference in the geographies inscribed across the map of China by foreigners and by *tongbao*, who favor the southeastern destinations.

Nationality

Where do the tourists come from? The leading tourist markets for China are Japan, USA, United Kingdom, USSR (now CIS), Germany, Philippines, Thailand, Singapore, Canada, France, and Australia. We can really divide this into two groups of tourists. Many of the visitors coming from USSR, Philippines, Thailand, and Singapore are visiting relatives: they can be grouped as *huaqiao*, the overseas Chinese. In contrast, the visitors from Europe, Japan, USA, and Canada are not necessarily visiting relatives. There is an essential difference in the motivations of these two sets of visitors.

Where a tourist comes from largely determines where the tourist goes. Whether tourists are from the USA, Japan, France, or UK, the top five destinations are Beijing, Shanghai, Guangzhou, Xian, and Guilin. There is some variation in ranking of destinations among these countries: for example, UK exhibits a stronger preference for Guangzhou. All of these cities are on the standard tourist itineraries.

For countries that supply mostly overseas Chinese as visitors, there is a strong differentiation. The preferred destinations for travelers from the Philippines are Shanghai, Xiamen, Beijing, Quanzhou, Guangzhou, and Shenzhen. Xiamen (Amoy) and Quanzhou are major cities in Fujian Province; most Philippine Chinese migrated from this province. For visitors from Singapore, the major destinations include Guangzhou, Xiamen, Shantou, Shanghai, and Beijing. Shantou, in Guangdong Province, was a major source for Chinese out-migration to mainland Southeast Asia.

Visitors from USSR (now the CIS, or Commonwealth of Independent States) inscribe a much different geography. The leading destinations are Beijing, Shanghai, Urumqi, Harbin, and Dalian. Urumqi, capital of China's Xinjiang Uyghur Autonomous Region in the Northwest, has some Russians in its population. There is an even far larger population of Kazaks, Uzbeks, and Uyghurs in Urumqi who have relatives across the border. Air, rail, and bus connections bridge the border. While Harbin and Dalian, in China's Northeast, also have Russian populations, there are also growing tourist opportunities for people coming from the Russian Far East.

A nationality visiting China that is not always revealed in official statistics is the Taiwanese. The year 1989 saw a loosening of the restrictions for visitors from Taiwan. There were twice as many tourists coming from Taiwan as coming from Japan in 1990. Their preferred destinations are the cities in Fujian (Xiamen, Quanzhou), Zhejiang (Hangzhou) and Shanghai, since many were born in or have ancestors from those areas. Taiwan's business investments have also focused on those places.

The Impact of Tiananmen

All the major tourist destinations suffered strong decreases ranging from 30 to 40% in numbers of tourists in 1989 following the repressive events of June, especially the Tiananmen Square massacre on June fourth. Shenzhen suffered the least with a drop of 18%, while Beijing dropped 46%. Some coastal centers in China actually increased their tourist traffic in 1989. These were places with overseas connections such as Quanzhou and Zhangzhou in Fujian Province, Nantong in Jiangsu Province.

Figures suggest that by 1990 China's tourism market had effectively recovered from the 1989 decline. In general, levels of activity in 1990 reached that of 1988. Complete statistics for 1991 are not available as of this writing, but indications are that the Chinese tourism industry is back on its previous pace of growth.

Nonetheless, Americans, Europeans and Japanese are not coming to China in the numbers that they were previously. The China Tourism Administration is making an all-out effort to bring back these well-paying tourists. The increase in numbers comes partially from Taiwan, Philippines, Singapore, and the CIS; these tourists are not spending as much money as China would hope for and came to expect from its wealthier visitors.

Another way to look at the impact of Tiananmen is to consider the cost and availability of accommodations. The hotel industry is overbuilt in areas such as Guangzhou, Shanghai, and Beijing. The boom in the economy focused on the construction industry; as the supply of big spenders has dried up, hotels can no longer command $100 per night. Rooms can be had at fancy locales for perhaps $20–40 per night.

A key for China will be to bring in repeat customers. China was a hot destination in the 1980s, but if people's first experience in China was a negative one, then there will be no second experience. That repeat customer will come back because of the high quality of sites, sights, and service, or to trek further afield in China.

This year China's National Tourism Administration has a major campaign, "Visit China '92." The goal is to encourage a continual stream of tourists, to fill the hotels and enhance the image of China.

Conclusion: A Myriad of Geographies

Who is a tourist in China? A Wall Street broker on a $10,000 cross-the-continent grand tour from Berlin to Beijing by train and camel. An accountant from London visiting relatives in Guangzhou. A restaurant owner from Seattle sampling Shanghai vegetarian cuisine on a package tour. A Japanese college student backpacking through the Tian Shan. We are all tourists in China. It's grand, it's wonderful, it's China.

The geographies of tourism in China are as myriad as all of us as we inscribe our routes on our maps of China. Does your map match others? Is it a map of the other? A journey through China begins with a single step.

III. THE UNITED STATES AND CHINA

EDITOR'S INTRODUCTION

Since the 19th century, China has preoccupied American policymakers. This section explores current U.S. political and economic policies with the world's most populous nation. In the first article, reprinted from *Current History*, Tufts University professor Daniel Zweig analyzes the complexities of U.S.-China relations and suggests a policy agenda for the Clinton administration. In the following article, published in *Foreign Policy*, and discussing a debate which continues to the present, former State Department official Roger W. Sullivan argues that the Bush administration should have abandoned its "hands off" policy and actively pressured the Chinese government to respect human rights, as well as reduce its reported $16 billion worldwide arms sales.

The annual renewal of the Most Favored Nation (MFN) status for China often raises an intense debate in Congress. Critics charge that China's policies on human rights, arms sales and emigration should disqualify the autocratic Beijing regime from receiving the lucrative benefits derived from this special trade relationship. In the last article, President Clinton outlines why his administration approved the MFN renewal in 1993 and discusses the conditions for renewal in 1994.

CLINTON AND CHINA[1]

In devising a policy toward China, President Bill Clinton's administration faces a series of important questions. The president's overall foreign policy goals are relatively clear: promote democracy and freedom worldwide, resuscitate the American

[1]Article by David Zweig, associate professor of international relations, Fletcher School of Law and Diplomacy. From *Current History* 92:245–252 S '93. Copyright © Current History, Inc., 1993. Reprinted with permission.

economy and America's international economic strength, and ensure American and global security. But what should be the hierarchy among these issues? Should one issue dominate? Can one pursue all three at the same time and still maximize the national interest?

The end of the cold war has drastically reduced American concerns with military security while increasing those regarding economic issues. Clinton was elected president precisely because he could best articulate the American public's anxiety about the changing global economic environment. No doubt, he also reflects concerns with human rights and democratization that are deep within the American body politic. But right now, Americans want jobs and a better position in the global marketplace.

And herein lies the problem. Economic growth, particularly trade-based growth, is an interdependent process; without markets for exports, there is no growth, and without imports there is no comparative advantage. If pursuing a foreign policy based on expanding human rights globally undermines access to markets, leads to large increases in the prices Americans pay for goods, and complicates security relations with a major global and regional power, what is a president to do?

The lack of a clear hierarchy is not the only problem confronting a president who must govern in an interdependent world. The tools of his trade, the weapons of statecraft, have changed as well. As he moves into the realm of economic policy, Clinton will rapidly discover that America's military power is not the key determinant of bilateral policy conflicts, especially those involving economic issues. (If it were, the United States could, for example, use its superior military might to force the Japanese to open their markets.) In the case of China, the leverage to make it respond to United States concerns is based more on the degree to which China needs access to American markets, investment, and technology. How long it would take China to find new markets and the costs of doing so greatly enhance the leverage the United States has over China.

But can one successfully use economic power to affect another state's political agenda? Can influence in one area be used to affect outcomes in another? As the president contemplated his decision on whether or not to grant China Most Favored Nation (MFN) status this spring, whether to apply conditions to it, and how to deal with China for the rest of his administration, he found that those issues clouded the horizon. If he withdrew

MFN, what would have been the effect on the United States economy? How many American jobs would be lost? What would have been the impact on the price of basic consumer goods? How to calculate the opportunity costs to American businesses—to the economy—if the United States were the only country excluded from competition in the fastest growing economy in the world? Moreover, with the United States trying to legitimize the role of the UN as a regional peacekeeper, could the United States afford bad ties with a rising global power, one that is a permanent member of the Security Council? Yet without threatening China's economic growth, without using America's most potent leverage over China—access to the United States market—how could he also press forward his goal of bringing greater freedom to the people of China?

What Does the US Want from China?

America's agenda toward China is based on what the United States wants from that country. One can start from the assumption that American foreign policy should serve American interests. But what are United States interests in China?

Let us start with the tough ones, human rights and democratization. Many constituencies in the United States, including the president, liberal and conservative members of Congress, human rights groups, Chinese students, and perhaps many average American citizens, are particularly exercised by the human rights abuses, mistreatment of prisoners, repression in Tibet, and arrests of political activists that continue to occur in China. But why do Americans care whether China turns democratic and throws off its Communist mantle? First, a democratic China would ensure the same high standard of human rights for its citizens that Americans have. It is a fundamental belief among Americans that the Chinese should have the right to speak their minds on political issues without fear of incarceration. Second, because democracies have internal restraints on military expansion, it is assumed that a democratic China would be a peaceful China, which would help guarantee the security of China's neighbors and the United States. Third, it is assumed that a democratic China would be more stable politically, easier to negotiate with, and more likely to fulfill its global commitments on issues such as arms control and nonproliferation, environmental degradation, and population control.

While some of these assumptions are questionable—could a democratic China stem the rapid growth of the country's population?—we must still ask a basic question: how fast do we want change to occur in China? And what are the risks involved in pushing for rapid change? Some members of the United States Congress believe that the collapse of the Chinese Communist party will lead to a democratic alternative. However, the most likely scenario would be a takeover by a Chinese military no longer constrained by a Communist party. This could be even more destabilizing for the region, since there would be little internal opposition to further expansion of the military budget. One of paramount leader Deng Xiaoping's greatest contributions to regional stability in the 1980s was the demilitarization of Chinese society and China's foreign policy. Only in the wake of Tiananmen, when the military saved the regime, has it successfully flexed its political muscle to get a larger share of the national budget. [*Author's note:* It is also important to remember that the Persian Gulf War, with its display of American military technology, heightened the Chinese military's awareness of the great technical gap between it and the Western militaries. Some of the growth in defense spending must be seen as a response to these concerns for national security, rather than simply seen as reflecting Chinese expansionist tendencies.] The collapse of the party could also exacerbate human rights abuses—witness the cruelty meted out during the post-Tiananmen crackdown to those who were arrested by the martial law troops.

An alternative scenario would be the situation that has emerged in the former Soviet Union. When freedom suddenly explodes without the development of proper political institutions, political chaos is likely. But where will the United States be when China tries to put the pieces of a collapsed system back together? Look how slowly the United States has responded to the needs of the former Soviet republics. Unlike the Soviet Union, which was a direct military threat to the United States, China does not directly threaten American security. A collapse leading to chaos may be of less benefit to the United States than such an outcome was in the former Soviet Union. Collapse and disorder could trigger a massive flow of refugees into Hong Kong, or a new stream of boat people onto the shores of Japan, South Korea, and Taiwan. While Deng has raised this fear to frighten the world into not pressing China for political reform, one cannot underestimate the costs to all of East Asia if internal chaos in

China demolishes the floodgates controlling more than 1 billion people.

Yet, if the United States does not press the Chinese to adopt democratic institutions for China's own benefit, China will continue its cycle of liberalizations and crackdowns, which alienate the population and undermine economic growth. Without strong popular institutions, China's leaders increase the possibility of chaos when the political system does weaken further, which it eventually will. No doubt, rapid economic growth and expanding income inequality are placing great pressures on the Chinese system. But what type of system can best handle these strains? While Westerners believe democratic institutions are the solution, the examples of Singapore, Taiwan, and South Korea lead many Chinese to believe in the utility of a "new authoritarianism" that would maintain stability as the country goes through its rapid growing pains. (In fact, one more decade of political authoritarianism and rapid economic growth may be the perfect formula for the emergence of a moderately wealthy, politically modern Chinese state).

But the 1980s also shows that without stable, reliable institutions through which people can express their concerns about official corruption, unequal development, and fears of inflation, the Chinese people, especially students, will take to the streets and subvert political stability. It is therefore in everyone's interests to press the Chinese government to gradually create real institutions for the democratic expression of popular concerns.

The United States Economic Agenda With China

In Bill Clinton's search for a formula to reinvigorate the United States economy in the short term and strengthen its underlying qualities in the long term, China will be an important element. The United States has become more export-oriented, in search of new international markets. Since China will become the fastest growing market in the world in the next 20 years, United States firms must be able to sell their goods there. Bilateral trade has expanded dramatically; by 1992 China was America's ninth-largest trading partner. Trade soared last year, with the United States exporting $7.5 billion to China, and China exporting $25.7 billion to the United States. China's direct exports to the United States account for 9.2 percent of total Chinese exports, a figure that continues to grow.

As the quality of China's work force improves, American firms must consider offshore production in China a necessary part of their Asian economic development strategies. However, the president's agenda of increasing jobs at home may run counter to such strategies. But as more and more of America's competitors for market share in East Asia use China's labor force to produce higher quality products at relatively low prices, American firms will have to follow suit. Even the president's desire to increase the number of higher value added and high-tech jobs at home runs counter to market forces that will pull United States producers of technological products into China. [*Author's note:* It is estimated that there are at least 50,000 highly talented software engineers in China; Taiwanese and Japanese firms have already begun to forge close links with Chinese software firms. If American businesses do not employ some of them to produce American brands of software, they will not remain competitive.]

The United States also needs cheap Chinese exports to keep the price of its own goods down. Personal income in the United States is declining as more and more people shift from higher paying manufacturing jobs to lower paying service sector jobs. But lower salaries need not lead to a lower standard of living if the costs of Chinese-made household appliances decline as well.

But the United States also wants fair trade with China. While it imports billions of dollars of Chinese goods, the United States also wants access to China's more than 1 billion consumers. The Commerce Department and the United States trade representative pushed the Chinese to sign a Memorandum of Understanding (MOU) on market access last October, which will greatly reduce tariff barriers on hundreds of goods.

Other obstacles remain, however, including protecting American copyrights and intellectual property. American trade unions also want an end to prison labor exports to the United States, which contravene United States trade laws such as Section 307 of the 1930 Tariff Act. These latter issues loom as potential points of confrontation in the trade realm.

The International Agenda With China

A broad set of global issues also shape United States policy toward China. At the top of this list is the desire that China stop selling long- and medium-range missiles to countries in unstable regions and to enemies of American allies, such as Syria. China, which has agreed to abide by the Missile Technology Control Regime (MTCR), has a moral obligation to restrict its missile sales. The United States would like China to be far more circumspect in transferring nuclear technology, especially to countries, such as Iran and Algeria, that are trying to build nuclear weapons, and it desperately wants the Chinese not to employ military measures to resolve its territorial claim on Taiwan. For decades Taiwan has been a divisive issue in American politics; should the People's Republic resort to force, the United States would find itself in a situation where it might have to intervene.

For financial reasons, the United States hopes that Britain will successfully transfer sovereignty over Hong Kong to China in 1997 and that China will not destabilize the Hong Kong economy. The United States has over 60,000 expatriates living in Hong Kong and is the colony's third-largest investor, after China and Japan. As a measure of its concern, the United States Congress has passed legislation calling on China to resolve the transfer of sovereignty in a prudent manner. Under the 1992 United States-Hong Kong Policy Act, the secretary of state is to monitor Hong Kong's democratic institutions, while the president is to ensure that they function autonomously after China takes over.

On issues of East Asian security, the United States needs high-level Chinese cooperation if any kind of regional arrangement is to be built. Unless there is international cooperation in East Asia, a new era of nationalism will emerge. And President Clinton may see a regional security arrangement as one way to decrease American military obligations in East Asia, which are a drain on the economy.

As the United States contemplates building this East Asian security system, it must deal with a "rising China," whose economy is growing rapidly and whose military is in a stronger position domestically than at any time since 1971. The rapid growth of China's GNP will put more funds in the hands of the Chinese military. Continuing unresolved territorial claims, such as Hong Kong, Taiwan, and the Spratly and Paracel islands in the South China Sea, require China's enmeshment in a host of multilateral agreements that will limit its external actions and ensure responsible behavior. China, however, is likely to resist such efforts. Already, the perception of Chinese military expansionism has alarmed China's neighbors, particularly the members of the Association of Southeast Asian Nations (ASEAN) and Japan, and could fuel a growing arms race in the region, which is not in America's interests. [*Author's note:* According to some Chinese sources, China's military buildup is aimed at Taiwan, with plans already drawn up for an immediate invasion of Taiwan when it declares independence. A more likely scenario would involve various Chinese threats as Taiwan moved toward independence, ending with a possible attack if Taiwan persists.]

Similarly, the United States needs Chinese support for resolving many global crises, including the war in Yugoslavia, the tenuous Cambodian peace accords, and the ongoing nuclear threat on the Korean peninsula. With its seat in the United Nations, China has a great deal of power over the UN's development into a multilateral peacekeeping force and over the Security Council's ability to become a real center for negotiating solutions to crises. On North Korea, China is seen as the only state that has direct access to top Korean leaders. While the United States may also wield great leverage over North Korea, a united strategy may be the only way to ensure a nuclear-free Korean peninsula.

The United States also has a strong interest in China's environmental policy. As Douglas Murray has argued in *America's Interests in China's Environment,* China's "ecological problems [are] so severe that they constitute a collective crisis with global consequences and powerful implications for America." According to Murray, helping China avoid the globally harmful effects of its rapid industrialization, rising consumption levels, and relative neglect of its environmental problems would be extremely cost-effective—more so than the investments the United States must make to correct its own. Also, cooperative research involving Chinese facilities and scientific talent would be less costly and more productive than projects based solely in the United States and relying primarily on American scientific know-how. Moreover, investing in cleaning up China's environment means China will become a major market for environmental products—another plus for the United States, since it is a leader in clean energy technologies. Already by 1991, about 20 percent of China's $200 million in purchases of environmental equipment came from American firms, and the United States is well positioned to participate in contracts funded by the World Bank, United Nations Development Program (UNDP), Global Environmental Facility, and Asian Development Bank.

What Does China Want from the United States?

The end of the cold war has diminished the need for the United States to maintain a strategic alliance with China; for China, it means that it no longer needs a security understanding with the United States since the Soviet Union no longer poses a threat to it. Thus, China does not have to make major concessions in its dealings with the United States. However, less strategic dependence has not translated into a loss of United States leverage over China on other policy issues. Since 1979, China, too, has responded to the increased global salience of economics, and as it presses its agenda of growth and development, it finds itself again vulnerable to United States foreign policy pressures, some of which directly challenge its sovereignty.

Several internal factors in China require it to maintain good relations with the United States. The adoption of an export-oriented industrialization strategy has made China highly vulnerable to shifts in external markets. With over 25 percent of its exports going to the United States, and with markets in Europe and Japan relatively closed, China will have to depend on United States acquiescence in order to maintain its successful growth strategy.

Coastal areas are growing rapidly through community-led, export-oriented strategies. In a desire to bring in joint ventures and gain access to foreign technology and foreign capital (previously available only to state-owned firms), local coastal governments are slowly undermining the government's import substitution strategy and giving foreigners access points to the domestic market. Many coastal villages are becoming home to offshore production for Hong Kong, Taiwanese, and South Korean firms using the cheap labor to maintain their position in the United States market. Should the United States market become closed to Chinese exports, much of this investment would dry up as producers moved to Thailand, Indonesia, or Malaysia.

China also needs access to American technology. The Chinese have discovered that joint ventures with Japan, Taiwan, and Korea bring in little new technology; the United States is perceived to be much more willing than most of China's other trading partners to share relatively new technology. The growth of China's high-tech industries, including computers, space vehicles, and electronics, will require United States technology; moreover, to gain access to it, China will need United States support in lifting Western restrictions on the transfer of "dual use" technology to it. But so long as China does not allow foreigners to compete in China with its high-tech industries or participate in some of its high-tech programs, that technology should not come so easily.

Educational exchanges have been another conduit through which China has received access to American technology. Even though the percentage of overseas students and scholars returning to China has decreased dramatically since the mid-1980s, the Chinese government has chosen to keep the door open for many who want to go abroad and have the funds to do so. The government believes that even if these people do not return immediately, many will eventually do something useful for China. Difficult Sino-American relations would greatly complicate these exchanges.

Another issue that requires China to maintain good ties with the United States is its role in the world community. Branded by the United Nations as an "aggressor" nation for its confrontation with the United States in North Korea in 1950, China suffered for several decades as a pariah nation. Although it moved into many international organizations in the late 1970s, it again faced international opprobrium after crushing the pro-democracy movement in Tiananmen in 1989. China is thus highly sensitive about its international stature and strongly wants to take what it sees as its rightful place near the top of the community of nations.

Two events are high on China's international agenda, and both give the United States some leverage. First, China's entrance into the General Agreement on Tariffs and Trade (GATT) passes through Washington, and the Chinese know it. One of the terms of last fall's MOU on market access was that the United States would work "enthusiastically" for China's entry into GATT. But the recent visit of Assistant United States Trade Representative for GATT Affairs Douglas Newkirk to Beijing, where he said that China would probably not gain access to GATT for at least another 5 to 7 years, created great consternation in the Chinese government. Linking criticism of China's restrictive trading practices and its ability to gain entrance into GATT is one way for the United States to press China to further lower its tariff barriers.

China also strongly desires to host the Olympics in the year 2000. Billboards throughout Beijing exhort the people to present a good face in order not to undermine China's chances of being the site of the Olympics. While the United States has no veto in the International Olympic Committee, American pressure against China's hosting the Olympics could be problematic. [*Editor's note:* The International Olympic Committee voted in 1993 to award the 2000 Olympic Games to Sydney, Australia.]

Finally, while the Chinese would never admit that they need

help in solving an issue deemed an "internal affair," they do need the United States to maintain its "One China Policy," and its pressure on Taiwan not to seek independence. Recent conferences by China scholars and presentations before congressional hearings have called on the people of Taiwan to remain patient. For China, a declaration of independence by Taiwan would be the worst possible scenario; the inevitable use of military force would, at the very least, scuttle the current economic boom.

Pursuing The Foreign Policy Agenda

While the United States needs to confront China directly on an array of critical issues, American political leaders must not jettison the relationship because China pursues its own interests in a manner that challenges world trends. They must confront that behavior and work to affect it. The best strategy for the Clinton administration is a mixed strategy that combines efforts at strategic enmeshment; continued economic, cultural, and political involvement, which will allow the United States to benefit from the "open door" China cannot afford to close; and direct confrontations on human rights, arms sales, unfair trade, and nuclear proliferation when China's actions are inimical to United States global and national interests. The "easier" partner of the mid-1980s is gone for now, but one should not assume that a mix of quiet diplomacy, public protestations, and hard negotiations cannot gain results.

As has been noted, China's trade dependency on the United States market leaves China highly vulnerable to American trade pressures. If China lost access to the United States market, its economic boom, particularly in south China, would stumble badly. No other market of similar proportions exists for its exports. Foreign investment that relies on re-exports to the United States would also decrease. But the degree of vulnerability for both the United States and China varies across policy arenas. The United States has great leverage when directly confronting China over specific economic and trade policies. And United States firms benefit from trade pressures that improve access to the Chinese market. For a president who must worry about jobs, directly challenging China to open its market, using clear guidelines and indicators of compliance, may be a far more effective strategy than a broadside on the trade relationship because of a political agenda. Even Clinton has recognized that the Bush administration's strategy of threatening economic sanctions to gain movement on economic policies, rather than using economic threats for political purposes, has led to significant agreements with China on a host of economic issues, including MOUs on prison labor, intellectual property rights, and market access.

Still, implementation mechanisms and monitoring systems are a problem, since Beijing appears unwilling or unable to enforce these commitments. The United States trade representative must continue to pressure the Chinese to meet agreements they have made under the MOUs. The Voice of America must play a role in informing local officials of the content of these agreements—the Chinese government, it seems, may not fully inform local governments of their obligations under the MOUs— and consular officials must meet with local trade officials and warn them that their export market is at risk if they do not conform to these agreements. The Chinese must be warned that if direct, issue-specific trade negotiations do not open China's markets, lower the trade imbalance, and end trade violations, pressure could build in the United States for widespread trade confrontations. Asia scholar Ross Munro has suggested a trade agreement that would compel China to increase its imports from, or decrease its exports to, the United States whenever China's trade surplus approached a target zone. Such "managed trade" may not be unwelcome by the current United States trade representative.

Conditional MFN: The Thin Edge of the Wedge

How can the United States push its agenda of improving China's human rights behavior? Was making MFN conditional the right strategy? There are enormous economic costs and political risks in linking MFN to China's human rights behavior. If MFN is ended next year because China does not meet the human rights conditions, China could raise tariffs from the "minimum" category to the "general" category for a host of United States imports and shift to other suppliers from Europe and Japan. The American aircraft industry, producers of chemical fertilizer, exporters of wheat and other grains, and producers of industrial and construction machinery would suffer most. These four industries comprise much of the $7.5 billion in imports China bought from the United States in 1992. The United States–China Business Council estimates that ending MFN would cost 100,000 United

States jobs, a difficult pill to swallow for a president who has made employment expansion "job one." Hong Kong, as Governor Christopher Patten told the president, would suffer badly, since many of its products exported to the United States are now produced in mainland China and would therefore face much stiffer tariffs in the United States market. Similarly, many Taiwanese and Korean firms producing offshore on the Chinese mainland would be forced to relocate to other parts of Southeast Asia.

Second, few in the United States business community support linking trade policies and human rights. This community believes that expanding business is a liberating force in itself. Moreover, the examples of Taiwan and South Korea suggest that economic development and the creation of free markets help generate support for democratic transitions. One potential fallacy in this argument, however, is the assumption that economic development inevitably leads to the creation of an autonomous middle class, which then presses the state for political liberalization. In China, where private property rights are still unclear, much of the economic growth is due to local government industrialization, which may weaken the central state's control over the localities, but need not generate a middle class, as it has in South Korea and Taiwan.

Third, jeopardizing trade relations for improvements in Chinese domestic behavior is risky. By making MFN conditional, the president will be in a bind next year not to appear weak on human rights: unless China makes *very* significant progress, it will be hard for him to certify that it has. This fact will shift the debate to whether or not to withdraw MFN. The political stakes and pressures at that time will dwarf anything we have seen to date in the recurrent discussions on MFN. Also, given the current pace of economic growth, the problems in rural China, and growing inequalities and corruption, major protests could reemerge in the next 12 months. China will meet that challenge forcefully, and if necessary with brutality. No doubt, massive arrests of peaceful demonstrators and secret executions of labor activists, as in 1989, would and should not be tolerated; but should we condemn China for trying to maintain some semblance of social order as it undergoes this historic growth spurt? And tying MFN to China's domestic behavior, rather than to external acts such as arms sales which the central government should be able to control, puts the initiative in the hands of people who want to see MFN taken away. One might anticipate massive riots in Tibet next spring as young monks become aware that triggering a military crackdown in Tibet will force the president's hand to end MFN.

Fourth, despite the president's desire to preserve Sino-American ties, conditional MFN will undermine bilateral business relations. In the eyes of businessmen in both China and the United States, conditional MFN may have been the first step down the slippery slope of taking away MFN, given that next year's debate will not be about imposing conditions but instead will focus on whether or not to remove MFN altogether. So conditional MFN dramatically increases the risk for Americans of doing business in China. Similarly, Chinese businessmen may hesitate to establish joint ventures with American firms, now that the United States administration is one step closer to canceling MFN. Two years ago, an American businesswoman cold not get the best silk producer in Nantong to meet with her; he felt that the possible withdrawal of MFN made working with American firms too risky. Today many Chinese firms must perceive the risks to be even higher.

It is continued economic engagement that keeps China trapped in its tango with the United States. Without access to the United States market, China could not grow as rapidly as it has, but without that engagement the United States would have less leverage over China's internal affairs. While threatening to withdraw MFN may appear to be the best tool, doing so will undermine the leverage the United States has over China. But because of the linkage between economic growth and the United States market, China cannot disengage from the United States, even as the United States presses China on human rights, democratization, and arms control. Moreover, continued economic expansion will allow for the slow emergence of social forces—the civil society—that may eventually lead to a democratic transition. External pressure can create the context within which liberalization will occur; but unless society is ripe, as it was in South Korea in 1988 when hosting the Olympics prevented the Korean military from cracking down on popular protests, it cannot be the critical force triggering democratic change. [*Author's note:* Another mistaken belief in the United States is that China was on the verge of a democratic transition in 1989; one need only recall the numerous predictions after June 4 that the system was about to collapse. Even now there is no real opposition force in China that could step in and govern. Today many Chinese look back with some relief that the students did not take power in 1989.]

Moreover, prodding China to release political prisoners and build democratic institutions is far short of making human rights the pillar of United States policy toward China. In the current context, where American popular opinion, presidential views, and congressional concerns so strongly favor democratization in China, support for a "peaceful evolution" of the Chinese political system seems the most appropriate public policy. According to a recent suggestion from the Atlantic Council and the National Committee on United States–China Relations, a bilateral human rights commission may be one useful forum for a "quiet dialogue on human rights at senior levels." The United States government should also press China in many multilateral forums, such as the UN Human Rights Commission, to improve its human rights record. It should use the Voice of America as a tool to help Chinese understand the outside world. It must engage government officials and Chinese research scholars in a debate about the benefits of democratization, and the opportunities that exist for peaceful transitions that leave ruling parties in power—noting that this has been the outcome in Taiwan and South Korea. But Americans must also make it clear that they call for liberalization in order to avoid the breakdown of political authority in China, not to trigger it. Given China's experience of the past 90 years, few Chinese, outside a sector of intellectuals and working class activists, support foreign efforts to destabilize their country. A gentler, less corrupt and more equitable system, with rising incomes would satisfy most Chinese today.

An Alternative Scenario

Despite the important constraints imposed on United States–China policy, events may not follow the logic dictated by this theory for several reasons. First, ideological commitment to human rights by the president, plus his need to maintain strong ties to his party's liberal wing, led him to favor conditional MFN. But using an executive order warning China about its human rights and arms proliferation abuses to replace congressional legislation conditioning MFN has created the perception that this is a declaratory policy with too few teeth for a president who sharply criticized the former administration on its policy, and who needs the support of Congress for his domestic agenda. Second, China's own behavior, especially its inability to abide by its pledges and legal commitments not to sell intermediate-range missiles, fuels the furor in Washington against China. Third, the inconsistency between United States political and economic ties with China complicates the relationship. In the past the two were always in balance: in the 1950s the United States and China hated each other and had no trade; in the 1970s the two nations were cautiously interactive both politically and economically; the mid-1980s saw the heyday of political, military and economic ties. But since Tiananmen, political ties have remained at best cool, while economic ties have heated up. But American foreign policy often struggles with such dissonance; efforts by politicians to bridge this moral and economic gap will cause them to restrict economic ties.

On the Taiwan issue, the administration must recognize that despite the numerous Sino-American confrontations since the 1950s centering on Taiwan, Americans have consistently underestimated the importance of Taiwan to the Chinese government. Despite an apparent amelioration in relations with Taiwan, the Chinese government will not tolerate an independent Taiwan; and if an invasion follows a declaration of independence, the United States will be forced to confront the Chinese militarily. Thus, while it asserts that it has no position on this "internal affair" between the Chinese, the real challenge for the United States will come if Taiwan proclaims its independence.

Finally, if we are to arrest China's possible expansion into the South China Sea, work for a peaceful solution to the Taiwan issue, prevent a Sino-Japanese arms race, and establish some kind of security arrangement in East Asia, the United States must be involved in direct talks with the Chinese military. The Chinese cannot dismiss American and Asian concerns about an expanding Chinese military by innocent protestations of misunderstanding. China's "peaceful" and "just" foreign policy positions (as the Chinese call them) are not apparent to all. Serious concerns are emerging about Chinese great power aspirations, and until China responds to those issues through greater openness, there should be no lifting of the sales embargo on "dual use" technology. An engaged United States policy, which tries to enmesh the Chinese military in a stronger bilateral or preferably multilateral security arrangement, rather than one that seeks to dismantle China's Communist system, will garner strong support from America's Asian friends.

Dealing with China in the near and distant future will not be easy. A system under stress—with weak political institutions, a succession looming, and with dramatically different cultural traditions—will continue to challenge American policymakers. But strong economic ties can limit China's freedom of movement, even as they limit America's own. A careful policy that asserts American and global interests can succeed, if the United States is patient and has the will to pursue it.

DISCARDING THE CHINA CARD[2]

In the current debate over China policy, there is one point of general agreement: The pre-Tiananmen bipartisan consensus is gone. President George Bush defends a policy that was already outdated when he took office, while the Democratic majority in the Congress calls for change but offers no positive alternative beyond punishing the People's Republic of China (PRC) for the June 1989 massacre at Tiananmen Square. If U.S. policy toward China is to be rebuilt around a new consensus, Americans must first understand why the old consensus fell apart. The reason was no Tiananmen Square: If revulsion at the televised violence had been the force that destroyed the domestic consensus, the sense of outrage would have blown over quickly and America would have returned to a policy that treated China as a special case—a "friendly, non-allied" state. Tiananmen, then, was only the alarm bell that made Americans wake up and ask whether their China policy still made sense. For most Americans, the answer was "No."

It was not so much that China had changed, but that the world had changed. During 1989, reform in the Soviet Union and radical changes in Eastern Europe made many Americans question China's supposed strategic importance to the United States. The subsequent collapse of communism in Eastern Europe and the Soviet Union and the dissolution of the Warsaw Pact made the old anti-Soviet basis of U.S.-China policy irrelevant.

With America's overriding geopolitical concern removed, it was no longer possible to conduct relations with China by managing most issues with ambiguous language in order to further the main interest the two countries had shared: deterring and discomfiting the Soviet Union. The Bush administration was slow to

[2]Article by Roger W. Sullivan, former president of the U.S.-China Business Council, from *Foreign Policy* 86:3–23 Spring '92. Copyright © 1992 by the Carnegie Endowment for International Peace. Reprinted with permission.

recognize this change and even denied it for a time. It has yet to understand the implications of this change for policy.

The administration certainly understands that it makes no sense to focus on the Soviet threat in the post-Cold War environment; it does not see, however, that this change makes its China policy unworkable. Instead, it argues that China's strategic value to the United States has not been reduced but merely transformed. The administration assumes that it can simply plug in new issues—such as bilateral trade, the proliferation of missile and nuclear weapons technologies, the peace settlement in Cambodia, and stability on the Korean peninsula—to replace the old anti-Soviet emphasis while maintaining the old policy paradigm.

This thinking is misguided and policies based on it will not work. To be of value to the United States in deterring the Soviet Union, China did not have to do very much; it just had to be there. As former national security adviser Zbigniew Brzezinski once put it, China was "a key force for global peace simply by being China." But China can no longer be of value to America on these new issues simply by "being China"; it must change its behavior. Yet the current regime has demonstrated that it is unwilling or incapable of cooperating productively on these issues.

Before the demise of Soviet communism, issues in Chinese–U.S. relations were handled by a technique that in government came to be called "creative ambiguity": framing issues in language that each side could claim represented its position, while refraining from correcting or contradicting the other side's interpretation. The Shanghai Communiqué of 1972 was the prototype, and the December 1978 communiqué announcing the establishment of U.S.-Chinese diplomatic relations followed the same form. When the United States "acknowledged" the Chinese position that there is "but one China and that Taiwan is a part of China," the PRC was able to claim that the United States had accepted the position that Taiwan was a domestic Chinese matter. Meanwhile, the United States could respond to domestic criticism by claiming that it had merely stated the American understanding of the Chinese position. Just as earlier administrations did not require China to do much toward deterring the Soviet Union except "being China," neither did they expect Beijing to move beyond its cooperative rhetoric and be accommodating on other issues.

Indeed, it was the Nixon administration's insight that Taiwan need not be divisive. China did not seriously plan to take military action against Taiwan, but sovereignty concerns and national pride prevented the Chinese from agreeing to a formal renunciation of force. The United States had no serious interest in keeping Taiwan separate or making it independent, but it could not simply abandon Taiwan and concede that it was part of the PRC. In 1982 the Reagan administration adopted a similar approach— papering over a basic disagreement with an essentially meaningless diplomatic formulation—in its successful effort to put aside the issues of arms sales to Taiwan. And so the Taiwan problem did not have to be solved; it could be managed and avoided.

Ambiguity and Bluff

Now, however, trying to deal with China on post–Cold War issues the way earlier administrations coped with secondary issues like Taiwan is doomed to failure. Ambiguous communiqués deceptively assuring Washington that China will not sell missiles to Middle Eastern states, for example, cannot be a foundation on which to build a productive bilateral relationship. China's subsequent behavior will demonstrate that there was no substance to the assurances, making it appear that the Bush administration either fell for a Chinese lie or perpetrated a hoax on the American people by allowing the Chinese to act against U.S. interests under the cover of soothing rhetoric. Post–Cold War issues such as nuclear, biological, and chemical weapons proliferation are real. They call for substance, not spin control. And so the bluff implicit in any attempt to manage these issues with ambiguity will certainly be called. Indeed, it already has been.

The controversy over China's 1987 Silkworm missile sales to Iran illustrates the point dramatically. With the Cold War already winding down, China's sales to Iran suddenly became the first of the new post–Cold War problems in Sino-American relations. Beijing apparently did not comprehend the issue's seriousness and tried to finesse it. Yet, despite valiant efforts by the wordsmiths in China's Ministry of Foreign Affairs, the sales defied easy management. The United States wanted them stopped. The problem was only made worse by the fact that the Reagan administration mistook China's ambiguous words for a real commitment to resolve the problem.

An irate secretary of state George Shultz orchestrated a postponement of export control liberalization for China. Then, in November 1987, China announced that it had stopped selling the missiles that a month earlier it had denied selling at all. In March 1988 the State Department told the press that the Chinese "have been living up to [their] pledge" not to sell more Silkworm missiles to Iran, and Shultz told the Chinese foreign minister in Washington that the United States was prepared to lift the restriction imposed in October 1987 and "to do more" to liberalize controls on high-technology exports to China.

In 1988, persistent reports of planned Chinese sales of missiles to Syria and an actual sale to Saudi Arabia, both acknowledged by the State Department, prompted the Senate to pass a resolution calling for an end to Chinese missile sales and threatening new restrictions on high-technology trade if China refused. Chinese missile sales thus became the major item on the agenda during Shultz's July 1988 trip to China. This time the Chinese denied having sold "ballistic missiles" to any country other than Saudi Arabia and agreed "to study" Shultz's request for in-depth discussions of the missile proliferation issue.

Secretary of Defense Frank Carlucci raised the issue again on his September 1988 Beijing visit. This time the Chinese at first were prepared to say only that China "will not sell armaments in large quantities." Carlucci nevertheless said after the conclusion of his talks that he was "fully satisfied" that China would behave in a "thoroughly responsible way" in its weapons sales. He offered no basis for his confidence, but State Department officials hinted that the Chinese had promised to abide by the Missile Technology Control Regime (MTCR) guidelines. Whatever words the Chinese employed to give that impression, the commitment clearly did not hold.

When National Security Adviser Brent Scowcroft visited Beijing in December 1989, he also came home convinced that he had won Chinese assurances on missile sales to Middle Eastern countries. But when new shipments were reported the following spring, administration sources suggested that there might have been some confusion over exactly what had been promised. China apparently said only that it "had no plans" to sell intermediate-range missiles in the Middle East—a classic creative ambiguity formulation.

If the Chinese understood that creative ambiguity would no longer work, they showed no sign of it—perhaps because even after Tiananmen they found that it still seemed to work. In June 1991, Secretary of State James Baker, reacting to intelligence reports that China was once again planning missile sales to Syria and Pakistan, warned of "potentially profound consequences" if China were to go ahead despite earlier promises. The Bush administration further acknowledged to Congress that China had apparently been cooperating on nuclear technology with Iran despite Chinese statements "made repeatedly to us . . . that they will not support or encourage nuclear proliferation." However the Chinese phrased their statements, they apparently believed, or more likely hoped, that the administration was still prepared to play the ambiguity game. And why shouldn't they? It was the message given by former president Richard Nixon and other "friends of China" who went to the PRC in October 1989 and called for a "return to the formula that has served us so well since [Nixon's] first journey to China in 1972." That was the message conveyed by Scowcroft's trips and his handling of the missile sales issue.

It was also the message delivered by Baker's November 1991 visit to Beijing. Once again the Chinese were praised for agreeing to vaguely worded proposals on missile sales, trade, and human rights. Particularly shocking was the administration's apparent willingness to cite "clear gains" on the missile proliferation issue and to accept at face value China's "commitment" to observe the MTCR, a pledge that administration sources concede the Chinese have made—and broken—before. Two months later, administration sources acknowledged that the Chinese were resisting demands from Washington to put their vague verbal assurances in writing. Further, there were hints that China was seeking to reopen the anti-proliferation issues that Baker thought had been settled during his November visit.

On trade, Beijing proposed a formulation on patent and copyright protection that Baker initially called "positive." On November 26, 1991, however, U.S. Trade Representative Carla Hills announced that China's proposals had turned out to be "insufficient" and that negotiations to avert imposition of punitive tariffs against China under Section 301 of the 1988 Trade Act had collapsed. U.S. negotiators commented privately that the two sides were never even close. An agreement was nevertheless reached in January 1992, but a judgment on whether these Chinese promises will be kept will be kept will have to await the outcome of scheduled "consultations" between the two sides on implementation. A second round of negotiations on other obstacles to market access is expected to continue into the fall of 1992.

Human rights is a different kind of issue. American policy

treated it as a secondary issue during the Cold War because there seemed little to be done. For the most part, Chinese human rights violations were simply ignored. In fact, before the 1989–91 worldwide collapse of communism, few questioned two key assumptions guiding Washington's China policy: first, that communist regimes cannot be fundamentally reformed or overthrown; and, second, that the Chinese communist government was firmly in control and that it enjoyed the support of the Chinese people. Events in Eastern Europe and the Soviet Union have done much more to undercut these assumptions than has the massacre at Tiananmen.

The administration does not seem to understand this. When Deputy Secretary of State Lawrence Eagleburger testified before Congress in February 1990 in the first comprehensive presentation of Bush's China policy after Tiananmen, he could not understand why people were making so much of China's human rights behavior. There was repression in the 1970s as well, he said, but "somehow [the repression] received scant attention here." The complaint misses the point. It is not 1971 anymore. In 1971 the United States could and did justify holding its nose and dealing with Romanian dictator Nicolae Çeausescu, but certainly no one suggested it do so again in 1989.

The Geopolitics of Yesterday

American overtures to China in 1971 made sense for a number of reasons, none of which apply today. Achieving normal relations with the PRC enabled the United States to end military support for South Vietnam, which had become politically insupportable in America. It also put the United States in a position to exploit the Sino-Soviet split and reap the obvious benefits of blocking the advance of Soviet influence in Asia and drawing Soviet forces away from Europe.

In addition, Americans had come to accept the Nixon-Kissinger view that since communism in China was there to stay, Washington should replace the old policy of seeking a collapse of Chinese communism with the supposedly more realistic approach of seeking to strengthen moderates like Zhou Enlai and Deng Xiaoping in hopes of encouraging the emergence of a kinder, gentler communism.

There was, nevertheless, unease about supporting such a repressive Chinese regime and particularly about appearing to abandon Taiwan. But most government officials involved in China policy suppressed their ambivalence. The geopolitical argument that relations with China enhanced U.S. national security was persuasive. Even President Ronald Reagan, who had criticized President Jimmy Carter's China policy during the 1980 campaign, was soon persuaded. In an April 1982 letter to China's paramount leader, Deng Xiaoping, Reagan wrote that it was "particularly important" that Chinese-U.S. relations resume their broad advance because "we face a growing threat from the Soviet Union . . . in Afghanistan and Iran [and] in Southeast Asia."

In all three areas the threat has been transformed. On February 15, 1989, the Soviets completed the withdrawal of their troops from Afghanistan. In Iran the threat no longer derives from the Soviet Union, but from China's willingness to sell missiles and nuclear technology. In Southeast Asia the United States need not fear a Soviet naval presence in Vietnam or Soviet-backed aggression; instead, the United States must ensure that China does not wreck the U.N.-brokered peace settlement in Cambodia through renewed support for the Khmer Rouge. While these changes do not make China irrelevant, they certainly demand a different policy.

Immediately after Tiananmen, it was not clear how the administration would respond. Bush announced sanctions, including withholding support for World Bank loans and suspending military sales to China. In general, though, these sanctions were not strictly applied for long enough to do any real damage. The one exception was the suspension of high-level visits. In the 10 years after the establishment of diplomatic relations, the frequent exchanges of high-level visits were an important part of the old way of conducting U.S. relations with China. These visits were highly valued by Beijing because they raised China's status in the world and the government's reputation at home. The high-level meetings were not necessary to conduct serious business—on the contrary, they were frequently scheduled without serious substantive purpose—but were intended to symbolize the great importance both governments placed on the continued expansion of the relationship. Because of that history, Bush's decision to suspend such visits appeared to convey a strong message: that the United States was no longer prepared to conduct its relations with China on the old basis.

Within a month of the ban's announcement, however, that message was only clear to Americans. To the Chinese, the administration was saying, in effect, "ignore the rhetoric; nothing has really changed." That was the business-as-usual message in the administration's decision, despite its own publicly announced ban on high-level visits, to send Scowcroft and Eagleburger on their secret trip to Beijing in July 1989 and again in December 1989; it was the message when, on the latter occasion, they toasted Chinese leaders and called for "bold measures" to "overcome [the] negative forces" in both countries who seek to "frustrate [U.S.-Chinese] cooperation."

Despite criticism from Congress and the press that these gestures amounted to kowtowing to the Chinese, the administration reverted to the old approach to China. The annual process of renewing non-discriminatory [Most Favored Nation, or MFN] tariff treatment for China became the outlet for congressional frustration and the vehicle for engaging the administration in a general policy debate. Renewal had been routine every year since MFN treatment was first extended to China in 1980 because Congress was well aware that MFN treatment is not a special benefit but is considered standard for almost all trading partners. Congress even let Bush's decision to renew MFN treatment for China immediately after Tiananmen pass without a vote. But when Congress saw no change in administration China policy, despite the collapse of communism in Eastern Europe and the Soviet Union and the clear evidence that China was becoming more repressive, congressional opposition to China's MFN status mounted.

Congress questioned the double standard that denied MFN treatment to a reforming Soviet Union while extending it to an increasingly repressive China. Each year since 1989 a majority of Congress has favored conditioning renewal of MFN status on a significant improvement in human rights. Some specific conditions have included the release of all those detained—and an accounting of all those killed—during the peaceful demonstrations leading to and following Tiananmen, as well as the elimination of such abuses as forced labor, religious persecution, detention without trial, and heavy restrictions on domestic and foreign press. After trade figures showed that China, a non-market economy that severely limits foreign access to its market, had nearly doubled its trade surplus with the United States in 1990 to $10.4 billion, Congress promptly added "significant progress" toward opening the Chinese market to its conditions for renewing MFN treatment.

The president has been able to retain MFN status for China

by the threat of his veto. A blocking third of the Senate has supported the administration's position that conditional renewal would be tantamount to withdrawing MFN status because Beijing would refuse to comply with the conditions, and that withdrawal would be too costly. It would raise tariffs on Chinese goods to prohibitive levels, causing severe damage to American consumers and businesses as well as hurting the people of an already beleaguered Hong Kong, which earns a significant portion of its income as an entrepôt for U.S.-Chinese trade. In China, loss of MFN treatment would hurt the very people America wants to support: the entrepreneurs and reformists in south China who dominate the country's export trade.

The annual threat to withdraw MFN status has produced a few small concessions and cosmetic improvements in China. These are important because they can mean freedom for at least a few Chinese dissidents. Unfortunately, though, threats to reduce trade are not going to bring about substantial change in China. Many Americans believe that Beijing so desperately needs foreign exchange that it would have no choice but to accept conditions along with MFN treatment. This assumption is dangerously wrong. The Beijing leadership makes a convincing case that the benefits of foreign trade and investment go largely to Hong Kong and Taiwanese investors in export-oriented businesses. The leadership would probably strangle the south if it could, even if that would mean sacrificing what the central government claims is only a small percentage of the foreign exchange it earns from business enterprises in the south.

Nor would Chinese leaders compromise in any substantial way to secure continued MFN status. They are convinced that compromise and reform brought down the communist parties in Eastern Europe, and they have no intention of suffering the same fate. The Chinese leadership also does not believe compromise is necessary because it thinks the MFN threat is a bluff. As Premier Li Peng put it, taking MFN status away is "a card" China knows the United States cannot afford to play, because then it "won't have the card anymore." Li may be wrong. As congressional frustration grows with the obvious failure of the administration's China policy to encourage change in China, the odds increase that some new outrage in Beijing might just change enough votes to override the president's veto.

In response to the criticism, administration rhetoric has shifted away from the stance long advocated by Henry Kissinger,

Nixon's secretary of state and the architect of the opening to China, that the United States must accept and deal with China as it is. Now Bush has adopted a tougher-sounding formulation that depicts the current Chinese regime as an anachronism and argues that the United States must be on the side of change. In a major policy speech at Yale University in May 1991, the president noted that no country has yet found a way to import the world's goods and services while stopping ideas at the border. He expanded on that theme in a November 1991 speech to the Asia Society, saying that America cannot "retreat from the challenge of building democracy [in China]."

When this bold rhetoric was translated into policy, however, "building democracy" in China turned out to be nothing more than a recasting of the traditional "let's not isolate China" line. That in turn became the justification for sending Baker to Beijing despite the president's own ban on high-level visits. Baker's claim that "unless we were to keep U.S.-China relations in a deep freeze forever, we had to start talking" misses the point; it also reflects a profound misunderstanding of the political situation in China. Of course the United States needs to talk with the Chinese; the argument is about what Washington should say and where.

The administration clearly has not abandoned its hope for a productive post–Cold War relationship with China based on the old formula of creative ambiguity. The assumption that engagement must mean salvaging the relationship with the current regime in China is a fundamental flaw in administration policy. The current regime is incapable of making real progress on any of the critical outstanding issues.

The great paradox of the Chinese "totalitarian" regime is that it does not fully control its subsidiary power structures. In a real sense, the Chinese leadership resembles nothing so much as the Mafia. The "dons" maintain an uneasy truce with one another, avoiding conflict in order to put themselves at best advantage when the next death occurs and the power cards are again reshuffled. In this way, those who formally speak for China are frequently not the people who can effect major policy changes.

This closed and archaic system of decision making is what has made Bush administration efforts to curb China's weapons sales and nuclear technology assistance so futile. Clearly, the Chinese are generally reluctant to curtail a trade that Western intelligence agencies estimate generates profits of some $16 billion a year. More seriously, China's deceitful record over the past several years shows that neither the Chinese minister of foreign affairs nor even Premier Li can guarantee the PRC would honor commitments to end such trade.

In the spring of 1991, for instance, as Chinese government officials assured Under Secretary of State Robert Kimmitt that they were serious about curtailing missile sales and nuclear proliferation, a senior Foreign Ministry official conceded privately that if a decision to sell Chinese weapons technology were nevertheless made, the ministry would not be consulted or asked for permission. Indeed, the ministry would probably first learn about such sales from the *New York Times*.

Li, who in the Mafia analogy is a lieutenant rather than a don, would not be able to stop a sale and probably would not even be consulted about it. Whether even a "don" like the aging president Yang Shangkun could stop such sales is an interesting theoretical question. As a practical matter, it is unlikely he or any other top leader in this regime would be willing to use up the political chits to do so. Military sales abroad are conducted by trading companies that are often run by children of the Communist party elite on behalf of the People's Liberation Army (PLA), which is allowed to keep all of the substantial foreign exchange earned from these sales. Chinese officials say privately that the New Era Corporation, Polytechnologies, Great Wall Industries Corporation, and similar PLA-connected arms exporters are permitted to retain the foreign exchange they earn to enable them to finance the PLA's modernization program off budget. No one is likely to be prepared to break those rice bowls or risk antagonizing important elements of the military, whose support will probably be critical in the final stage of the power struggle to replace Deng as China's paramount leader.

The current regime is also incapable of making significant progress on the country's egregious violations of human dignity, all of which have worsened considerably since Tiananmen; China resolutely maintains that "there are no human rights in abstract terms. . . . The rights acknowledged and protected by a state are in fact civil rights in this country." In other words, the human rights the Chinese people can expect to enjoy are whatever the Chinese Communist party decides to grant them. These do not include freedom from torture, from arbitrary detention without charges or trial, from the suppression of peaceful protest, or from the religious persecution of Tibetan monks and Christians—despite a guarantee of religious freedom in China's constitution.

How can the United States expect to influence a regime that says it is prepared to discuss human rights only to educate foreigners on the meaning of "socialist human rights"? As long as China is ruled by a clique whose overriding concern is survival, which sees peaceful demonstrations as "counterrevolutionary rebellion" aided by "anti-China forces in the United States," and which dismisses even such a moderate summary of human rights abuses as the State Department's 1990 human rights report on China as slander, flagrant interference in China's internal affairs, and "expressions of out-and-out hegemonism and power politics," foreign government attempts to talk to Beijing about human rights will prove fruitless and perhaps even counterproductive.

On economic issues the picture is no more hopeful. Although China had begun reducing access to its market in the fall of 1988, after Tiananmen the process became increasingly politicized, resulting in significantly more pronounced restrictions on trade and foreign investment. It has raised tariffs significantly, tightened its complex import licensing system, and imposed quotas and import bans on a wide range of foreign goods. Despite repeated promises going back to the 1979 U.S.-China Trade Agreement to protect foreign copyrights and patents, China has not done so. Its reasons appear more ideological than economic. China sees foreign contact of all kinds as potentially subversive—an instrument in the supposed foreign plot, headed by the United States, to overthrow the communist system using such nefarious tools as trade, aid, and even embassy receptions. Beijing is also determined to reduce foreign competition in order to protect its inefficient state enterprises. The Chinese leadership appears convinced that communism collapsed in Eastern Europe and the Soviet Union because those societies allowed their state sectors to fail; the Chinese have no intention of making that mistake. Through subsidies as well as control over credit, energy, and raw materials, the central government works to protect the state sector against its competition, both foreign and domestic. There is no chance that China will take substantial steps toward opening its economy when the country is ruled by a party that considers outside companies to be a threat to the state enterprises that are the very essence of the socialist system.

Finally, Chinese cooperation on the key environmental issue of slowing global warming is doubtful. Chinese officials predict that in 50 years China will consume more coal, much of it of heavily polluting high-sulfur content, than did the entire world in

1990. The collapse of communism in Eastern Europe has fully revealed that communist regimes, because they are accountable neither to their own people nor to the world outside, routinely produce environmental nightmares. In the absence of any effective expression of domestic concern over environmental problems, the regime can ignore the costs and emphasize production at the expense of pollution control. Until a more responsive and responsible leadership assumes power, Chinese officials are likely to respond to international pressure on environmental issues the same way they deal with other issues the leadership is unwilling or incapable of addressing: by bluster or by obfuscation.

The Bush administration may be hoping for more progress on such politically sensitive issues as China's export of goods made with prison labor and its deliberate mislabeling of goods to evade U.S. customs regulations, both of which have resulted in substantial seizures of Chinese products. But in this area, as in China's arms export industry, one has to wonder how much control the central authorities can, or would want to, exercise over enterprises run by the favorites of the party elite, including their children. What the United States is likely to see, then, is more Chinese promises and announcements of "regulations," which the administration will be able to tout as progress but which will turn out in practice to be little more than creative ambiguity. As this becomes obvious—to the Congress, to companies, and to others who expect real change—dissatisfaction with the policy and with the entire relationship will mount.

The most recent addition to the list of new strategic issues that supposedly require the United States to maintain a close, friendly relationship with China is the continued danger that North Korea will develop nuclear weapons. Despite the December 1991 compact between North and South Korea to forgo the pursuit of offensive nuclear capability, U.S. intelligence estimates that North Korea may have the capability to produce weapons-grade plutonium by June 1992. It is argued, therefore, that China is needed to pressure North Korea, and administration officials point to Chinese assurances that they encouraged North Korean president Kim Il Sung to place his nuclear facilities under international inspection. An official Chinese source also said that, in conveying the message, Beijing argued that international inspection would not be to Pyongyang's disadvantage. And, indeed, Baker noted in a November 1991 speech in Japan that international inspection did not stop Iraq and that such inspections "cannot ensure that a renegade regime will not seek to acquire nuclear weapons." That is exactly right.

So why is a close U.S. relationship with China a key element in American strategy to block North Korea from developing nuclear weapons? If the December agreement breaks down, only direct U.S. pressure—and the threat to take military action if necessary—would have any chance of persuading North Korea to abandon its nuclear program. And if North Korea chooses to pursue nuclear technology, and the United States shrinks from the military option, North Korea will have nuclear weapons no matter how many high-level Americans visit Beijing.

In Cambodia as well, China's active cooperation is not needed: China remains important in both Korea and Cambodia only to the extent that it chooses to pursue an active spoiler role. China's policies in Asia are intended to advance its own national interests; and the nature of the Chinese-U.S. relationship—whether friendly or cool—is unlikely to change that fact or prevent any mischief making if the Chinese are so inclined.

The End of Chinese Communism?

What policy makes sense in such difficult circumstances? The first requirement is that it be bipartisan. What pressure the United States has tried to exert on the Chinese government has doubtless been less effective because Chinese officials calculate that Bush understands them and will save them from their American critics. The administration, the Congress, and the public need not agree on tactics. Reasonable people can still differ about whether to renew MFN, for example, but support for or rejection of proposals should be based on the evidence of their effectiveness; proposals should not be rejected out of a concern that they might offend or annoy the octogenarians in Beijing. Finally, whatever differences of opinion there are on tactics, Congress and the administration should agree on a common strategic goal: the end of communist rule in China.

A second requirement is to abandon the pre-Tiananmen assumption that the Chinese government is somehow permanent or that the United States must act as if it were because there are so many important problems that can only be resolved by dealing with the current regime. That turns reality on its head. The Beijing government is not here to stay, and it cannot help resolve anything. China's communists are preoccupied with staying in control and enhancing their own power. Out of touch with the world and discredited in the eyes of their own people, they will in all likelihood remain in office through the rest of Bush's current term in office, though probably not beyond another three to five years. This is not to say that the death of Deng Xiaoping will prompt a rapid return to reform and progress toward a more open society. The process will be long and difficult, though less so than in the more ethnically diverse former Soviet Union; the assumption of power by a new generation committed to greater openness, respect for human dignity, and a free-market economy may well take the rest of this decade. But it will begin relatively soon. Americans must do what they can to encourage this process.

Third, the United States should build relationships with the people of China, not its government. Since Tiananmen, the Chinese central leadership has sought to expand official governmental contact and recognition while attempting to restrict private contacts. The United States should turn that around and stand with the people, encouraging as much cultural and business exchange as the government will allow. At the same time it should minimize prestige-building, high-level government contact. Such a policy will hurt the regime, encourage the people of China, and above all maintain the flow of "subversive" ideas. It is time to seriously consider providing financial support for a Radio Free China. This approach was effective in Europe; perhaps it would be in China.

Another instrument of change is the business sector. No one can visit the booming, entrepreneurial south China provinces of Guangdong and Fujian without being impressed by how revolutionary the introduction of market principles can be. Just by being in China, businesses introduce new ideas and subvert the system. The United States should be encouraging such interchange, not seeking to cripple it by withdrawing China's MFN treatment. Companies could, however, do more. Foreign companies, particularly those operating factories, have extensive direct contact with the Chinese people. These companies could make a major contribution to change in China, and incidentally earn the gratitude of the next generation of leaders, if they would adopt a set of corporate principles reminiscent of the Sullivan Principles used against South Africa.

Human rights groups have already proposed that all companies operating in China sign an agreement refusing to accept a military presence in their factories or party representation on their boards of directors, and to oppose government attempts to force the firing of an employee for political reasons. Similarly, companies should not permit the scheduling of party indoctrination sessions on company time. These are all reasonable proposals consistent with good business practice. Congress has considered imposing such a set of principles on American companies operating in China, but that would be unwise. Legislated guidelines would make American companies agents of the U.S. government in the eyes of Chinese bureaucrats and expose them to discrimination—if indeed they were even allowed to continue operating. If the principles were adopted by the companies themselves, emphasizing sound business practice and not politics, it would improve the chances that non-U.S. companies would also sign the principles and present a common front to the Chinese government.

While legislation is inappropriate and unnecessary, American companies would need to be assured that they were not acting contrary to U.S. policy. The Bush administration could satisfy business on that point by calling together a representative group of responsible companies involved in investment in China to explore the concept and assure them that such an initiative would not be inconsistent with government policy. China would still charge that the companies were just doing their government's bidding, but there would be no denying that the initiative was voluntary. Some companies would probably elect not to participate, but if the larger ones did, and were able to persuade some non-American firms to join in, Beijing would have to deal with them. If there were legislation, the matter would simply add one more government-to-government issue to the other irritants.

None of these sanctions will bring down the Chinese Communist party, but they will ensure that the United States does not, by act or omission, undercut those in China who will bring about the change Americans hope for. As has become clear after the collapse of the Berlin Wall, it is shortsighted to minimize the importance of standing with oppressed peoples.

U.S. policy, then, should try to make life as uncomfortable for the current leadership in China as it can. This does not mean the government should refuse to talk with Chinese leaders. The United States should talk when it has something to talk about, but at the lowest appropriate level and at sites outside of Washington and Beijing. That is what Bush's much-criticized ban on high-level visits after Tiananmen should mean: not a straitjacket, robbing the administration of its flexibility to act in the national interest, but a statement that Americans regard the current regime as a pariah. The administration ought to state clearly that it has no intention of returning to the high-level visits that characterized the pre-Tiananmen period, with all their hype and symbolism.

Sending cabinet-level officers to Beijing or welcoming their Chinese counterparts at the White House does not gain concessions from a grateful PRC. On the contrary, it confirms their belief, as Deng is reported to have said after Tiananmen, that China is "too big a piece of meat," and that if the Chinese wait, relations will return to normal. Worse still, as Li bragged to a domestic audience, such kowtowing proves "that the number of friends [China has] is increasing and that [the Chinese regime's] international status is on the rise." Undoubtedly, Bush's January 31, 1992, meeting with Li at the U.N. not only increased the status of the regime and Li himself; it also said in effect that the administration has abandoned any pretense of trying to change the Chinese regime. The United States would convey a powerful message if the world saw that Chinese leaders are not welcome at the White House but that the Dalai Lama is.

On human rights, the United States should not shrink from criticism for fear of offending the current Chinese leaders. They will act in their own interest whether or not Washington is nice to them. In any case, American policymakers should be more concerned with how the successors to this government will judge U.S. words and actions during this period of transition. Nor should the United States be deterred by those who charge that criticism of the ways in which the Chinese leadership crushes the spirit of its people is a naive attempt to impose "American values" on the Chinese. The United States needs to be clear that it is pressing for China's adherence to human values, not for its adoption of American political or economic structures. And the U.S. response to China's standard line, that the "people of a country should be free to choose the social system . . . ideology and morality" they deem appropriate, should be that the only obstacle preventing the Chinese people from making their choice is the Chinese Communist party and its leadership.

In economic relations the United States must keep its strategy clearly in mind: to make life difficult for the current Chinese leadership. Cutting off MFN status is not the way to press that aim. By continuing China's MFN treatment, the United States strengthens the market-oriented south, introduces new ideas, and undermines the communist system. This is the "peaceful evolution" that worries the leadership in Beijing so much.

Foreign trade and investment do not in fact prop up the current Chinese leadership, as some in Congress fear. Americans should be more concerned that the regime will succeed in tightening controls over trade and investment in order to minimize their subversive effects, while still satisfying the state's essential needs for technology, capital, and markets. To counter this effort by Beijing, U.S. policymakers should consider selective economic sanctions that target the central government and its state enterprises, not shotgun sanctions that hit all Chinese and will bankrupt the entrepreneurial south. Appropriate measures include restricting technology transfer, reducing China's textile quotas, selectively raising tariffs under Section 301 of the Trade Act on those Chinese exports manufactured in state enterprises, and actively opposing (not just abstaining from with a wink) any World Bank or Asian Development Bank loan that would strengthen state enterprises or the central planning system. The administration has already moved on some of this agenda, but not as elements of a considered new policy. Instead, the administration has remained reactive, doing the minimum necessary to preserve Bush's blocking third on Senate MFN votes.

Will pressure from the outside speed the inevitable collapse of communism in China? No one can be sure. However, such pressure hastened the process in the Soviet Union and Eastern Europe. As Czechoslovak president Václav Havel told Congress in 1990, "You . . . helped us to survive." But China is different, some say, and Americans should recognize Asian realities. What realities are these? That Asians do not place the same value on life as we do, as General William Westmoreland said about the Vietnamese? Or is it that they do not value freedom and human dignity as Americans do? In fact, Americans can learn much about freedom and human dignity from the thousands of Chinese who were willing to die or go to prison to protest the suppression of their political, economic, or religious freedoms, even while protest seemed hopeless.

Americans can also learn from another Asian, Burmese opposition leader Aung San Suu Kyi, the winner of the 1991 Nobel Peace Prize. As she wrote in an unpublished essay:

Within a system which denies the existence of basic human rights, fear tends to be the order of the day. . . . A most insidious form of fear is that which masquerades as common sense or even wisdom, condemning as foolish, reckless, insignificant or futile the small daily acts of courage which help to preserve man's self-respect and inherent human dignity.

Surely those of us outside that system—in China and elsewhere—need not be corrupted by fear of failure. We can be courageous and practical enough to stand with the Chinese people, and to support the emergence of a responsive and responsible government in China.

RENEWAL OF MFN STATUS FOR CHINA[3]

President [Clinton's] Announcement, May 28, 1993

Yesterday the American people won a tremendous victory as a majority of the House of Representatives joined me in adopting our plan to revitalize America's economic future.

Today, Members of Congress have joined me to announce a new chapter in United States policy toward China.

China occupies an important place in our nation's foreign policy. It is the world's most populous state, its fastest growing major economy, and a permanent member of the United Nations Security Council. Its future will do much to shape the future of Asia, our security and trade relations in the Pacific, and a host of global issues, from the environment to weapons proliferation. In short, our relationship with China is of very great importance.

Unfortunately, over the past four years our nation spoke with a divided voice when it came to China. Americans were outraged by the killing of prodemocracy demonstrators at Tiananmen Square in June of 1989. Congress was determined to have our nation's stance toward China reflect our outrage. Yet twice after Congress voted to place conditions on our favorable trade rules toward China, so-called Most Favored Nation (MFN) status, those conditions were vetoed. The annual battles between Congress

---

[3]Reprint of an address by William J. Clinton, from *Foreign Policy Bulletin* 4/2: 44–47 S/O '93.

and the Executive divided our foreign policy and weakened our approach over China.

It is time that a unified American policy recognize both the value of China and the values of America. Starting today, the United States will speak with one voice on China policy. We no longer have an executive branch policy and a congressional policy. We have an American policy.

I am happy to have with me today key congressional leaders on this issue. I am also honored to be joined by representatives of the business community and several distinguished Chinese student leaders. Their presence here is a tangible symbol of the unity of our purpose. I particularly want to recognize Senate Majority Leader George Mitchell of Maine and Congresswoman Nancy Pelosi of California. Their tireless dedication to the cause of freedom in China has given voice to our collective concerns. I intend to continue working closely with Congress as we pursue our China policy.

We are here today because the American people continue to harbor profound concerns about a range of practices by China's Communist leaders. We are concerned that many activists and prodemocracy leaders, including some from Tiananmen Square, continue to languish behind prison bars in China for no crime other than exercising their consciences. We are concerned about international access to their prisons. And we are concerned by the Dalai Lama's reports of Chinese abuses against the people and culture of Tibet.

We must also address China's role in the proliferation of dangerous weapons. The Gulf War proved the danger of irresponsible sales of technologies related to weapons of mass destruction. While the world is newly determined to address the danger of such missiles, we have reason to worry that China continues to sell them.

Finally, we have concerns about our terms of trade with China. China runs an $18 billion trade surplus with the U.S., second only to Japan. In the face of this deficit, China continues practices that block American goods.

I have said before that we do not want to isolate China, given its growing importance in the global community. China today is a nation of nearly 1.2 billion people, home to one of every five people in the world. By sheer size alone, China has an important impact on the world's economy, environment, and politics. The future of China and Hong Kong is of great importance to the region and to the people of America.

We take some encouragement from the economic reforms in China, reforms that by some measures place China's economy as the third largest in the world, after the United States and Japan. China's coastal provinces are an engine for reform throughout the country. The residents of Shanghai and Guangzhou are far more motivated by markets than by Marx or Mao.

We are hopeful that China's process of development and economic reform will be accompanied by greater political freedom. In some ways, this process has begun. An emerging Chinese middle class points the antennae of new televisions towards Hong Kong to pick up broadcasts of CNN. Cellular phones and fax machines carry implicit notions of freer communications. Hong Kong itself is a catalyst of democratic values, and we strongly support [Hong Kong] Governor [Christopher] Patten's efforts to broaden democratic rights.

The question we face today is how best to cultivate these hopeful seeds of change in China while expressing our clear disapproval of its repressive policies.

The core of this policy will be a resolute insistence upon significant progress on human rights in China. To implement this policy, I am signing an Executive Order that will have the effect of extending Most Favored Nation status for China for twelve months. Whether I extend MFN next year, however, will depend upon whether China makes significant progress in improving its human rights record.

The order lays out particular areas I will examine, including respect for the Universal Declaration of Human Rights and the release of citizens imprisoned for the nonviolent expression of their political beliefs, including activists imprisoned in connection with Tiananmen Square. The order includes China's protection of Tibet's religious and cultural heritage and compliance with the bilateral U.S.-China agreement on prison labor.

In addition, we will use existing statutes to address our concerns in the areas of trade and arms control.

The order I am issuing today directs the Secretary of State and other Administration officials to pursue resolutely all legislative and executive actions to ensure China abides by international standards. I intend to put the full weight of the executive behind this order. I know I have Congress's support.

Let me give you an example. The Administration is now examining reports that China has shipped M-11 ballistic missiles to Pakistan. If true, such action would violate China's commitment to observe the guidelines and parameters of the Missile Technology Control Regime. Existing U.S. law provides for strict sanctions against nations that violate these guidelines. We have made our concerns on the M-11 issue known to the Chinese on numerous occasions. They understand the serious consequences of missile transfers under U.S. sanctions law. If we determine that China has in fact transferred M-11 missiles or related equipment in violation of its commitments, my Administration will not hesitate to act.

My Administration is committed to supporting peaceful democratic and promarket reform. I believe we will yet see these principles prevail in China. For in the past few years, we have witnessed a pivotal point in history as other Communist regimes across the map have ceded to the power of democracy and markets.

We are prepared to build a more cooperative relationship with China and wish to work with China as an active member of the international community. Through some of its actions, China has demonstrated that it wants to be a member of that community. Membership has its privileges, but also its obligations. We expect China to meet basic international standards in its treatment of its people, its sales of dangerous arms, and its foreign trade.

With one voice, the United States Government today has outlined these expectations.

President's Report to Congress, May 28, 1993

Pursuant to section 402(d)(1) of the Trade Act of 1974 (hereinafter "the Act"), having determined that further extension of the waiver authority granted by section 402(c) of the Act for the twelve-month period beginning July 3, 1993 will substantially promote the objectives of section 402, I have today determined that continuation of the waiver currently applicable to China will also substantially promote the objectives of section 402 of the Act. My determination is attached and is incorporated herein.

FREEDOM OF EMIGRATION DETERMINATION

In FY [Fiscal Year] 1992, 26,711 U.S. immigrant visas were issued in China. The U.S. numerical limitation for immigrants from China was fully met. The principal restraint on increased emigration continues to be the capacity and willingness of other nations to absorb Chinese immigrants, not Chinese policy. After considering all the relevant information, I have concluded that continuing the MFN waiver will preserve the gains already achieved on freedom of emigration and encourage further progress. There, thus, continues to be progress in freedom of emigration from China; we will continue to urge more progress.

Chinese Foreign Travel Policies

In FY 1992, 75,758 U.S. visas were issued worldwide to tourists and business visitors from China, a 35 percent increase over FY 1991 and a 76 percent increase over FY 1988. Foreign travel by Chinese Government-sponsored businessmen alone increased by 48 percent in FY 1992, reflecting Deng Xiaoping's policies of accelerating China's opening to the outside world.

In FY 1992, 18,908 student visas (including exchange students) were issued, a decline from FY 1991 of 14 percent but still 8 percent greater than FY 1988. The decline was probably the result in part of a recent new directive requiring Chinese college graduates educated at state expense to work for five years before applying for privately-funded overseas study. A drop in funding from recession-strapped U.S. schools and relatives may also have played a role.

Chinese students continue to return from overseas for visits without any apparent problem. With the exception of student activist Shen Tong, we are not aware of any case in which Chinese living in the U.S. who returned to China for visits after June 1989 were prevented from leaving again. Shen was detained in September 1991 and then expelled from China two months later for trying to establish a Beijing chapter of his Fund for Chinese Democracy.

Human Rights Issues

As detailed in the Department's annual human rights report, China's human rights practices remain repressive and fall far short of internationally accepted norms. Freedoms of speech, assembly, association, and religion are sharply restricted.

China understands that the Clinton Administration has made human rights a cornerstone of our foreign policy. We have already repeatedly raised our concerns with the Chinese authorities and we intend to press at every opportunity for observance of internationally accepted standards of human rights practice.

We have made numerous requests for information on specific human rights cases. China has provided information on some of these cases but further and more complete responses are necessary. The Chinese recently released, prior to completion of their sentences, several prominent dissidents whom we had identified on lists provided to them. These included not only Tiananmen-era demonstrators but also Democracy Wall (circa 1979) activists. We hope this is the first step toward a broad and general amnesty for all prisoners of conscience.

The Chinese promised then Secretary Baker in 1991 that all Chinese citizens, regardless of their political views, have the right to travel abroad. The only exceptions are citizens who are imprisoned, have criminal proceedings pending against them, or have received court notices concerning civil cases. A number of prominent dissidents, despite long delays, have been able to leave China. Some others have not. Those who have been able to obtain exit permits in the past year include labor leader Han Dongfang, writers Wang Ruowang and Bai Hua, scientist Wen Yuankai, journalists Wang Ruoshui, Zhang Weiguo, and Zhu Xingqing and scholar Liu Qing. Others, like Hou Xiaotian, Yu Haocheng, and Li Honglin, continue to face difficulties in obtaining exit permission. We continue to press the Chinese on these and other cases.

Our goal is the release of all those held solely for the peaceful expression of their political and religious views. In November 1991, the Chinese confirmed to Secretary Baker the release of 133 prisoners on a list presented them earlier in June of that year. Since then, the Chinese have released additional political prisoners, including Xu Wenli, Han Dongfan, Wang Youcai, Luo Haixing, Xiong Yan, Yang Wei, Wang Zhixin, Zhang Weiguo, Wang Dan, Wang Xizhe, Gao Shan, Bao Zunxin, and a number of Catholic clergy and lesser known activists. We continue to press for a general amnesty and for permission for international humanitarian organizations to have access to Chinese prisons. We have also pressed for improvement in the conditions of those in Chinese prisons.

China has recently and for the first time admitted publicly that domestic human rights policies are a legitimate topic of international discussion. China has hosted human rights delegations from France, Australia, the U.K., and Germany. China sent several delegations to the U.S. and Europe, as well as Southeast Asia, to study foreign human rights practices and issued a "white paper" maintaining that basic human rights are observed in China and arguing that a country's human rights record should be viewed in light of its own history and culture. We reject this limited definition of human rights but believe it is a significant step forward that China is willing to debate human rights issues with its international critics.

The U.S. continually raises with the Chinese Government the need for protection of Tibet's distinctive religion and culture. We are concerned about China's heavy-handed suppression of political demonstrations in the Tibetan Autonomous Region. Demonstrations, on a smaller scale than in past years, continue to result in instances of brutal beatings and long detentions. China has admitted some foreign observers to Tibet and to the main Lhasa prison. Diplomatic reports state that the Chinese Government is providing funds for rebuilding monasteries and that monks are now provided more leeway in their religious practices. In recent years, an increasing number of non-Tibetan Chinese have moved to the Tibetan Autonomous Region in search of economic opportunity. We will continue to monitor closely reports that the PRC is encouraging involuntary emigration by non-Tibetan Chinese to areas traditionally settled by Tibetans. So far, we have found no evidence of a Chinese Government policy to this effect.

NONPROLIFERATION ISSUES

China's support for global nonproliferation initiatives has increased substantially since the beginning of 1992. In March 1992, China acceded to the Nuclear Non-Proliferation Treaty (NPT) and adhered to the Missile Technology Control Regime (MTCR) guidelines and parameters. In January 1993, Beijing became an original signatory to the Chemical Weapons Convention (CWC). China now is a party to all of the leading nonproliferation agreements. These commitments have influenced Chinese behavior: Beijing has refrained from selling certain sensitive items because of proliferation concerns, and nonproliferation as an issue appears to receive more senior consideration in Chinese policy-making circles.

At the same time, certain sensitive Chinese exports raise questions about PRC compliance with these commitments. At present, the greatest concern involves reports that China in November 1992 transferred MTCR-class M-11 missiles or related equipment to Pakistan. Such a transfer would violate China's MTCR commitment and trigger powerful sanctions under U.S. missile proliferation law. There also are reports that China is exercising inadequate control over sensitive nuclear, chemical, and missile technology exports to countries of proliferation concern. Even if these sales do not violate PRC obligations, they raise questions about China's appreciation of the importance of preventing the proliferation of weapons of mass destruction and their ballistic missile delivery systems.

We are also concerned that China has withdrawn from the Middle East arms control (ACME) talks. The U.S. holds that, as a permanent member of the U.N. Security Council, China has a special responsibility to continue these talks.

Seeking full Chinese compliance with multilateral obligations and support for international nonproliferation goals is a top Administrative priority. The U.S. is prepared to employ the resources under U.S. law and executive determinations—including the imposition of sanctions—if the PRC engages in irresponsible transfers.

TRADE ISSUES, INCLUDING PRISON LABOR

Reciprocal granting of MFN tariff status was a key element cementing the normalization of Sino-U.S. relations by providing a framework for major expansion of our economic and trade relations. In 1992, bilateral trade topped $33 billion, with Chinese exports of $25.8 billion and U.S. exports of $7.5 billion. China was our fastest growing export market in Asia in 1992 as U.S. exports to China rose by 19 percent. In turn, the United States remains China's largest export market, absorbing about 30 percent of China's total exports.

China maintains multiple, overlapping barriers to imports in an effort to protect noncompetitive, state-owned industries. China also has recognized that its development goals cannot be achieved without gradually reducing protection and opening its domestic market to the stimulus for change brought by import competition.

Our market access agreement, signed October 10, 1992, if implemented by the PRC, will increase opportunities for U.S. exports by phasing out 70 to 80 percent of China's nontariff trade barriers over the next four years. The regular consultation process required by this agreement allows us to monitor implementation and take appropriate action should China violate its commitments. Progress has been made in opening the market to U.S. products but we still need to resolve several issues regarding implementation.

Recently, the Chinese have indicated an interest in doing more business with U.S. companies. As U.S. corporate executives are arriving in droves to explore new commercial opportunities in Beijing, at least eight Chinese delegations have been or will soon be dispatched to the U.S. with orders to "buy American." These missions have the potential to generate billions of dollars of export of aircraft, autos, satellites, oil drilling equipment, aviation electronics, wheat, fertilizer, and other U.S. products.

Still, the large and growing U.S.-China trade deficit is unacceptable. The over $40 billion trade surplus China has accumulated with the United States since June 1989 has been very destructive to American industries, particularly the textile and footwear sectors, resulting in loss of American jobs. It is therefore essential that the PRC implement the market access agreement we have negotiated, which would produce a much greater equilibrium and fairness in Sino-American trade.

China officially banned the export of products produced by prison labor in October 1991. In August 1992, we signed a Memorandum of Understanding [MOU] under which the Chinese agreed to investigate cases we presented and to allow U.S. officials access to suspect facilities in China.

The U.S. has presented the Chinese Government information on 16 cases of alleged use of prison labor. The Chinese have reported back on all 16 cases, admitting that in four cases they were forced to correct the fact that prisoners were being used to produce goods exports in violation of Chinese law. U.S. officials have visited three prisons and have standing requests to visit five others, including a revisit to one facility.

In the past two years, U.S. Customs has aggressively expanded its enforcement of U.S. laws banning the import of prison labor products. Customs has issued over twenty orders banning suspected Chinese goods from entering the U.S., achieved one court conviction of a U.S. company for importing prison made machine tools and seized suspected equipment in another case.

Since the Prison Labor Memorandum of Understanding was signed last August, there has been no indication that goods allegedly produced by prison labor have entered the U.S. Talks with China will continue on the full enforcement of the provisions of the prison labor MOU.

CONDITIONS FOR RENEWAL IN 1994

China has made progress in recent years in the areas of human rights, nonproliferation, and trade. Nevertheless, I believe more progress is necessary and possible in each of these areas. In considering the optimal method of encouraging further progress on these issues, I have decided to issue the attached Executive Order which outlines the areas in the field of human rights with respect to which China, in order to receive positive consideration for a renewal of MFN in 1994, will have to make overall, significant progress in the next 12 months.

In considering extension of MFN, we will take into account whether there has been overall, significant progress by China with respect to the following:

• Respecting the fundamental human rights recognized in the Universal Declaration of Human Rights, for example, freedoms of expression, peaceful assembly and association.

• Complying with China's commitment to allow its citizens, regardless of their political views, freedom to emigrate and travel abroad (excepting those who are imprisoned, have criminal proceedings pending against them, or have received court notices concerning civil cases).

• Providing an acceptable accounting for and release of Chinese citizens imprisoned or detained for the peaceful expression of their political views, including Democracy Wall and Tiananmen activists.

• Taking effective steps to ensure that forced abortion and sterilization are not used to implement China's family planning policies.

• Ceasing religious persecution, particularly by releasing leaders and members of religious groups detained or imprisoned for expression of religious beliefs.

• Taking effective actions to ensure that prisoners are not being mistreated and are receiving necessary medical treatment, such as by granting access to Chinese prisons by international humanitarian organizations.

• Seeking to resume dialogue with the Dalai Lama or his representatives, and taking measures to protect Tibet's distinctive religious and cultural heritage.

• Continuing cooperation concerning U.S. military personnel who are listed as prisoners of war or missing in action.

• Ceasing the jamming of Voice of America broadcasts.

The Administration will also use tools under existing legislation and executive determinations to encourage further progress in human rights.

In addition, I wish to make clear my continuing and strong determination to pursue objectives in the areas of nonproliferation and trade, utilizing other instruments available, including appropriate legislation and executive determinations. For example, various provisions of U.S. law contain strong measures against irresponsible proliferation of weapons of mass destruction and nuclear weapons technology. These include missile proliferation sanctions under the National Defense Authorization Act. Using these tools as necessary, we will continue to press China to implement its commitments to abide by international standards and agreements in the nonproliferation area.

In the area of trade, the Clinton Administration will continue to battle for full and faithful implementation of bilateral agreements with China on market access, intellectual property rights, and prison labor. Section 301 of the 1974 Trade Act is a powerful instrument to ensure our interests are protected and advanced in the areas of market access and intellectual property rights. The Administration will also continue to implement vigorously the provisions of the Tariff Act of 1930 to prevent importation of goods made by forced labor.

IV. HUMAN RIGHTS

EDITOR'S INTRODUCTION

The 1989 massacre at Tiananmen Square focused worldwide attention on human rights abuses in China. This section discusses the human rights practices in China, and their ramifications for U.S. foreign policy. First, Christopher P. Carney, an instructor at Pennsylvania State University, argues the U.S. is inconsistent and hypocritical in criticizing China's human rights record while not condemning other countries such as El Salvador, or examining the deaths of innocent civilians during the U.S. invasion of Panama. Writing in *Asian Affairs,* he urges the U.S. "to improve relations with the PRC [People's Republic of China], not punish it for its human rights record."

Repression, however, continues to be reported. In an article from *The Sciences,* the exiled Chinese astrophysicist Fang Li Zhi and his co-author, human rights activist Richard Dicker, condemn the imprisonment of Chinese scientists and intellectuals. The suppression of Chinese Christians and the crackdown against their churches is the focus of the following article, reprinted from *Christianity Today.* Finally, China's occupation of Tibet and its repressive human rights policies are examined in a background report prepared by the State Department for the U.S. Senate Foreign Relations Committee.

HUMAN RIGHTS, CHINA, AND U.S. FOREIGN POLICY[1]

One of the most perplexing questions in the development of U.S. foreign policy is the importance of human rights. By making

[1]Article by Christopher P. Carney, instructor at Pennsylvania State University-Scranton, from *Asian Affairs: An American Review* 19:123–132 Fall '92. Copyright © 1992 by Helen Dwight Reid Educational Foundation. Reprinted with permission.

human rights an issue of high salience, U.S. policymakers have placed themselves in a paradoxical situation. On the one hand, promoting global human rights is seen as the morally and politically correct approach. On the other hand, geopolitical and geostrategic realities have, at times, caused the United States to turn a blind eye to certain chronic abusers of human rights. The irony of the Gulf War is an obvious example: the United States was perfectly willing, for political expediency, to join in an alliance with an old enemy and human-rights abuser, Syria, in order to liberate the personal kingdom of the Al-Sabah family. As another example, states such as Sudan, Somalia, Pakistan, El Salvador, Honduras, Indonesia, the Philippines, Kenya, and Guatemala receive or have received tens of millions of dollars in aid from the United States—and their human rights conditions are as bad or worse than those in Syria. Such inconsistency between stated policy and actual practice seriously erodes America's credibility and simultaneously sends the message that the United States is not really serious about human rights.

Defining relations with states based on their human rights records is flawed for at least three reasons. First, as stated above, the United States fails to evenly apply the same standards to every state. Some nations are arbitrarily punished for not meeting U.S. standards whereas other abusive states face no sanctions whatsoever. Second, the measures used to determine human rights conditions are inconsistent and subject to debate. Moreover, they tend to be value laden with Western ideals and pay little attention to a nation's unique cultural experience. Various groups, using different subjective criteria, create the scales and reports which policymakers use to judge human rights conditions in each nation. The discrepancies in these measures create a confusion and disagreement that is eventually reflected in policy. Finally, it might be reasonably argued that U.S. focuses upon the wrong kind of human rights. Rather than concentrate solely on a state's civil and political freedom, U.S. policy should also consider how well a nation provides the more fundamental human necessities— wholesome nutrition, pure water, adequate housing, proper health care, education. United States policy might be more effective and less contradictory if it were grounded in universally accepted ideas of human suffering and actual physical well-being rather than some theoretical notion of civil and political "correctness." The inherent flaws in U.S. human rights policy create situations that needlessly constrain policy options. Moreover, tensions with so-called "abusive" nations often arise, further limiting U.S. choices instead of providing opportunities for constructive changes.

In this article, I will explore the three problems mentioned above and discuss their implications for U.S. policy in general and U.S.-Sino relations in particular. It seems to me that because of its tenacious adherence to the human rights canon, the United States is missing many opportunities to expand its influence within the People's Republic of China (PRC).

Inconsistency of Application

By almost any standard, civil and political rights in El Salvador have been abysmal. Between 1985 and 1990, however, the United States gave the Salvadoran regime an average annual sum of over $102 million in military assistance plus another $348 million in economic assistance (which includes Security Supplemental Assistance, which, although reported as "economic aid," is really paramilitary in nature). Human rights in El Salvador did not improve during this period. Nonetheless, so long as the Sandinistas controlled neighboring Nicaragua, El Salvador received the aid. During this same period, Pakistan received an average annual sum of $279 million in military aid and over $370 million in economic aid. Somalia's military aid package during these years averaged nearly $12 million per year, and Sudan's military assistance accounted for another $12 million; their average annual economic aid packages were $43 million and $111 million, respectively. Egypt, whose civil and political rights have clearly not been exemplary, received a yearly average of nearly $1.3 billion in military aid and $1.1 billion in economic help. In addition, the United States granted each of these nations Most Favored Nation (MFN) trade status despite the 1973 Jackson-Vanick Amendment's prohibition of trading with nations that abuse human rights.

This pattern of assistance by the United States can be partly explained within the context of the Cold War. Despite stated U.S. human rights policy, Cold War tensions and the zero-sum balance-of-power mentality of the Reagan and early Bush administrations relegated human rights to a secondary issue in aid-allocation decisions. Moreover, in order to promote free and normal trade within a capitalist system of nations, MFN status was granted to these abusive states, even though a congressional amendment technically prohibited it. Yet other states with poor human rights conditions, but whose geostrategic positions were not as critical to American interests, did not fare quite so well in either the military/economic aid category or the MFN category.

With the end of the Cold War, however, and the loosening of the tight bipolar global structure, perhaps the United States will be more evenhanded in its application of rewards or sanctions to human rights abusers. If not, it will continue to miss opportunities for improving relations with former rivals. This is especially true with China.

During the latter part of the Reagan administration, and very early in Bush's first term, the PRC was gaining favor with the United States. Close trade relations were being discussed in light of Beijing's new brand of economic liberalism, fewer people were concerned about China's military, joint U.S.-Chinese listening posts monitored Soviet weapons tests, and the Chinese government made concessions on the sale of Silkworm missiles to Iran—all of which seemed to indicate a more willing player in the international system, particularly with regard to United States' interests. The 1989 tragedy of Tiananmen Square, however, shocked and embarrassed the United States into a hard-line position with the Chinese regime. As a result, high-level diplomatic ties were cut and, perhaps more important for China, trade restrictions were imposed and its MFN status jeopardized.

For the United States, Tiananmen Square was less an example of Chinese brutality than it was an event that jarred policymakers into seriously rethinking the value of China in a world absent the Soviet threat. It must be remembered that the PRC never was an ally of the United States, but China's geographic locale and common concerns about the Soviet Union made for a certain coziness that might not have existed otherwise. As long as the PRC could fulfill U.S. goals vis-à-vis the Soviet Union, civil and political rights in China were never a concern. But once the global television audience witnessed the tanks crushing the student uprising, the United States had no choice but to decry the act, as well as the regime and political system that perpetrated it. In essence, without a Soviet threat, Tiananmen Square was the event that shattered America's bipartisan consensus over playing the China card. Since that time, for international political reasons, those in Washington, D.C., (especially Congress) have felt compelled to punish the PRC for this most egregious of human rights violations. Once again, although this instinct might be understandable, it is inconsistent with America's own human rights behavior.

The world was outraged by the Chinese gerontocracy's wanton display of brutality, but few noticed the hundreds of innocent civilians who, later in 1989, were killed by U.S. troops during the invasion of Panama—and were then hastily buried in mass graves. Perhaps 1989 was simply a year for imperfect decision making. At any rate, one must wonder if the United States or the world would have reacted so sharply against China if the people killed at Tiananmen Square were crying out for more food rather than more democracy. And though one certainly cannot condone the action of the Chinese leadership, one might well ask what Washington's response would be if a communist movement based in its own neighborhoods suddenly gained increasing national support and international media coverage. The world did see how an Ohio National Guard unit reacted to a minor student protest at Kent State University in 1970.

The point is clear: the United States, as the self-proclaimed defender of human rights, does not apply standards evenly. Post-Tiananmen U.S.-Sino relations have been distinctly cool, bordering upon antagonistic, and the United States has lost an opportunity to promote its interest in a strategically and commercially vital East Asian nation. It is crucially important for the United States to regain that lost opportunity.

Difficulty of Measurement

Perhaps the most fundamental concern of those interested in the promotion of human rights is how to measure them. After all, how can one judge how bad or good conditions are in a given country unless there is some standard to use as a benchmark? More to the point, how does one even know what human rights are? In his seminal essay, "A Critique of 'Human Rights Development' and an Alternative," John McCamant attempts to address these questions.

McCamant contends that human rights, as a concept, are not susceptible to measurement. Nonetheless, many attempts have been made to quantify, for scholarly and/or policy purposes, the level of human rights conditions in a given state. As such, several scales and reports of human rights conditions have been developed by various groups. These include the annual *Amnesty International Report*, Freedom House's annual "Comparative Survey of Freedom," the Department of State's *Country Reports on Human Rights Practices*, and Lars Schoultz's survey of human rights experts. McCamant argues that each of these measures is methodologically deficient and conceptually inaccurate. For example, although the Amnesty International report provides a stark assessment of rights in a large number of nations, it only focuses upon prisoners of conscience, torture, and the death penalty; it does not report data on other types of human rights conditions. Freedom House, McCamant asserts, is vague, does not accurately specify the dimensions of its survey, and suffers from political bias (an unusual claim, given the fact that all human rights reporting seems to be very subjective). The State Department's country reports are weak because they do not cover nations that are not U.S. aid recipients and make no attempt to compare nations' human rights conditions. Schoultz's survey of experts, which establishes a criteria of evaluation, is based upon very subjective opinions and largely inconsistent notions of which human rights have been violated and where. McCamant demonstrates further flaws in each of these measures, but exploring them is well beyond the scope of this work. At any rate, it is plain that consistency in the measures of human rights does not exist at present. Which measure an analyst opts to employ is purely a matter of individual choice. Each measure has its strengths, but each also has its weaknesses. Policy that is based upon any one measure is bound to be weak as well.

McCamant points out that "the concept of 'human rights' has been extracted from the proper moral and legal context dealing with the individual and has been applied to countries as a whole." If this is truly the case, does it mean that measures of human rights are taken out of context? And if policies are based upon these measures, are they not then already flawed? As McCamant correctly argues,

The concept of human rights emphasizes evaluation—the moral worth of actions. Moral condemnation—and outrage—needs to be cultivated in this increasingly jaded world, but if we go no further than moral condemnation, we will be consigned to impotence. Even where sanctions back up condemnation, this approach greatly limits policy alternatives. It is possible that it will even be counterproductive, making the situation condemned worse than better. . . . For suitable policies that do more than applaud the good guys and denounce the bad guys, it is necessary to develop a theory about how and why the bad guys are bad, and the good guys, good. We need a causal theory about violations of human rights. Here we run into another contradiction: because "human rights" is an evaluative rather than an analytical concept, its use discourages the analysis needed to develop a causal theory. For reasons of policy, then, it is also necessary to shift from "human rights" to different but related analytical concepts.

Yet McCamant's invective to find a new analytical concept, though timely, is flawed as well. In fact, it suffers from the same fundamental problems as all the rest of the measures discussed above—they are all culturally biased. Inherent in their respective premises are traditional Western, Judeo-Christian values. This begs a basic question: Can Western, Judeo-Christian values be fairly applied to assess "human rights" conditions in non-Western, non-Judeo-Christian states? I think not. Applying Western values to those in the Orient is as wrong as applying Oriental values to the West. Nonetheless, American policy with all nations is based upon its conception of human rights. Not only will some states never pass muster, those that eventually do will likely have to make some profound cultural transformations. Such transformations are likely to be disruptive and might well lead to a popular backlash—such as Iran felt in the 1970s when fundamentalists resisted the Shah's attempts to Westernize. Moreover, such backlashes might produce human rights conditions that are even worse than those the U.S. policy was attempting to affect.

Therefore, given the built-in cultural bias and the myriad flaws with human rights measures, is it fair or even wise to penalize China for its human rights conditions? Has the overall cultural insensitivity of the United States caused it to miss a chance to bring change, albeit gradually, to the PRC? It must be remembered that China's human rights values are largely based on Confucian ideology, which can be traced back to at least 221 B.C. This ideology did allow for a legalist tradition (in the Western context) but did very little in the way of legal codification and protection of civil and political rights. As Steven Thomas writes, "responsibility for criminal activity and debts was collective; individual legal protections were nonexistent." This system, despite challenges, survived over two thousand years until 1911, when it was replaced by revolutionaries with a Western system. The Chinese legal system then suffered many convolutions, always falling back on the previous two thousand years as a guide, until 1949, when Mao assumed power.

[B]ecause of traditional Chinese and Leninist-socialist policies toward human rights, China's post-1949 Communist leadership has not granted high levels of civil and political rights such as freedoms of speech, press, religion, association, and dissent. Instead, following socialist principles adopted in 1921, Chinese Communist leaders have supported health care, education, housing, food, and employment programs designed to provide at least a minimum level of social and economic rights. As a result of this commitment, China since 1949 has achieved one of the most impressive social and economic rights records in the Third World and attained a relatively high level of economic growth.

In this light, it seems somewhat unrealistic that U.S. policy makers should expect dramatic shifts in human rights conditions any time soon: American policy is bucking 2,100 years of Chinese tradition. Further, the above passage suggests that certain kinds of social and economic rights are at least as important and compelling as the civil and political rights the United States ascribes to. In fact, in a certain sense, it could be argued that social and economic rights are more fundamental and practical than political and civil rights.

If this is the case, perhaps the United States should reward the Beijing regime, not punish it, for, as I will show in the next section, the Chinese government has done a fairly respectable job of promoting the kinds of rights that enhance social, economic, and physical well-being.

Misdirection of Focus

China's preference for providing social and economic rights at the expense of civil and political rights cannot be criticized too harshly by those in the West. Every government must make choices for itself and its nation and these choices tend to be based upon cultural evolution and national experience. Over two thousand years of Chinese culture and experience have reinforced the notion of collective rights rather than individual ones. Providing adequate and wholesome nutrition, clean water, health care, housing, and education are the most important tasks of any government. These are the human rights that are most fundamental, the rights that China does a reasonable job of providing for its 1.1 billion citizens.

It would seem that reducing human suffering is essentially more important than granting political enfranchisement and individual rights. If one accepts the premise that the hungry would rather eat than vote, then one cannot fault too greatly any government that provides these essentials for its citizens. China does a comparatively good job of providing those basic needs that ease human suffering, [according to a Population Crisis Committee report in which] sixty nations have human suffering conditions worse than the PRC's. Many of these nations are still recipients of large amounts of official U.S. economic and military assistance and enjoy a MFN status. Further, by Western standards, most of these nations have civil and political human rights conditions that are as "bad" as the PRC's.

This begs two fundamental questions. First, rather than focus upon a nation's civil and political conditions, why not also judge a state by how well it eases human suffering? Easing human suffering would presumably be a way to create social harmony and political stability, especially if it is accomplished within the cultural context of each nation. The promotion of social harmony and political stability are clearly in the geopolitical interests of the United States and are also consistent with the national values it espouses. However, many nations in [the Population Crisis Committee report] do a comparatively worse job of providing civil and political rights, and economic and social rights, than does China. Second, why is the United States rewarding nations who are more abusive than the PRC, given their human suffering scores? What message does this send, not only to abusive nations, but to those struggling to maintain a modicum of civil and political liberties and economic and social ones? In some cases, one might be inclined to suggest that the United States' policy of rewards and sanctions ignores both the civil and political conditions of a nation as well as its economic and social ones. This is clearly not consistent with American national values.

By focusing on other kinds of human rights besides those civil and political, one obtains a more balanced perspective of a nation's internal condition. Is a nation more or less abusive if it provides enough food, water, medicine, and housing to its people than those nations that do not provide those basics but who allow their citizens to vote? Perhaps the United States should ask the hundreds of thousands of homeless people within its borders, or those with no (or inadequate) health care: Which is fundamentally more important?

As I suggested earlier in this article, basing U.S. policy with China on human rights is naive at best and just plain stupid at worst. It limits options, paralyzes new initiatives, and makes America seem very hypocritical. The United States can no longer afford to punish China for Tiananmen Square for two thousand years of cultural inertia.

The Future of U.S.-Sino Relations

As the world emerges from the cold war and heads into the twenty-first century, China could play an increasingly prominent role in promoting U.S. interests. There are at least four reasons why warmer U.S.-Sino relations are vital for the United States.

First, renewing China's MFN status would continue to foster the nascent entrepreneurial spirit that already exists in the country—especially in the southern provinces. This would increase contacts with the West and could lead to a gradual, yet natural, softening of China's civil and political rights policy. One must not underestimate the political influence that Western capital, modes of production, and daily contact can have. Moreover, once relations are more cordial, China can provide U.S. exporters with a vast market. Japan, by pursuing a more pragmatic policy with Beijing, has already seen the benefits of the Chinese market. These same economic benefits can be realized by the United States.

Second, as a member of the United Nations Security Council, the PRC is in a position to block U.S. initiatives for global policy, especially sanctioning rogue states. The "new world order" envisioned by the United States could be profoundly altered by Chinese resistance in the United Nations. Moreover, normalized diplomatic relations might enable the United States to persuade the Chinese to halt or reduce arms sales and nuclear weapons technology transfers to unstable third world nations. In the same vein, concerted U.S.-Sino pressure might also persuade the North Korean regime to cease its quest for a nuclear capability and stop exporting ballistic missiles to regions of the world already beset by high tension.

Moreover, one should not forget that China will be able to exert more regional influence as the United States gradually removes its military bases from the Western Pacific. Given its reduced military presence in the region, it becomes vital to United States regional interests that relations with Beijing remain cordial. One would hope that the same sorts of geopolitical dynamics that led to the events in the 1930s and 1940s will not reappear in the face of a diminished United States presence.

Third, future generations of Chinese leaders might be more inclined to cooperate with the United States if the current relationship improves and is deemed to be mutually beneficial.

Finally, it is ridiculous to not have a normal diplomatic relationship with a nation of 1.1 billion souls. The implications for the global environment alone make friendlier relations essential.

Given these reasons, America must seek to improve relations with the PRC, not punish it for its human rights record. As I have shown, basing U.S. policy on a concept such as human rights not only displays the inconsistency and hypocrisy within decision-making circles, it demonstrates a narrow perspective of the world and its peoples. Though clearly very important, the emphasis on civil and political human rights tends to cloud the American view of how well nations provide the even more fundamental economic and social rights to their people. U.S. policy with the PRC can promote Western conceptions of human rights, but it must also be sensitive to Chinese values. More importantly, U.S. policy needs to be far more consistent and pragmatic than in the past. Otherwise, America will continue to miss opportunities, until there are no more.

PORTRAITS OF OPPRESSION[2]

Early last November [1991] an appeal was released to foreign correspondents in Beijing by supporters of ten pro-democracy activists held prisoner at what is euphemistically called the Lingyuan Auto Factory Training Brigade. The statement announced that on the fifteenth of the month six of those inmates, including Liu Gang, a thirty-year-old graduate student in physics, would begin a hunger strike. The drastic action was intended to protest the "inhumane persecution" of China's political prisoners and to rally worldwide support for the dissidents' cause. The timing of the strike made it all the more dramatic: U.S. Secretary of State James A. Baker 3d was due to arrive in Beijing on the same day. Baker would be the highest-level American official to visit China since June 4, 1989, the day the Chinese army killed hundreds of pro-democracy student demonstrators around Tiananmen Square.

The risks of the hunger strike—severe punishment, for one—were serious. And they underscore the conditions that pushed Liu Gang and his companions to their desperate actions: extremes of treatment that are typical throughout the vast network of Chinese prisons and labor camps. At Lingyuan all but the

[2]Article by Fang Li Zhi, exiled Chinese astrophysicist and Richard Dicker, a lawyer. From *The Sciences* 32:17–21 S/O '92. Copyright © 1992 by *The Sciences*. Reprinted with permission.

most aged and infirm prisoners are made to do heavy work for fourteen hours a day. If one does not complete an assignment or fails to show enough enthusiasm in the mandatory political study sessions—in which inmates are inundated with Communist party dogma—one is beaten by guards wielding electrified batons and leather belts.

Supporters of the dissidents attest that typically more than forty inmates at Lingyuan are crammed into a 215-square-foot cell and denied medical care. The daily prison diet, if one can call it that, is vegetable soup and a steamed bun made of corn flour. And there is little food for the mind, aside from the daily barrage of party doctrine: the men are forbidden to keep any reading or writing materials. And as if that were not enough, the warden has evidently encouraged the hardened criminal offenders to harass the political activists.

And so the hunger strike began. Exactly how it played out is not known, although there are reports that Liu Gang was force-fed by guards and that he suffered a broken arm while resisting nourishment. More specific information is hard to come by. Relatives of the six political prisoners have been denied access to Lingyuan, though they have been told by the authorities that their loved ones are "in one piece." Given the track record of bureaucratic assurances in China, there is now grave concern for the dissidents' lives.

Liu Gang and his cohorts, unfortunately, are not unique. Since June 4, 1989, many other Chinese scientists, science students, and other thinkers have been imprisoned, blacklisted or otherwise persecuted in the purge of democratic sympathizers. One of us (Fang) and his wife were forced to take refuge for more than a year at the American Embassy in Beijing. Branded as criminals guilty of "counterrevolutionary propaganda and instigation," the couple now live in exile in the United States.

The wave of government repression has had a chilling effect on science in China. Research at every level in every discipline has suffered to some degree. In the post-Tiananmen environment Chinese students have become demoralized. Many of them who are studying abroad have lost their desire to return home or to use their skills to build up the country. A great number of students inside China have lost the incentive to do scientific work. In short, an enormous intellectual resource has been buried under conditions that should appall anyone who has ever tasted freedom. There are limits, of course, to the effect outsiders can have on the state of scientific research and discourse in China. But there is much that can be done, far more than the mere wringing of hands, to help those who share the fate of Liu Gang.

The massive crackdown that began three years ago was not the first assault on the scientific and academic community in China. Thirty-two years earlier the government had launched a propaganda campaign aimed at critics of the Chinese Communist party. In that so-called antirightist movement many intellectuals were pressured to renounce any previous statements or actions that conflicted with party doctrine. In effect, it was a much more extreme version of the McCarthyism that had plagued the U.S. earlier in the 1950s. By the end of 1957 at least 300,000 Chinese—perhaps as many as half a million—had been condemned to labor camps or banished to remote areas of the countryside. Many of those people were jailed or interned solely on the basis of their "class background." Others, who were not imprisoned, including some of China's finest scholars and scientists, were persecuted. Among the more prominent victims of the witch hunt were the chemist Fu Yin and the innovative sociologist Fei Xiaotong. Each lost the right to teach, publish and conduct research. Fu was expelled from the Chinese Academy of Sciences, and Fei was pressured into making a demeaning public confession before the National People's Congress.

After a few years the antirightist fervor subsided and conditions stabilized. In 1966, however, Mao-Tse Tung and a faction in the Communist party unleashed the Great Proletarian Cultural Revolution, a titanic, bloody struggle to dislodge the people they accused of "taking the capitalist road." Mao summoned China's youth into the streets to assault individuals and institutions alike, and during the next several years violence and chaos enveloped the country. Once again scientists and intellectuals were prime targets of the struggle. Indeed, a recurring theme in Mao's thought was the desire to blur the distinctions between what he saw as a bookish, urban elite and the workers of China's rural breadbasket. In any event those intellectuals who did not toe the Maoist line were sent to what the party, with its customarily euphemistic turn of phrase, called cadre schools. The schools were nothing more than labor camps, the curriculums of which included backbreaking physical work and forced ideological "remolding"—parroted self-criticism and the study of Mao's written works. As special punishment, recalcitrant intellectuals were locked in *nuipengs*—cow sheds. Among them, again, was one of

us, the "reactionary" Fang, who remained in his nuipeng for
more than a year.

Intellectuals who were lucky enough to avoid the cadre
schools were sent to work as laborers in the countryside.
Schools—the real ones—and libraries were closed, and all non-
Marxist volumes were removed from circulation. Admission to
universities, when it took place, was determined by what then
passed for political correctness. Indeed, during the cultural revolution all scientific work was dictated by political dogma. Thus
research projects in physics, genetics, chemistry and so forth were
deemed justifiable only if they advanced the Maoist idea of ending all distinctions between mental and manual labor. How such
disciplines could be evaluated along those lines remains mysterious to us. Nevertheless, Linus C. Pauling's Nobel prize–winning
theory of molecular bonding and the entire discipline of
computer science, for instance, were roundly attacked. Under
such absurd constraints it is no wonder that research and academic study in China came to a virtual halt.

In 1970 the University of Science and Technology [UST],
China's counterpart to MIT or Caltech, was moved from Beijing
to Hefei in the rural province Anhui. Lin Biao (Mao's heir apparent until his suspicious death in a plane crash—while fleeing
China—the following year) justified the change by noting that in
Hefei, which lies far from the Chinese border, the university
would be safer in the event of a Soviet invasion. In truth the move
was another step in the campaign to close the gap between town
and country and to raze the class wall between practitioners of
mental and manual toil. Effectively exiled, many famous professors at the university—including Fang, freed from his cow
shed—were made to do physical labor, such as road and railroad
construction and, of course, farming. On the new UST campus,
now an Orwellian nightmare, laboratories and libraries were
closed, and the only book available was the celebrated volume of
Mao's quotations. Faculty members were "encouraged" to spy on
politically suspect colleagues. At that point Fang, among others,
could continue to publish only under a pseudonym.

Although the excesses of the cultural revolution abated by the
1970s, the years of intimidation and oppression had sapped the
creativity and the will of an entire generation of China's best
minds. According to *Intellectual Freedom in China After Mao*, published by the human-rights organization Asia Watch, those older
intellectuals who have managed to survive the political turmoil

"are content with stability. . . . They worry above all about bringing trouble upon themselves by unorthodox behavior or unwelcome initiative." And now, in the wake of the slaughter at Tiananmen Square, a new generation of Chinese scholars and scientists may be doomed to the same fate.

The story of Liu Gang, and how he went from a peaceful life in research to one of unimaginable horror, fairly represents the plight of pro-democracy activists throughout China's scientific community. Liu came to the pro-democracy movement in the mid-1980s, when he was an undergraduate at UST, still located in Hefei. He helped organize campus gatherings, which became known as democracy salons, in which participants exchanged ideas on political reform. Refusing the security of the "iron rice bowl"—a lifetime job with the state—he went to work for the Beijing Social and Economic Sciences Research Institute [SERI], an independent think tank founded by the economists Chen Ziming and Wang Juntao. SERI conducted pioneering studies on the potential effects of economic change and the possibility for political pluralism in China.

Liu played a key role in the massive pro-democracy demonstrations that began in the spring of 1989. He advocated a moderate course, calling for pacifism and the gradual democratization of China under the leadership of the Communist party. Nevertheless, he was ranked number three on the Chinese government's list of the "most wanted" student activists. And shortly after Tiananmen, Liu was arrested. He was detained in Qincheng Prison, on the outskirts of Beijing, for nearly twenty months before going to trial. Variously placed in solitary confinement, shackled with leg irons and subjected to other forms of extreme physical abuse, he endured and became known as "the Iron Man of Qincheng."

In February of last year, while world attention was focused on the war in the Persian Gulf, Liu was finally placed on trial. In a judicial burlesque lasting just three and a half hours the state claimed that he was one of the so-called black hands behind the democracy movement. Liu was found guilty, of course, and the court imposed an apparently predetermined six-year sentence.

Many other scientists, like Liu Gang, are languishing behind bars. Consider the young marine biologist Chen Lantao, who was sentenced to eighteen years in prison for "counterrevolutionary propaganda and agitation" and "disturbing the social order and traffic." Among the criminal activities listed on his indictment was that he listened to the Voice of America. Wen Yuankai, a distinguished chemist and cancer investigator, was placed under house arrest for more than a year. Others, who were not arrested, have lost the right to teach, to publish and to direct the work of graduate students. At many institutions, consequently, research has slowed to a crawl.

No academic area has been more affected by the events of the past three years than the social sciences. In those disciplines faculty firings and reorganizations have become commonplace. Some departments, such as the history department at the prestigious Chinese People's University [CPU], have been closed altogether. Other courses at CPU have been modified beyond recognition, to eliminate all "bourgeois liberal" tendencies. In that way, supposedly, it has been possible to preserve the "revolutionary and scientific" character of Chinese education. Just after the Tiananmen massacre SERI was closed. Wang Juntao and Chen Ziming were arrested as they tried to flee the country. With characteristically skewed logic the government has now ordained that for a social scientist to obtain official approval for research he must summarize his conclusions. Only if those "results" are consistent with the Communist party line can the work proceed.

It goes without saying that the government's stranglehold on the life of the mind has had a profound effect on Chinese students in all disciplines. Students associated with the 1989 movement were actively prevented from finding appropriate employment. For example, Shao Jiang, a mathematics student who was arrested after Tiananmen, spent a year in prison, even though he had never been charged with or tried for a criminal offense. After his release he made repeated job applications but was rejected for all teaching and research posts. Now he works as a computer salesman. His story is a common one. Other democratically inclined members of the class of 1989 have been sent to the countryside where, in the Maoist tradition, they have been forced to work on farms.

In the fall of 1990 the State Education Commission issued a set of new restrictions on speech and political activities to be enforced across the thousand or so institutions of higher learning in China. The rules ban unauthorized meetings and all other means whereby students might organize protests. Beginning early last year the government placed some 800,000 university graduates in summer jobs on defense projects and in research institutes all along the Chinese border and in remote areas of the country. The point was to avoid a concentration in the cities of university alumni, regarded as the people most likely to participate in protests.

One alarming trend has been an infusion of militarism into student life. In the past, freshmen at Beijing University received a few weeks of military training; now they are sent away for a year to experience the grueling rigors of training at a military base in Shijiazhuang, the capital city of Hebei Province, south of Beijing. Last year a permanent military facility was established on the outskirts of Beijing, the purpose of which was to impose doctrinaire Marxist concepts on university students. Young men and women from seventy-one institutions have been forced to attend the facility so far, which Xiao Qiang, a former physics student, now with the organization Human Rights in China and living in exile in the U.S., describes as "basically for brainwashing."

Students were forced to repeat the slogans and dogma. This is very frustrating. Most students don't believe it. They would write self-criticisms. It's very depressing to do. This had no effect in changing people's minds—it just made them cynical.

Indeed, all the government measures have demoralized Chinese students at home and abroad. Inside China there is a widespread feeling of alienation over the political crackdown, and students are scarcely motivated to do serious academic work. For many years Chinese students could look forward to pursuing their work overseas: in 1989, for example, some 42,000 Chinese were studying in the U.S., the vast majority of them in the sciences. But severely restrictive regulations enacted in 1990 now make the prospects daunting for students who hope to pursue their work on foreign soil. For one thing, college graduates must complete five years of work (two years if they have finished graduate school) in industry or a government agency in China before they are allowed to go abroad. Moreover, it must be certified that students applying for exit visas have been politically "rehabilitated"—meaning that they are demonstrably free of any anti-Marxist taint. The new rules have aggravated an already substantial brain drain on China. For example, only 32 percent of the 80,000 students and scholars who came to the U.S. between 1978 and 1989 returned to China after the completion of their studies. And that was *before* Tiananmen. More recent figures estimate that at least 150,000 Chinese students have gone abroad since 1978, most of them to the U.S., Japan, Australia, France, or the United

Kingdom. One can only speculate about how many of them will not go home until the political climate eases.

One could reasonably ask why an American should care that Chinese intellectuals do not return home. After all, from the American vantage is it not better that the U.S., rather than adversarial, totalitarian China, reap the benefits of all that expertise? Perhaps, if viewed in a narrow way. Yet it is important to remember that a China that respects human rights is much more in the interests of the American people than one that does not. And a Chinese scientist can make a far greater contribution to that goal living in China than he can living in, say, Arizona.

For American scientists watching from afar, the maddening state of affairs in China may bring profound sorrow as well as feelings of enormous frustration. What, one wonders, can be done? Not enough, perhaps. Nevertheless, U.S. scientists are in a position to play an important role in behalf of their imprisoned and persecuted colleagues. The reason lies in a paradox of sorts. While the Chinese leadership is keeping ideological and political controls fastened very tightly, it is moving to modernize the economy. Because scientific exchange is extremely important to economic development—not to mention global prestige—Beijing has welcomed international meetings and conferences.

Thus American scientists traveling to China, receiving Chinese visitors in the U.S. or attending conferences attended by Chinese scientists must seize the moment and voice their concerns about oppressed intellectuals in China. In particular, if individual cases are raised in a firm—but not overtly hostile—manner, there can be a real impact. One cannot overstate the importance of repeatedly inquiring about specific prisoners. The tactic, which puts authorities on notice that there is international interest in a certain case, has proved very effective in similar human-rights campaigns, such as the one aimed at the former Soviet Union. Certainly there is some awkwardness inherent in such a direct approach, but the plight of some of China's most creative thinkers far outweighs any temporary social embarrassment. And there are techniques that can serve to minimize discomfort. For instance, a scientist attending a conference in China can discreetly place a written list of imprisoned activists in the hands of his hosts or of any nearby government officials. No lengthy dialogue is required and the scheduled agenda is not disrupted. Petitions can be circulated and other written statements of concern can be posted on bulletin boards.

Somewhat more dramatic, scientists delivering papers at conferences can dedicate their presentations to one or more harassed or incarcerated Chinese colleagues. The impact of that gesture was shown to be powerful in the effort to free dissidents imprisoned in the former Soviet Union. And there are less flamboyant ways to integrate concerns about political prisoners into the framework of a conference. At a business session, for instance, one can introduce a resolution stressing the importance of freedom of expression, opening the way for debate on the topic. Or, perhaps, a special session on the issue can be requested. In either circumstance the matter of persecuted intellectuals will become a major focus of discussion.

Another option is to boycott a conference altogether, on the basis of a principled objection to Chinese human-rights practices. That approach is of little use, however, unless the decision to boycott and the reasons for it are publicized—in letters to the conference organizers and the appropriate professional journal, and, if there is sufficient interest, through a press conference.

It is important to remember that, in spite of the government's efforts to suppress it, the pro-democracy movement in China is not dead. Rather it survives, at great risk, in a number of underground organizations throughout the country. Meanwhile a host of groups supporting the activists have arisen among Chinese living in the U.S., notably the Independent Federation of Chinese Scholars and Students, Human Rights in China, and the Committee of 100. Those groups and others have maintained constant contact with people inside China, through telephone calls, letters and occasional visits. Outside the American-Chinese community several human-rights organizations are working in behalf of the dissidents. The Committee to End the Chinese Gulag, in which we are both active, has labored to publicize the mistreatment of political prisoners and other abuses in China and Tibet. Closely affiliated with Asia Watch (a division of Human Rights Watch), the committee has informed and advised the scientific community about prisoner cases and helped organize appeals and responses. Asia Watch has issued reports with unprecedented documentation on the crushing of the democracy movement in Hunan Province, prison conditions there, the suppression of dissent in Inner Mongolia, and the use of prison labor for the production of goods exported to the U.S.

In the past year there have been distinct signs that concerted international pressure has had an effect on the Chinese approach to human rights. A few prisoners have been released when foreign-policy needs have demanded it. Shortly after Secretary Baker left Beijing last November, the Chinese government freed Wang Youcai, an imprisoned student leader who had been on the most-wanted list. Early this year the regime announced the release of nine people held in connection with the pro-democracy movement. And recently Beijing began to issue photographs of prominent imprisoned dissidents, a move designed to deflect criticism—though the pictures have not been subject to independent verification.

The experience of Wang Juntao and Chen Ziming also reflects some modification in the Chinese position. Wang and Chen were branded by Beijing as the masterminds of the 1989 democracy movement. After their arrest they were held for more than a year without formal charges and then were rushed to trial, a week after Liu Gang. Their sentence was even more severe than Liu's: thirteen years' imprisonment.

The next month, Wang requested medical treatment after blood tests confirmed that he had the dangerous and highly contagious disease hepatitis B. He wrote thirty appeals for care, but officials of the Beijing Corrections Department kept insisting that Wang was not ill. Meanwhile, both he and Chen were held in punitive solitary confinement, locked in tiny, airless cells, with vermin-infested mattresses and open toilets that generated an overpowering stench. After a few months of that, Wang was unable to stand erect or take deep breaths.

As international protests mounted last summer, officials of the Chinese Ministry of Justice insisted that Wang was in fine health. In August both Wang and Chen went on hunger strikes to protest their mistreatment—yet the justice ministry firmly asserted that both men were eating well and gaining weight. To undercut a worldwide wave of concern, Beijing went so far as to release television footage to the Cable News Network showing a healthy-looking specimen alleged to be Wang. But the international community was not assuaged. Last September British Prime Minister John Major pressed the case of Wang and Chen when he traveled to Beijing, as did a visiting U.S. congressional delegation. Chinese students in Washington, D.C., began a hunger strike, human-rights organizations protested and several scientific associations in the U.S. (including the New York Academy of Sciences) wrote appeals to Li Peng.

Eventually Beijing bent, though it did not break. Last fall

authorities finally announced that Wang had been moved to a prison hospital and acknowledged that he was, indeed, suffering from hepatitis. Chen, meanwhile, was transferred from the hell-hole of solitary confinement to a cell among the general prison population. The Chinese response was at once an answer to international concern and a cynical gesture to defuse attention. Understood in both those contexts, the move makes clear the need for intensified pressure on Beijing from all who believe men and women have a fundamental right to speak, write and think as they please.

THE BLOODY SEED OF CHINESE PERSECUTION[3]

The recently concluded fourteenth Congress of the Communist Party of China confirms that the country is moving toward a form of "social capitalism" that party cadres no doubt believe will lead their country into greater affluence than ever before. *"Nei jin wai sung,"* a commonly used four-character phrase, best describes the reforms: economic release, political tightening.

But not all of China's citizens are basking in the prospect of economic prosperity. What is not amplified in the international press is the fact that China remains politically entrenched in policies that repress individual freedoms. Most Chinese Christians would say that 1992 ranks as one of their more difficult periods since the Cultural Revolution ended in 1976.

For Wang Wai Yee (her name has been changed to protect her identity), a young Christian woman arrested September 8 for attending a house-church meeting, the economic reforms are meaningless.

After spending 12 exhausting days in a filthy prison cell, the days and nights marked by endless hours of interrogation, she was finally allowed to return home.

Some 120 believers arrested together with Wai Yee that fateful day in the village of Guo Fa in Central China, were reportedly

[3]Article by Andrew Wark, correspondent, News Network International, Hong Kong. From *Christianity Today* 36:54+ N 23 '92. Copyright © 1992 by News Network International. Reprinted with permission.

beaten, intimidated, and threatened by Public Security Officers, who attacked the group en masse. Wai Yee was fortunate, considering that most of her fellow Christians may remain in detention for months—simply for having attended an unregistered church service.

When Wai Yee returned home in mid-September, it was to a house she barely recognized. The authorities had stripped her home bare of all her belongings. Furniture, clothing, blankets, and cooking utensils were gone. Items deemed of little worth had been carried outside and burned, as were her Bible and Christian books.

Wai Yee was left with little more than the frame of her house and the clothes on her back. But she told an interviewer that she believed the church would recover. It was not the first police raid the fellowship had endured, and it most certainly would not be the last.

The Persecution Gets Worse

Today China's churches are teeming with reports like Wai Yee's. A new chapter of the Chinese church is being written with accounts of great courage in the face of mounting persecution. Regrettably, most individual accounts will probably never be known outside of China. But those that do filter out confirm that persecution continues to be an undeniable reality for millions of Chinese Christians.

In the past year, authorities have launched a significant and widespread crackdown on unregistered house churches, resulting in hundreds of arrests and numerous reports of Christians being intimidated, harassed, and beaten.

Most Chinese Christians worship in house churches, although there is a network of officially recognized churches. But because of government restrictions on how those churches are managed, most Christians opt to worship under the cloak of secrecy, where they are free from official interference and control.

Many international observers argue that China's economic reforms are essentially a ploy by the Chinese Communist party to consolidate control over a disillusioned society.

"What indications do we have that things are any better?" asked Lesley Francis, director of Overseas Missionary Fellowship's Hong Kong–based China Study Department. "Persecution has increased, leftist political control is still in force, and, in many respects, China is worse off sociopolitically than it was three years ago."

According to Ross Paterson, British author and director of Chinese Church Support Ministries, nowhere is the growing repression more evident than in China's religious arena.

"There is no doubt that the situation [facing] the church in China has significantly deteriorated in the past year," Paterson said. "The 1989 Tiananmen Square massacre, the historic changes in Eastern Europe [in the late 1980s], and the equally historic events in Russia in 1991 have led to a clampdown in China, which makes many Chinese Christians live nearer to the Cultural Revolution than to a post-Marxist China."

In February, provincial directors of the Religious Affairs Bureau (RAB) met in Beijing behind closed doors to discuss national religious policy. During the course of their meetings, the RAB directors reportedly formulated a plan that called for the closure of unregistered religious meeting points throughout the country and a wide-scale crackdown on itinerant evangelists.

Since then, many provincial and district governments have issued their own directives, encouraging party cadres to monitor church affairs more stringently and to restrict or eliminate house-church activities.

Elsewhere in China, the signs of a government crackdown are irrefutable. According to church leaders, up to 50 Christian meeting points in Beijing were forced by authorities to close between January and June. In mid-March, 30 house-church members were reportedly arrested in Suzhou, Jlangsu Province, for conducting "illegal religious activities."

In late April, up to 80 unregistered church leaders and lay workers in Queshan County, Henan Province, were arrested and held for several months. In June, authorities in Chang Zhi, Shanxi Province, raided an "illegal" house church, lashing out at worshipers with electric batons and arresting 12 church leaders.

While repression appears to be primarily targeted at churches remaining outside the state's religious system, some church leaders from the "official" church, the government-sanctioned Three Self Patriotic Movement (TSPM), have also faced harassment. In September 1991, some 300 Public Security officers massed around a registered church in Datong, Shanxi Province, and broke up a service.

After being ordered to evacuate the church, worshipers watched in horror as authorities razed the building with bulldozers. When church leaders protested, they were curtly told by an official that the building's location was too prominent for their liking. To this day, the church remains a mass of rubble.

Problems From Within

According to the Hong Kong–based Chinese Church Research Centre, a recently completed unpublished survey by the State Statistical Bureau indicates there are 63 million Protestants and 12 million Catholics in China today.

This figure far exceeds previous estimates of the China Christian Council and Chinese Catholic Patriotic Association, which officially claim there are 5.5 million Protestants and 3 million Catholics.

Christianity's rapid growth, however, has clearly outstripped the church's ability to disciple its new converts. High levels of illiteracy among rural church members and a lack of theologically trained teachers have given rise to a dangerous upswing in the number of indigenous heretical movements.

"In many rural areas, the churches are growing quickly, but the people are often uneducated peasants, with backgrounds steeped in folk religion, ancestor worship, Buddhism, and the occult," said China expert Anthony P. B. Lambert.

Acute shortages of Bibles and Christian literature have only compounded the problem. While Bibles in simplified Chinese script are now more readily available through the China Christian Council's Nanjing-based Amity Press, the number published annually falls far short of the actual need.

It is unlikely that China's political climate will allow the church to address such needs effectively while the Communist party's octogenarian leadership remains firmly in power. The order in which the old men of Chinese Marxism are phased out of party leadership may have a profound effect in determining the future of the country. Who or what will follow remains an enigma, even to the most experienced China-watchers.

U.S. AND CHINESE POLICIES TOWARD OCCUPIED TIBET[4]

Historical Background

Tibet defined itself as a unique culture and predominantly Buddhist civilization during its "imperial age" which lasted for

[4]Testimony before the United States Senate Committee on Foreign Relations, 102nd Congress, 2nd Session, July 28, 1992.

two centuries and ended soon after 800 A.D. During this time Tibet was united under one ruler and extended its influence over neighboring countries and peoples. China's own historical records and the treaties concluded during this period refer to Tibet as a state on equal footing with China. In other periods, like other states, Tibet came under the influence of powerful foreign rulers—the Mongol Khans, the Gorkhas of Nepal, the Manchu emperors and the British rulers of India. China's present claim that Tibet is an integral part of China is based entirely on the influence that Mongol and Manchu emperors exercised over Tibet in the thirteenth and eighteenth centuries, respectively.

As Genghis Khan's Mongol Empire expanded toward Europe in the west and China in the east in the thirteenth century, the Tibetan Buddhist leaders promised political allegiance and religious blessings and teachings in exchange for patronage and protection. This relationship became so important that when Kublai Khan conquered China and established the Yuan dynasty, he invited a Tibetan Lama to become the Imperial Preceptor and supreme pontiff of his empire. Tibet broke away from the Yuan emperor before China regained its independence from the Mongols with the establishment of the Ming dynasty. Not until the eighteenth century did Tibet once again come under a degree of foreign influence.

The Manchus who conquered China and established the Qing dynasty in the seventeenth century embraced Tibetan Buddhism as the Mongols had. The Dalai Lama agreed to become the spiritual guide of the Manchu emperor and accepted patronage and protection in exchange. Manchu emperors sent imperial troops into Tibet four times between 1720 and 1792 to protect the Dalai Lama and the Tibetan people from foreign invasion or internal unrest. Manchu influence did not last for very long and was entirely ineffective by the time the British briefly invaded Tibet in 1903–04, and ceased entirely with the overthrow of the Qing dynasty in 1911.

Independence (1911–50)

With the end of the Manchu period, Tibetans expelled the small Chinese garrison from Tibet and, in June 1912, the 13th Dalai Lama reproclaimed Tibetan independence. In 1914, the UK, China and Tibet negotiated the Simla Convention, which recognized Chinese "suzerainty" over Tibet as long as the

Chinese agreed to respect Tibetan autonomy. The Chinese never ratified the Convention, and the British (who themselves had invaded Tibet briefly in 1903–04) therefore never felt that the bargain had been struck. In any event, the term "suzerainty" is imprecise in international law and is not synonymous with "sovereignty."

That question aside, the Tibetans were in charge of their government and controlled their own territory during this period. The Tibetan government maintained independent international relations with all neighboring countries, most of whom had diplomatic representatives in Lhasa. The British view, expressed during World War II, was that "Tibet is a separate country . . . entitled to exchange diplomatic representatives with other powers. The relationship between China and Tibet is not a matter which can be unilaterally decided by China." A more expansive view of the British position, officially conveyed in June 1943 through the Dominion Office to Canada, Australia, New Zealand and South Africa is instructive:

Tibetans are a different race from Chinese and have a different religion, language and culture. They have never been absorbed culturally by the Chinese. . . . For over thirty years they have enjoyed de facto independence and do not wish to be resubjugated. Their memories of Chinese rule are those of disorder and incompetence, whereas the Dalai Lama's administration has great moral authority. . . . [T]here appear to be few grounds on which China can justifiably assert unqualified control over a nation isolated by geography, already self-governing and determined to retain the same independence that China now advocates for other countries of the Far East such as Burma and the Malay States.

The U.S. position throughout this period recognized Chinese suzerainty *and* an autonomous Tibet. At times, however, we stated our policy as one of not questioning China's claim, rather than one of accepting China's right to rule Tibet as a protectorate or suzerain. When we sent a mission to Lhasa in 1943, the U.S. did not apply to the Chinese Nationalist Government for permission to travel and conduct business with the Tibetan Government. Ambassador Loy Henderson, our envoy to India during the Chinese invasion, cabled the Secretary of State in December 1950, reminding him that Tibet's de facto autonomy was universally recognized. He continued by stating that the United States "believes that the Tibetan people have the same inherent right as any other to have the determining voice in its political destiny," and recommended that the U.S. consider recognizing an independent Tibet "should developments warrant."

PRC Invasion of Tibet (1949) Through Departure
of Dalai Lama (1959)

In early 1949, Mao Tse-Tung's Communist forces consolidated their victory over Chiang Kai-Shek's Nationalists, who subsequently fled to Taiwan. The Chinese Communist Party had maintained since 1922 that Chinese recovery of Mongolia, Sinkiang and Tibet were primary goals. During 1949, tension increased between Lhasa (the capital of Tibet) and Beijing, and Tibetans feared imminent invasion after the Chinese vowed to "liberate" Tibet on September 3, 1949. In November, People's Liberation Army (PLA) forces moved toward the PRC-Tibetan frontier, and began to infiltrate into eastern Tibet.

Negotiations between Lhasa and Beijing began in 1950, punctuated by sporadic fighting that summer. Talks proved fruitless and by October 7th, the PLA invasion of Tibet was fully underway. After some early resistance, the PLA overcame the small and disorganized Tibetan resistance. The question of Tibet was proposed for UN debate in late November 1950, but India persuaded the UK and the U.S. that debate on the matter would not produce any useful results, so debate was put off. The Tibetans themselves appealed to the UN on December 13, 1950, but UN discussion of the invasion was never held.

In the spring of 1951, a Tibetan delegation traveled to Beijing to negotiate a settlement. PLA troops were poised outside Lhasa, and were occupying much of Tibet. On May 23, 1951, the Tibetan delegation signed the "17-Point Agreement," which allowed the PLA free rein in Tibet and gave the PRC control over Tibet's foreign affairs and defense in exchange for religious and political autonomy. The U.S. Government tried to persuade the young Dalai Lama, who was in India at the time, to repudiate the agreement and not return home. Secretary of State Dean Acheson cabled Ambassador Henderson two weeks after the agreement was signed that Tibet should not be "compelled by duress" to accept it, and offered light arms and political support, with the proviso that India agree. But the Dalai Lama did return home and reluctantly accepted the agreement, hoping that the Chinese would live up to their end of the deal.

This did not occur. The Chinese did not allow the Tibetans to run their internal affairs with any meaningful degree of autonomy, and as a result they had a difficult time ruling Tibet from the very first. Never high by Western measures, the Tibetan standard of living deteriorated rapidly in the 1950s. After much privation—including massive food shortages, arbitrary arrest, torture and detention, the destruction of more than 1,000 monasteries, constant attacks on Buddhism and the monastic structure of society, and according to the Dalai Lama, the death of more than 65,000 Tibetans—the Tibetan people grew increasingly restless. A number of bloody clashes in eastern Tibet bordering on open rebellion became more frequent, particularly after 1955. In March 1959, tensions between the PLA and the Tibetans boiled over and large demonstrations and riots occurred in Lhasa. Some estimates put the death toll at many tens of thousands throughout Tibet. By the end of the month, the Dalai Lama had fled to India, where he remains to this day.

U.S. Policy

In the early years of Chinese occupation, U.S. policy was clear in its refusal to accept the PRC's forced occupation of Tibet, but also continued to refer to Tibetan autonomy within Chinese suzerainty.

U.S. diplomats at this time started discussing publicly the idea of Tibetan self-determination, something that had been written about in State Department cables and position papers but not much discussed in open fora. After the Chinese crackdown in 1959, the United States often used self-determination when discussing Tibet. In February 1960, for example, Secretary of State Christian Herter stated our official position as follows:

While it has been the historical position of the United States to consider Tibet as an autonomous country under the suzerainty of China, the American people have also traditionally stood for the principle of self-determination. It is the belief of the United States Government that this principle should apply to the people of Tibet and that they should have the determining voice in their own political destiny.

Successive administrations also strongly condemned Chinese human rights practices, and joined in support of the three UN General Assembly resolutions of 1959, 1961 and 1965. Occasionally our policy went beyond calls for self-determination and human rights by referring outright to Tibetan sovereignty. Several months after the Dalai Lama fled to India, the State Department spokesman in September 1959 said that the U.S. "has never recognized the pretensions to sovereignty over Tibet put forward by the Chinese Communist regime."

During the debate on the 1961 UN resolution, our delegate referred to the Chinese as "foreign oppressors" in Tibet, and further cited the 1959 and 1960 reports by the International Commission of Jurists, which concluded that Tibet had been independent prior to the Chinese invasion. The 1959 report also concluded that there was a "prima facie" case of genocide to be made against the PRC, and the 1960 report found that the PRC had committed "acts of genocide . . . in an attempt to destroy the Tibetans as a religious group."

According to a variety of public sources, in the 1950s the CIA began a covert program of military assistance to the Tibetan resistance. The program involved a fairly small number of people, and never amounted to much more than a nuisance to the Chinese. The CIA program did, however, hand the PRC a propaganda tool to claim that Tibetan resistance to Chinese rule was simply the result of American manipulation. In 1971, we phased out the assistance altogether, as we began to improve relations with the PRC under President Richard Nixon. The Nepalese closed down the main Tibetan base at Mustang in 1974.

After the opening to China, our policy toward Tibet began to change. When the Cultural Revolution ended, a time in which Tibet suffered greatly, U.S. policy began to accede to the PRC's claim of sovereignty over Tibet. The first time we stated unequivocally that Tibet was a part of China, without mentioning the autonomy-suzerainty link, was 1978. Since then, official U.S. policy has fully accepted the PRC position.

The policy shift before the mid-1970s and the more recent comments are striking. In October 1987, then-Deputy Assistant Secretary of State for East Asian and Pacific Affairs and now U.S. Ambassador to China J. Stapleton Roy testified before the House Foreign Affairs Subcommittees on Human Rights and East Asian Affairs. His testimony followed the worst riots in nearly thirty years in Tibet. Roy said that it was important to bear in mind, when looking at China's treatment of Tibet, their "traditional Confucian stress on authority and obedience," their memories of China's weakness and the fear that democratization "in a country of a billion people, mostly poor, would lead to a breakdown of social order and anarchy." While condemning Chinese human rights practices in Tibet, Roy took the Dalai Lama to task for being granted a travel visa as a religious leader only to engage in political activities upon his arrival in this country. Adopting the Dalai Lama's political agenda, Roy testified, would be "contrary to

U.S. policy" and "would constitute interference in the internal affairs of another country."

More recently, in written answers by Secretary of State James Baker to questions submitted by Senator Simon at a February 5th, 1992 Senate Foreign Relations Committee hearing, the Administration position held simply that "U.S. policy accepts the Chinese position that Tibet is part of China."

Human Rights

Reports of severe human rights abuses have come out of Tibet since 1950. Numerous human rights groups, including the International Commission of Jurists, Asia Watch, Amnesty International and others have issued periodic reports on the abysmal human rights situation in Tibet. As mentioned earlier in this memo, the Chinese have assaulted virtually every aspect of the traditional Tibetan way of life. In their 1959 and 1960 reports, the Legal Enquiry Committee of the International Commission of Jurists wrote: "It would seem difficult to recall a case in which ruthless suppression of man's essential dignity had been more systematically . . . carried out."

Religious leaders inside Tibet have been a particular target, as the remaining monks and nuns tend to be in the forefront of opposition to Chinese rule. Refugee reports of arbitrary arrest and torture, summary executions, enforced or involuntary disappearances and long imprisonment are widespread. For most of the time since the Lhasa demonstrations of 1987, Chinese security personnel have come down hard on Tibetan protesters, and have reportedly made daily life more difficult and dangerous. One measure of this is the increase in Tibetan refugees, which in 1991 reached 3,395, a threefold increase from the level of 1,108 in 1987.

This year's State Department human rights report cited China for "persistent abuses in Tibet," including "frequent credible reports from Tibetan refugees of torture and mistreatment in penal institutions," "harsh sentences for political activities" and ongoing religious and cultural persecution. In August 1991, a Subcommission of Independent Experts of the UN Human Rights Commission passed a resolution on Tibet, criticizing China for numerous human rights violations and for denying Tibetans their religious and cultural identity. Estimates of Tibetans held in prison for political offenses are in the 3,000 to 4,000 range, although Chinese authorities claim much smaller numbers.

In April 1992, Senators Pell and Boren applied for visas to visit Tibet. The PRC denied them permission to enter Tibet, saying the visit would not be appropriate at that time. Speculation in the press was that the two Senators were denied entry because of their efforts to attach human rights conditions to renewal of China's Most Favored Nation trading status, and because Senator Pell has long been a vocal critic of Beijing's policies in Tibet.

In March 1992, at the annual meeting in Geneva of the UN Human Rights Commission (UNHRC), twenty-two nations led by the EC [European Community] submitted a resolution deploring the human rights situation in Tibet. The resolution did not mention questions of sovereignty. The United States delegation, according to numerous reports, expressed interest in an alternative resolution that implied China's sovereignty over Tibet, and a number of nations backed away from supporting the EC resolution. The PRC vigorously opposed this weaker draft as well as the EC draft, and its lobbying efforts were successful. Neither draft was considered, and the PRC was not censured.

The Role of the Dalai Lama

The present Dalai Lama, born in 1935, is the fourteenth. The title is a Mongolian-Tibetan phrase which loosely translates as "Ocean of Wisdom." He is both the spiritual and temporal leader of Tibet. His influence with Buddhists worldwide, and particularly Tibetan Buddhists, is enormous. He is the head of the Tibetan government in exile, and lives in Dharamsala, India, which has been his home since 1959.

Throughout his life in exile, the Dalai Lama has always preached a non-violent solution to Tibet's occupation. In September 1987, on Capitol Hill, he presented a five-point peace proposal featuring:

• removing Chinese troops and transforming Tibet into a neutral, zone of peace;

• reversing China's population transfer policy;

• respect for Tibet's human rights and democratic freedoms;

• protection of Tibet's environment;

• negotiations between Chinese and Tibetans on the future status of Tibet.

In Strasbourg several months later, the Dalai Lama added that Tibet should become a fully self-governing democratic political entity, with some form of association with China. The PRC rejected the plan, and refuses to negotiate on any part of it.

Chinese publications and radio broadcasts often refer to the Dalai Lama as a "splittist," an agitator who wants to split Tibet from the "motherland" and return the people to their pre-1950 feudal status.

The Nobel Committee awarded its 1989 Nobel Peace Prize to the Dalai Lama. The committee noted that his efforts to free Tibet have consistently stressed non-violence. In a speech at Yale University on October 9, 1991, the Dalai Lama proposed that he visit Tibet, in part to see conditions first-hand, in part to encourage his people not to abandon non-violence in their struggle. In this way, he hoped to "create the basis for a negotiated solution." To date, the Chinese have rejected the idea of a visit to Tibet by the Dalai Lama.

Population Transfer

One of the thorniest issues today, beyond human rights abuses, is the movement of Chinese into Tibet. A declassified CIA study from the late 1970s holds that the first thousand or so Han (i.e., ethnic Chinese) settlers began to arrive in an organized fashion in 1976. Since then, it has been very hard to come up with accurate numbers, but we do know that the number of Han settlers has greatly increased.

A major problem is identifying the boundaries of Tibet. The Tibetans in exile claim that historic Tibet extends into the Chinese provinces of Qinghai and Sichuan, and small parts of Yunnan and Gansu. Tibetans refer to these regions as Amdo and Kham. In 1965, the Chinese set up the Tibetan Autonomous Region, or TAR, in what used to be Central and Western Tibet, corresponding to an area roughly one-third the country's historic size and population. Tibetans in exile claim that the Tibetan population is six million; the Chinese claim a figure of slightly more than two million, but they are only counting Tibetans living in the TAR. Outside observers have put the total Tibetan population in historic Tibet as anywhere from 4.5 to 6 million, with similar numbers of Han Chinese (although the high range of the Han estimate is put by some at 7 to 8 million, which, if true, means that Tibetans are a minority in their own land).

These figures exclude the estimated number of PLA troops and other security forces, at about 50,000, although here again there is controversy: the Tibetans in exile claim the total number of security personnel is closer to 300,000.

One reason Tibetan development is now proceeding at an accelerated pace is that the once remote region is becoming linked to China with better roads and airports. The Chinese say that they are simply trying to develop the TAR, and in order to do so they need to send in skilled laborers, road workers, construction teams, miners, loggers, teachers and a variety of managers and bureaucrats. In order to attract people to what is considered an undesirable locale to Chinese, the PRC government offers bonus pay at several times the going rate in China and a number of incentives (including allowance for a second child, better medical care, more vacation time, etc.). Visitors to Lhasa and other urban areas throughout the 1980s reported that the influx of Han seemed to be on the rise. There does seem to be consensus that Chinese merchants dominate commerce throughout Tibet, particularly in Lhasa, and that living standards for the Han settlers are quite a bit higher than for the average Tibetan.

The Tibetans assert that the Chinese plan for Tibet to date has resulted in the destruction of rare wildlife, ecological disaster and the plunder of their natural resources. They further assert that the best farm land and the best materials and resources go to the Chinese colonizers. In addition, the Chinese attitude toward Tibetans is, at best, chauvinistic. Despite promises made over the years since the end of the Cultural Revolution to keep Tibet's unique culture and way of life intact, the Chinese have clearly tried to Sinocize the TAR. A principal method for achieving this goal is to treat Tibetans as second-class citizens, at least in part to encourage Tibetans to adopt Chinese ways. For example, while the Tibetan language is offered in some urban secondary schools, in many primary schools it is not offered. Even where Tibetan language is taught, there are very few textbooks available. In order to succeed in virtually any field it is now necessary to learn Chinese; almost all public institutions, from bus stations to post offices, conduct business only in Chinese.

Tibetans are a deeply religious people. In part because of this, the Chinese often write of the "backwardness" of the Tibetan people, and claim their "liberation" saved the Tibetan people from their status as serfs to the ruling, feudal monastic order. The PRC's assaults on Tibetan Buddhism are well documented, with more than 6,000 monasteries destroyed since the Chinese occupation. There are only a handful of historic monasteries remaining, although the Chinese often trumpet the building of new monasteries as evidence that they are allowing religion to flourish. In fact, religion is tightly controlled, and there are far fewer monks and nuns today than ever before in Tibet's history.

The transfer of population, whether it is occurring as a deliberate policy or simply as a consequence of a Chinese attempt to "develop" Tibet, is clearly having a devastating effect on the Tibetan way of life. Chinese attacks on Tibetan religion, education, language, the traditional economy and distinctive culture have led many observers to charge the Chinese with cultural genocide. These charges go back at least to the 1959–60 reports by the International Commission of Jurists, cited above. If one accepts that Tibet is an occupied country, as Congress declared last year, then China is in violation of several articles of the Fourth Geneva Convention of 1949, which forbid an occupying power to transfer or deport its civilian population into the territory it occupies. The PRC ratified this convention in 1956.

Legislation

Since 1987, a number of resolutions relating to the situation in Tibet have been passed by Congress. *In 1987,* Congress began providing funding for a small number of Fulbright scholarships for Tibetans. *In 1988,* Congress passed a resolution supporting the Dalai Lama's five-point proposal to promote peace and democracy in Tibet. *In 1989,* Senator Pell authored legislation establishing a Voice of America Tibet Service. Both the House and Senate passed separate resolutions condemning human rights abuses in Tibet. *In 1990,* $500,000 was provided to help Tibetan refugees overseas and 1,000 immigrant visas were set aside for Tibetans living in India and Nepal.

In 1991, the Senate passed a Moynihan resolution welcoming the Dalai Lama to the United States and urging freedom and human rights for Tibet. The State Department Authorization bill, signed into law by President Bush on October 28, 1991, contained a provision sponsored by Senator Pell declaring Tibet to be an occupied country whose true representatives are the Dalai Lama and the Tibetan government-in-exile. *So far in 1992,* Congress has appropriated $1.5 million for Tibetan refugees for [fiscal year 1992], and the Senate passed a Simon resolution urging the U.S. government to support Tibetan human rights in all appropriate international fora.

V. CULTURE AND SOCIETY

EDITOR'S INTRODUCTION

Is China becoming a more democratic and humane society? This section discusses recent trends, both positive and negative. In the first article, reprinted from *Nieman Reports,* University of Iowa journalism professor Judy Polumbaum discovers that "the most fascinating aspects of journalism in China pertain not to how the political aspects of authorities control the press, but rather to the myriad ways, both accidental and deliberate, that people and organizations have of interfering with the controls."

China's television is just beginning to present more options to the world's largest audience, according to Judith Marlane, a professor at California State University-Northridge. Writing in *Television Quarterly,* she presents a cautiously optimistic view, although she also acknowledges the presence of severe governmental constraints. Another potential bright spot is Chinese art. Art historian Joan Lebold Cohen, writing in *ARTnews,* describes several innovative artists who refuse to adapt to Communist aesthetics.

Finally, China—which so greatly suffered during the opium trade—is again experiencing drug trafficking. Testifying before the Senate Judiciary Committee, Robert C. Bonner, an administrator of the Drug Enforcement Agency, warns that China has become a major corridor for drug smuggling.

CHINA'S PRESS—FORGET THE STEREOTYPE[1]

The closest thing to a universal law of journalism may be the truism "He who pays the piper calls the tune." It is only common

[1]Article by Judy Polumbaum, assistant professor of journalism, University of Iowa. From *Nieman Reports* 46:48–53 Spring '92. Copyright © 1992 by *Nieman Reports.* Reprinted with permission.

sense to suppose that in a country where the state owns and operates news outlets, the state determines the content and presentation of the news. In China, one presumes, the Communist Party and government define what is newsworthy, control how that news gets covered and decide what gets published or aired. And what gets published or aired necessarily reflects the Party and government line.

The problem with this scenario is that it overlooks realities—realities of geography, history, politics and human nature.

True, journalists in China work under many more overt restrictions than journalists in the United States. True, most members of the press corps are technically government functionaries, charged with the mission of publicizing and promoting official programs and policies. True, censorship and self-censorship occur at many stages of the reporting and editing process. True, when a Chinese maverick offends the powerful or transgresses convention, the consequences can be severe.

And true, the high hopes generated during discussions of "journalism reform" in the late 1980s—with much talk about the need to report the bad along with the good, to act as a watchdog over public functionaries, to air diverse opinions and ideas—have dimmed since the night of June 3–4, 1989, when a frightened and out-of-touch core of aging leaders used troops and tanks to reclaim Beijing's Tiananmen Square from student protesters, killing hundreds and perhaps thousands of civilians en route, terrorizing the capital's populace and squelching the political protest movement that had spread across urban China that spring.

Nevertheless, China's media system is far more variegated, more informative and more subject to chance and human whim than the totalitarian model would lead one to suppose. This became clear to me while doing research in China in 1987 and 1988, when I interviewed journalists and media scholars in half a dozen cities and obtained the opinions of some 450 newspaper reporters and editors across the country using mail questionnaires. Fortuitously, this was an especially open time when people felt fairly unconstrained about expressing their views, and when griping about the media was tolerated, and sometimes even encouraged, by elements in China's leadership.

Younger Journalists Most Unhappy

I found dissatisfaction with orthodox propaganda pervasive throughout the press corps. As one might expect, disgruntlement was greatest among younger journalists who had come of age during the tumult of the Cultural Revolution or the openness of the post-Mao era, but even seasoned Party veterans were questioning the methods and premises of their work. Interestingly, desire for change was most marked among news workers employed at the very pinnacle of the propaganda apparatus—at national media such as People's Daily, official voice of the Central Committee.

Perhaps most importantly, I discovered that the most fascinating aspects of journalism in China pertain not to how the political authorities control the press, but rather to the myriad ways, both accidental and deliberate, that people and organizations have of interfering with the controls. For example, one seasoned editor of a daily paper in a city in northeast China got clearance to publish a story on police brutality by changing the lead to emphasize that an investigation was ongoing, thus making the authorities look good. An editor of a weekly paper planning to run an article by a foreign diplomat fended off bureaucrats who wanted to review the story by convincing them they didn't really want to take the responsibility for a foreigner's prose. Sometimes editors who anticipated that officials would be inclined to censor a certain story would simply forge ahead without bothering to seek authorization. Sometimes reporters would pass on news squelched at the local level to correspondents from national print or broadcast media who were not constrained by local officialdom. National news organizations occasionally exposed press suppression at lower levels, such as an incident in which the party head of a small city, irritated at comments mildly critical of his administration, had confiscated the entire press run of the local newspaper.

About 50,000 Real Journalists

These examples, and many more I collected, belie the stereotype of the enslaved minion in the Communist propaganda machine. Behind the facade erected by our own Cold War politicians and scholars—and admittedly reinforced by China's own official pronouncements about the role and power of the media under socialism—are, as one might expect, real human beings. Although exact figures are hard to come by, perhaps half a million people work in China's news media in various capacities, from managerial to production; probably about 50,000 of them are bona fide journalists in the sense of collecting, writing and editing the news. While it would be stretching things to say that everyone in this press corps is clever or admirable, individuals of intelligence, personality and imagination, including many in positions of responsibility, are not hard to find.

Discarding the totalitarian model is a necessary step toward explaining the dynamics of journalism in China, but only a first step. To even begin to comprehend the nature of journalism anywhere, its rules and standards as well as its vagaries and surprises, one must consider the particular circumstances in which selection, presentation and dissemination of news take place. In the case of China, the context of news work is especially rife with complexities and contradictions.

Mixed Messages in the Provinces

First of all, we should consider the country's physical dimensions. The sheer size and vast population militate against uniformity or exactitude in collection, transmission, and reception of information and ideas. The further one gets from the "center," Beijing, the more distortion, static and mixed messages one is liable to find. Balkanism is not a major dynamic in China; with the exception of Tibet, formal breakup of the sort that occurred in the Soviet Union is highly improbable. However, provincialism in a more general sense is a longstanding theme of Chinese history, and the devolution of economic authority and encouragement of local initiative, which are part and parcel of the post-Mao economic reforms, have accentuated centrifugal tendencies.

A second, related point is that China's ruling party itself is not a monolith, and even its top leadership has seldom been in total unanimity. News selection and emphasis in provincial papers reveal local interests at work, while factional or policy differences at the highest levels are reflected in contradictory messages emanating from nationally circulated newspapers. This is always evident in times of political strife, and is apparent even amidst the drive for conformity imposed since Tiananmen: Commentaries and editorials in People's Daily since late 1989, for instance, have swung between a shrill insistence on ideological purity and a conciliatory tone with stress on economic reform.

A third consideration is that from a purely descriptive standpoint, media in China are not monolithic. Certainly, the Party tries to maintain central management over the news; all media organizations and employees are expected to know and follow basic policies and guidelines emanating from a working group under the Politburo and further interpreted and disseminated by central party and government bodies such as the Propaganda Department, under the Central Committee, and the State Press and Publications Administration, a ministry-level agency under the State Council. Another force for homogeneity is the official Xinhua News Agency, which from humble origins in the Red China News Press of the 1930s has grown into a behemoth organization employing some 6,000 people. Besides dispensing news in English, Russian, Arabic, French and Spanish for overseas subscribers, Xinhua remains the dominant source of national and international news for China's domestic media, both print and electronic, and the major supplier of news photographs.

Media Expanding At Dizzying Pace

Nevertheless, China's news outlets are surprisingly numerous and offer considerable variety in both type and content. The country had more than 100 newspapers when the Communists came to power in 1949, and their numbers have waxed and waned with economic and political cycles—growing to nearly 1,800 by 1958, all but about 300 shutting down during the famine and hardship of the early 1960s, gradually rising again until the start of the Cultural Revolution in 1966. This ill-fated effort by Mao Zedong to instill perpetual revolutionary fervor saw both anarchic and restrictive extremes: For two years, unofficial Red Guard newspapers proliferated with abandon, while most official publications were either suspended or closed outright. Later, unofficial publication was suppressed, and the few dozen official papers that resumed publication were notable for their uniformity.

Since 1978, however, media outlets and activities have expanded at a dizzying pace. The first few years of the reform period saw the revival of scores of old publications and the founding of hundreds more; for five years running, new newspapers were being started at the rate of one every day and a half. By 1988 the country had more than 1,600 openly circulated newspapers published at least once a week; in addition there were some 4,000 limited-circulation or "internal" papers. Local and small papers accounted for most of the increase, but some newcomers were important on the national scene, among them the English-language China Daily, started in 1981; the Economic Daily, begun in 1983; and the weekly World Economic Herald, a bold tabloid of economic and political analysis put out by a Shanghai research institute, which with a circulation of about 300,000 by the late 1980s attained an influence far disproportionate to its size—gaining even more prominence when it became a casualty of the upheavals of 1989.

This period also saw the founding of thousands of literary and scholarly journals, the revival of the book publishing industry and the emergence of a smorgasbord of genres in print media—not only traditional publications aimed at youth, workers, women and peasants, but also new publications for senior citizens and children, ones devoted to science, economics, travel, or hygiene and health, television and radio guides, digests and in-house factory newspapers.

Chinese Relying More On Television

Radio had been probably the most important mass communication channel in China in the initial decades following the founding of the People's Republic in 1949, especially in the countryside, where 80 per cent of the country's populace live (the latest census, conducted in 1990, puts the total mainland population at 1.13 billion). The radio network developed rapidly from the 1950s on, and by the late 1970s reached all cities, more than 90 per cent of the villages through loudspeaker systems, and about 70 per cent of peasant homes. Broadcasting to provinces and major cities was centrally directed from Beijing; regional services offered programming in dialects aside from the national dialect, Mandarin. In addition, the government built up its equivalent of our Voice of America, Radio Beijing, with shortwave broadcasts in foreign languages directed overseas.

With the launching of the reforms, radio spun off new stations and offered livelier programming; particularly in southern China, where influences from Hong Kong are strongest, new call-in shows and programs devoted to social and economic affairs vied for listeners. But it was television, begun in 1958 and long in an embryonic state, that really took off. The central television station, broadcasting over two channels, remains dominant, but regional and local operations have proliferated and grown, and both domestic production and importation of television sets have greatly increased. From 1976 to 1987, the nation's television audience grew from 34 million to 590 million, with television set ownership in urban areas doubling and in rural areas rising about 20-fold. Installation of satellites and new receiving and relay stations had made television reception available virtually nationwide by the late 1980s. Surveys of the media audience have found that both urban and rural residents are relying increasingly on television as their main source of news.

In the spirit of diffusing authority, control of both airtime and revenues was greatly decentralized. Along with the introduction of advertising in the print media, radio and television began selling commercial time, spurring the growth of the advertising and public relations industries (from the audience perspective, the novelty soon gave way to the same sort of complaining about commercial breaks that goes on in U.S. homes). Central and local stations extended programming hours, and experimented with new formats and shows. Television began to import entertainment series and other material. In 1979, recently arrived in China to teach journalism, I watched "Man from Atlantis" in the home of farmers on the outskirts of Beijing; when I returned in 1987 I was seeing Disney cartoons, as well as ABC footage with voice-over in Mandarin on the evening news.

The content of print media became more diverse and colorful in the 1980s, in both serious and lighthearted directions. Investigative reporting, tentatively pioneered in the 1950s, made a comeback; numerous high officials in the petroleum industry, commerce, railways, and forestry were shamed into resignation by scandals disclosed in the press—ranging from taking free meals to negligence or bureaucratic bungling resulting in catastrophic loss of life. Greater time and space were devoted to readers' letters, economic affairs and international news. Meanwhile, shrinking state subsidies and the acceptance of long-rejected theories of supply and demand encouraged attention to human interest stories, advice columns for parents or consumers, forums for the despondent and lovelorn and other non-political matters.

Media Stressing Original Material

Although Xinhua continues to set much of the news agenda in China, and to provide the bulk of stories in certain categories, editors have a fair degree of discretion over placement and emphasis. Furthermore, numerous national newspapers and central broadcast units have developed their own net of national and international correspondents over the past decade, and media outlets at all levels have placed greater and greater emphasis on original material.

The most important category of newspaper is still official "party organs," which exist at all administrative levels down to county and municipality and are formally under the auspices of the Communist Party Committee at the corresponding level. These number about 400, represent a larger share of circulation than any other type of paper, and are extremely influential as purveyors of official policy. The circulation of the largest, People's Daily, exceeds three million and has an actual readership that is far higher—although this figure is down from a high of some six million more than a decade ago, due to various factors such as competition from other papers and television, subscription rate hikes and probably reader boredom (People's Daily was very popular for a few years after going through a revamping under new editorial leadership in the late 1970s, but the novelty was wearing off, and since Tiananmen the paper has become more subdued and monotonous).

PM Tabloids Provide Livelier Tone

The significance of lighter fare remains apparent, however, in the evening newspapers, which are usually in tabloid format and have a livelier tone and more entertaining content than conventional morning broadsheets. This category burgeoned after 1979 and evening papers now number about 40, up from 13 prior to the Cultural Revolution, with a combined daily circulation exceeding 10 million.

A marked change in many newspapers over the past decade has been the heightened importance of photographs, and the improved sophistication in their use. Visually oriented journalists used to complain that press pictures were allotted the space of "a square of beancurd." A pioneer in raising photojournalism to new heights was the English-language China Daily, which from its inception in 1981 used pictures prominently on both front and inside pages. People's Daily and other broadsheets soon followed suit. Along with growing popular interest in photography as both hobby and desirable vocation came the development of respect for candid and artistic photography. New publications devoted to photography were founded, and photo contests and exhibitions abound. Stilted shots of leaders and artificially posed pictures of happy workers or peasants are by no means a thing of the past; however, genuine documentary photography is now widespread and tremendously appreciated.

A fourth major point to be made about journalism in China is the existence of numerous supplementary and alternative channels of news. The vast array of internal publications mentioned earlier, which parallels the open information system, is one important channel. These may carry specialized, controversial, critical or investigative material, the main criteria for classifying something as internal being whether its authors or overseers assess it as sensitive. From a Western perspective it may not be the stuff of secrets at all. Internal publications may not be sold on newsstands and technically cannot be shown to foreigners, although scholars have been known to share such materials with foreign colleagues.

Most newspapers regularly publish internal reports with detailed information on subjects considered too touchy for open publication. Often these investigations are initiated by complaints to the "mass work department"—a peculiarly Chinese institution, found in virtually every news organization, which handles readers' letters, visitors and other matters involving the public. The internal reports go to political leaders, and occasionally may be approved for publication in the news columns, or published after the problems they raise are resolved. Xinhua puts out some of the most important internal publications, including detailed reports from the grass-roots and overseas bureaus and daily translations from foreign media for high leaders—a lesser version of which circulates among the general public in the form of the popular daily tabloid called Reference News. Press reformers favor delimiting the realm of this sort of insider journalism, so that more sensitive topics could be dealt with openly and in a timely manner; and this was the direction in which news coverage was going up to Tiananmen.

Another vibrant alternative medium is the rumor mill, or what the Chinese call "small path news," notoriously unreliable but invariably conveying at least some kernels of truth. And one should not forget the information that arrives from beyond China's borders. Voice of America and the British Broadcasting Corporation broadcast to China in both English and several Chinese dialects, and shortwave bands are standard on Chinese radios. Residents of the southern province of Guangzhou have relatively easy access to radio, television and press from Hong Kong. Add to this Chinese adeptness at discerning problems or conflicts between the lines in the official media. As a journalism professor told me gleefully years ago, "The Chinese people really know how to read the newspapers."

Fifth, perhaps the least obvious but possibly the most crucial aspect of journalism in China, press controls are not ironclad. Like most systems of authority, China's political system relies on both informal and formal controls—subtle, unarticulated, quixotic methods as well as expressly stated, institutionalized ones— and the role of informal controls is particularly apparent in the area of mass media. Coercion has always been a factor in keeping the media in line and came to the forefront for a time after Tiananmen; but the system is fluid rather than fixed, with the limits of the permissible largely defined by time, place, and personalities.

Party Apparatus Aims at Control

This is not to say that formal regulatory and structural constraints are meaningless. In line with the principle that journalism is answerable first and foremost to the party and government, periodicals must be formally registered. After a few lax years when unauthorized publications came and went fairly freely, this licensing system was tightened with the establishment of the State Press and Publications Administration in the spring of 1987. An extensive party apparatus is in place to help assure that media organizations adhere to propaganda guidelines issued by top officials, and that media content reflects policies and programs set at the highest levels. Party committees and party secretaries have authority to hire and fire leading editors of media under their purview, to oversee the broad outlines of the news, to scrutinize what they consider important stories and to review and even to write key editorials and commentaries. Such authority is enshrined in many formal directives as well as in conventional wisdom.

The State Press and Publications Administration has the power to close media outlets for a variety of rationales. The agency carried out its first nationwide review of publishing houses, newspapers and other periodicals in 1987–88, and ordered more than 600 publications shut down or merged. It also tightened authorizations for new publications, approving only 50 new newspapers in 1988, along with 35 that switched from internal to open publication. A second consolidation drive was launched in the fall of 1989, resulting in the closing or merger of 190 newspapers, nearly 12 per cent of the nationwide total; some 600 social science journals had to cease publication as well. It is interesting that the agency seldom cites politics as a rationale for closing down a publication; streamlining management or fiscal problems are the most common reasons given. In the first round of inspection, only five newspapers were said to have been closed for political errors, and in the second only eight shutdowns were acknowledged as political. The latter group included the World Economic Herald, whose distribution has been held back and its editor, the late Qin Benli, removed for his obvious sympathy with the student demonstrators: the Beijing-based Economic Weekly, two of whose editors, Chen Zemin and Wang Juntao, were convicted of spreading "counter-revolutionary" propaganda and are now serving prison terms; and the Beijing magazine New Observer.

However, China has no formal prepublication censorship apparatus, and how directives and guidelines are interpreted in practice is largely up to local party committees and news organizations themselves. Decisions about how broad a debate to air on an embarrassing social problem, whether or not to cover a crime, or how to portray a disaster may hinge on the indulgence of a party official, the audacity of a chief editor, or the persistence of a reporter. Naturally, people are more willing to take risks when the political climate seems relaxed. Even in tense times, however, the rules are not fixed. Topics covered at one time may be covered up at another. Propaganda authorities suppressed news of student demonstrations that broke out at the end of 1986 for four days, even though the VOA and BBC had already made the events widely known. Yet rioting in Tibet less than a year later was reported as breaking news. Officials initially tried to limit coverage of the 1989 protests but then lifted restrictions, although even stricter limitations were imposed after martial law was declared in parts of Beijing. Sometimes plane or rail accidents are reported immediately; other times the reports are delayed; some grave incidents are not reported at all, as one only learns serendipitously.

Ideas Old and New: Clash of Traditions

Sixth, the weight of tradition as an influence on Chinese journalism cannot be ignored. The philosophies and practices of journalism in the People's Republic are not simply creations of the Chinese Communists, but rather are hybrids of old and new. It could be argued that, despite all their discontents, Chinese journalists have a culturally inherited propensity to accept news management. The paternalistic and didactic character of modern propaganda has deep roots in the Confucian heritage and most journalists in China, being members of an intellectual elite, subscribe to the role of teacher and guide to at least some degree.

On the other hand, some elements of Chinese tradition are conducive to what we might see as democratic tendencies. It is certainly convenient for the Communists that the liberal Western ideal of an adversarial "fourth estate" is alien to the Chinese tradition. However, the notion of a "loyal opposition" is a familiar and time-honored concept and provides a mantle of legitimacy of sorts for journalists who criticize those in power from a patriotic stance.

Furthermore, China's official rhetoric itself provides some sanction for crusading journalism—justifying it in theory, if not in practice. Under guidelines set down by the Communists in the 1940s and reiterated constantly, the news media are supposed to function as the "eyes, ears and mouthpiece" of the Party and government, to tirelessly propagate current policies and unswervingly support the cause of socialism. At the same time, however, the media also are supposed to be "eyes, ears and mouthpiece" of the people, to expose and criticize wrongdoing and give voice to popular grievances.

The other side of the weight of tradition is, of course, the erosive force of non-traditional thoughts and examples. The rapid infusion of new ideas and practices into virtually all realms of public and private life, brought about by the reforms and open-door policies, has had a profound impact on all aspects of journalism, from intellectual debates on the definition of news and the relationship between journalism and politics, to the content of journalism education and the conduct of news work. One element of this process was exposure to the example of aggressive Western reporters, an example noted by the Chinese media audience as well as Chinese journalists. In the late 1980s, when television began broadcasting press conferences between Chinese officials and foreign correspondents, often live, the sessions were the talk of Chinese offices and living rooms. Other influences came through Chinese translations of foreign works on journalism theory and practice, and through international exchange programs for journalism students, educators and practitioners. Given the ever-expanding reach of modern communications technologies and the ever more porous nature of geographic boundaries, the world's encroachment was no doubt inevitable and no doubt continues.

Compliance may still be the rule within China's press corps, particularly amidst the political chill since Tiananmen, but defiance became a commonplace exception after the beginning of economic reforms and policies of opening up to the outside world in 1978. The experiences accumulated over the decade that followed have lasting significance. Journalists got a good deal of practice in pressing the limits, showing they can be thoughtful, wily, even daring, at the production end of the news. Meanwhile, the media audience got used to seeing greater diversity and controversy in the news, and grew increasingly sophisticated and persnickety at the receiving end.

The inexorable trend toward freedom of expression surfaced most dramatically at the height of the 1989 demonstrations, when for a few days in May news coverage was as abundant and unbridled as demands for political change. This development was not as extraordinary as much of the foreign media portrayed it. Like the demonstrations themselves, the media activism was a logical outgrowth of 10 years of experimentation, an outcome of newfound freedoms combined with mounting frustrations.

After the suppression, the leadership subjected the news media to "rectification," which meant public castigation of the press corps for supposedly fanning the flames of rebellion, arrests of a number of journalists seen as particularly troublesome, and reassignment of uncooperative editors. Yet it is obvious that habits of work and mind cultivated over years cannot be erased overnight. When I returned to China for a visit in the spring of 1990, a year after those horrific events, I found friends in the media and academia at once deeply troubled and surprisingly philosophical. "China always works this way," said one scholar. "Two steps forward, one step back. Or maybe three steps forward, two steps back."

Instructed to recriminate against those active in the demonstrations, people at news organizations and research institutes instead have been protecting each other—a situation far different from what occurred in political campaigns under Mao. People continue to voice privately what they were saying publicly a few years ago, even to a foreigner such as myself— also quite different from the paranoia that prevailed in the past. The brutality of what Chinese refer to simply as "six-four," June 4, seems to have deepened the convictions of those predisposed to reform, while greatly unnerving many onetime party stalwarts. The end result of the Tiananmen debacle may be to hasten the progress of change, in journalism and in political life generally.

THE WORLD OF CHINESE TELEVISION[2]

Three years after Tiananmen Square, there is renewed progress in Chinese television. The massive size and population of this country present the mass media with challenges of prodigious proportions. Chinese television is currently starting to evolve as a forward-looking symbol of China's move into the modern age. But the political repression continues, and the creative forces are wary of content, and tend to focus more on technique than substance.

China's recent open-door policy has resulted in a major change in television programming. After the decade lost to the Cultural Revolution (1966–1976) when television broadcast little but hokey revolutionary operas approved by the party, there are now fresh topics and foreign co-productions. Television performs a key social function in China. Education and entertainment form the top priorities. Programming includes variety shows, traditional dramas, documentaries, news, foreign imports, sports, cartoons, classroom courses, children's programs and even soap operas. The world's largest television audience is finding new choices.

When regular television broadcasting began on September 2, 1958, in Beijing, there were about one thousand television sets to receive the signal. In 1989, potential viewers numbered six hundred million, two and one-half times larger than the population of the United States.

The first broadcast of international news was received via satellite on April 1, 1980, permitting some live pictures of other cultures and nationalities to be seen in China. This began to bring the Chinese people new awareness of the world around them.

Although foreign news stories may show critical issues facing the country, domestic news will not. Domestically, all news on

[2]Article by Judith Marlane, professor at California State University-Northridge. From *Television Quarterly* 26/2:25–31 '92. Copyright © 1992 by the National Academy of Television Arts and Sciences. Reprinted with permission.

Chinese television is "good": irrigation projects; a dinosaur exhibition; students learning computer programming; medical care
for farmers; efforts to encourage seawater fish breeding. The
only way problems are presented is through a story dealing with
corrections and "solutions."

For example, if an error is remedied, that is a permissible
news story. But there is no dissent; no controversy. China's media
is singleminded in its need to project and protect only the most
positive images of its own world.

The broadcast industry in China is hoping to develop and
produce material that is acceptable by Western standards; it is no
longer sufficient to be judged by national or even Third World
standards. However, the cultural and historical need to insist on a
view of China that is positive impedes this progress, and takes a
heavy toll; it impacts adversely on the creative ability to use film
and television with emotional impact and to portray the realities
of life.

I was recently selected to serve as the only Western judge in
the preliminary documentary division of the Shanghai International Television Festival. Together with eight other judges, all
successful Chinese producers and directors, we screened 74 documentaries from all over the world, including entries from Australia, Japan, Hong Kong, Cuba, Belgium, Canada, United States,
China, West Germany, Czechoslovakia and Yugoslavia.

During our ten days of viewing and discussing these international films, a curious dichotomy became evident. Except when it
came to their own country, Chinese colleagues were able to respond positively to films with emotional impact based on universal themes that transcended political philosophies, such as love,
hate and greed. They willingly solicit criticism and are eager to
apply it in all categories except their own. When it runs counter to
their ingrained nationalism, it is rejected.

The Chinese judges chose as their winning entry a documentary with ordinary production values about a dating service for
the elderly. *A Marriage Bureau for Elderly People* was a static, distant
discourse on a theme of social service; they bypassed *The Home for
Abandoned Children,* a superior film with major emotional impact
that told the true story of a poverty-stricken couple who raise
abandoned children.

No amount of heated discussion could convince the majority
of Chinese judges that this deeply moving depiction of family love

far transcended possible negative implications of abject poverty, and the reality that sometimes children are left abandoned in their streets. *The Home for Abandoned Children* created division within the ranks of Chinese producers and directors who have often known the effects of censure, and the problems of portraying ideas and events that do not meet with government approval. This documentary was not a reality of life in China considered suitable to be seen and shared.

Tight controls on what people are permitted to view makes most Chinese documentaries static, unemotional and even clinical. Chinese filmmakers, including some who were judges with me, frequently have been hurt in their professional careers when they attempted to deal with material that is officially not acceptable. Sometimes, even advanced techniques of film art are taboo.

As a result, they are more comfortable dealing with unaltered factual events, even though the results are often antiseptic and ineffective. This inhibits the power of the Chinese documentary to make an impact, squelches creativity and diminishes its appeal to a Western audience.

Chinese media experts, however, are eager to learn the latest Western production techniques so they can more successfully compete in the world market. They are capable of recognizing and appreciating well-made documentaries that communicate universal human themes. In fact, they voted unanimously for *Promises to Keep*, by Durrin Productions, a powerful United States documentary about the homeless, a critical issue presented with passion and personal impact. Since the problem was not set in their own homeland, the theme and the production was both acceptable and appreciated here. The winning film was American—a National Geographic special, *Baka People of the Forest* from WQED, Pittsburgh.

The Shanghai Television Festival has become a bi-annual event in an orchestrated effort to spotlight their country and to provide an opportunity for Chinese writers, producers and directors to study innovative media techniques from all over the world. The opportunities for their own documentaries to have significant impact will increase as they continue to interact with the West. China someday hopes to achieve recognition and distribution as their films and videos compete on the international market.

The problem, as the Chinese see it, is to permit their culture to interact with the Western world without a sacrifice of their deeply ingrained political and social values. The Chinese regard themselves as one family. They believe in conformity and reconciliation by narrowing down differences. There is gradual progress being made on the creative front, despite China's turbulent history since the Civil War.

The uncertain course of Chinese politics coexists with the growing importance of television. Foreign programs have become a staple of daily programming. Since 1979 when Bob Hope taped his special *The Road to China*, one of the first entertainment programs made in China by a foreign company, the desire for programming from the United States has increased. Programs with nonpolitical content have been the most acceptable. American television series recently aired in China include *Dynasty* (reported to be the favorite of Deng Xiaoping, China's paramount leader), *Hunter, Falcon Crest, Remington Steele,* and *Matt Houston.*

The most popular programs on television generally are motion pictures. These have included *On Golden Pond, Death On the Nile, Oliver,* and *Kramer Versus Kramer.* These broadcasts are studied by Chinese viewers as a portrayal of our lifestyles and culture. Often, this is a mixed blessing.

While in China, I had the opportunity to speak with the woman who was responsible for dubbing all films for the Shanghai Television Station. Huang Qi, a senior member of the staff, told me she had seen many American movies, and she was confused about the need that Americans seemed to have to break up their family when they go out for a job: she was using the example of *Kramer Versus Kramer* which she had recently dubbed. In China, she told me, it is very natural for a woman to go directly to work after graduation. Although women in China share a sisterhood of problems, they do not face "a sensational choice between job and family."

Huang Qi asked why it was necessary for a woman "to sacrifice her family." Her questions reflected confusion and concern—largely based on her experience watching American films and the values they project to her. She felt a need to understand more about the lifestyles of American women; to reach out her hand in a bond of friendship and compassion.

In China, women evidently have less conflict in the choice between marriage and career. They believe it is natural to marry and to have a child. (The government has established a one child per family quota.) But it is traditional Chinese philosophy to have a baby, to run a home and yet have job responsibilities. This duality often brings women conflicts and guilt since they feel they cannot be good housewives as their husbands expect when they have to work long hours to fulfill job duties. Often, women in Chinese television choose to shift their job assignment so they will have more time to be with their families.

Women news reporters in China also experience difficulties coping with the travel that is required. (This, too, is a problem shared by their American counterparts.) The night shifts and the constant pressures of breaking deadlines often create havoc in their personal lives. Those Chinese broadcasters in their mid 30s or early 40s seem the most torn as they struggle to lay a strong foundation for their career while also caring for small children and, in most cases, aging parents. The extended family in China is a cultural tradition. Network and local newswomen working in television stations throughout the United States can empathize with the need to make hard choices; to establish priorities; to take on increased burdens.

The women I met in Chinese television spoke with candor about their professional lives. Chen Wen, for example, is a brilliant news reporter and editor working for the Shanghai Television Station. She was their first camera woman. She told me that when she was seventeen years old, she was forced to go to the countryside as part of the cultural revolution. Wen worked in a factory there for four years.

When she returned to Shanghai, she became a teacher of art. Then, she answered an advertisement in the newspaper for a job as a reporter, passed an examination and joined the Shanghai Television Station eight years ago. Of the twenty-eight people working in the reporting section, she was the only woman.

Wen explained to me: "Originally, there were three other women there, but they got transferred after having children. The travel required was too demanding with a family." Chen Wen remains single.

On all her assignments, Wen feels equal to men. She says she has never experienced unpleasant times. She was pleased to admit that men enjoyed working with her. She told me they often want to protect her and offer their help. But she never permits them to take over what she accepts as her share of the job.

Wen acknowledged that men receive more preferential treatment in television news than do women. Most of the technicians in Chinese television stations are men; the television equipment is considered too heavy for women. The prejudice against women in news remains.

There are distinct advantages to being a newswoman and Wen was quick to point out the benefits, as she sees them: women are more tactful in approaching people and are more sympathetic in handling human relationships, she claims, and are often able to discover details that male correspondents miss. Therefore, they are able to give their stories additional dimension and depth. Wen also believes that, "Sometimes a woman will be easier to talk to and they will get information that a man will not. A woman is easier to approach."

Probably the most powerful woman in Shanghai Television is Jin Min Zhu, Vice Director of the Shanghai Television Station where she is the administrative head. With twenty-five years of experience in broadcasting, she is a pioneer in the industry. Zhu served as the first generation anchorwoman at Shanghai Television. Married with two children, Zhu told me that she believes women are making a greater contribution to Shanghai Television than men. She says, "They have to take care of family while they have to work." This dual responsibility makes it necessary to shoulder heavier burdens and they most often make double or triple the effort of men in order to attain the same achievements.

During my conversations with some of the women who are now making important contributions to Chinese television, they were interested to learn how their experiences and frustrations compared with women who work in television in the United States. In so many ways, we are the same. The women I met in Chinese television were friendly and receptive to an exchange of ideas. They spoke freely of their personal goals and lifestyles, although there was little talk of politics.

Over the past ten years, China's open door policy despite retreats and repression has contributed to economic progress and some nationwide reforms. In the mass media, there are major reforms being made in order to meet the current challenge and to promote the country's modernization program.

Television has recently been the instrument used to try to replace old feudal ideas that create obstacles to marriage and happiness. The matchmaking program *Tonight We Meet* was launched in 1990 by the Beijing Television station. The idea is more than entertainment: it provides opportunities for single men and women to meet while creating new views on life, love and marriage. It is the Chinese form of free choice through advertising. The program has been a great success and has matched up many new couples.

One of the first women to appear on *Tonight We Meet* was an attractive divorced journalist, Ren Li, who was indignant to learn that other divorced women were more interested in a man's position and material wealth. Ren believed that a woman should not depend on anyone but herself.

She came on the matchmaking program in order to tell the audience about her own expectations of marriage, saying it was not important whether or not she found a husband.

"If a woman doesn't have self-respect, she can only depend on a man." Ren stated that men always demand a virtuous wife. But to her, it was just as necessary for the man to be a virtuous husband and father. Many Chinese who heard Ren Li speak out on television called her a "brave woman." Traditional Chinese matchmaking has been given a jolt by the program. Unfortunately, I never did find out whether Ren found a new husband.

The Chinese love to watch sports events. Each year there are over 100 games broadcasted live or taped. In 1985, CBS-TV traded a package of sports programs that included several national basketball all-star and playoff games in return for advertising time on China Central Television. (Television advertising has been a regular feature of Chinese television since 1979.) Our advanced broadcasting technology including multiple camera shots, instant replay and slow motion effects literally dazzled the Chinese audiences. They are eager to learn the newest production techniques from us and adapt them to their own programming.

In 1990, the 11th Annual Asian games in Beijing resulted in an expanded effort toward providing sports coverage that included more interesting and varied technical use of cameras. They are striving to compete more effectively with the imported programs now available in China.

The Asian games were being held during my last visit to Beijing, and I was invited to attend the opening ceremonies. The grandeur, color and pageantry that was on display was impressive. But the most interesting addition to the spectacle was the appearance of helium filled yellow balloons in the shape of packages of M&M's which floated slowly upward from the floor of the arena; the ultimate commercial injected into a socialist country. The potential market for products in China is truly beginning to transform its landscape and its economy.

Offices are now set up in Los Angeles and New York by the Chinese to buy the products of the studios and independent production companies. Joint ventures with foreign companies are courted and welcomed. The international broadcasting and [advertising] communities recognize the potential market of over a billion consumers.

Television advertising is considered an effective way to begin to reach the largest consumer market in the world. Local fifteen second and thirty-second spots include ads for household appliances such as refrigerators and television sets, shampoo, cosmetics, furniture and cookies. International companies and products appearing on Chinese television include Colgate-Palmolive, Coca-Cola, Tang, Sony, Hitachi and Jeep. Dupont, Boeing and McDonnell-Douglas have used television advertising to promote their corporate image in China's modernization. Cigarette and liquor advertising are not permitted.

The door that is now being cautiously opened from within China has resulted in a large number of television documentaries emphasizing the progress that is being made here. Yet as I found at the Shanghai Festival, social and political criticism are not permissible and are not portrayed. In China today, as in the past, it is not possible to be a patriot and a dissenter at the same time. Personal suffering is considered irrelevant when compared to the prosperity of the nation.

The men and women working in Chinese television have learned that being critical of China and Chinese contemporary life marks the person as a dissenter and this creates serious problems for their future work. Such a climate keeps a blanket of fear over the creative community and the intellectuals.

It is obvious, of course, that the Chinese government still regards television as a useful propaganda tool and as a potential instrument of foreign policy, in addition to its money-making potential. After Tiananmen Square, there is renewed care in what is presented on the air. No one ever talks of the events of that tragedy.

If a question is asked, it goes unanswered. To the people of Chinese television, it has become a non-event. It never happened. So while I find so much that encourages extending our hands in friendship, while there is so much I share in the feelings and concerns of the men and women working in broadcasting, there remains a distance that I found difficult to bridge.

The broadcasting community continues to go through intense introspection and self-criticism. In any case, the commitment of Chinese leaders to the development of the television industry is strong and the increasing influence of Western programming is undeniable. Moreover, the tremendous promise of the Chinese television market is gradually being recognized by multinational corporations. The opportunities for interaction in the international marketplace are creating global influences that someday will establish a fresh voice for the largest television audience in the world. As Chinese television prepares to enter a new era, it is my hope that by working with the world community, they will be able to recognize and achieve their true potential.

CHINESE ART TODAY: NO U-TURN[3]

Two years after the traumatic political clampdown in China, recent visits to two major art centers—Beijing and Wuhan—and to a gathering of expatriate artists in San Diego offer a dramatic view of Chinese art now.

Beijing is no longer the sleepy, remote capital it was in the 1970s with the Forbidden City as its principal attraction. In the 1980s it was transformed into a modern commercial metropolis with luxury hotels, traffic jams, and air pollution. Toward the end of the decade, Beijing's art too was becoming genuinely modern, as was demonstrated by landmark events such as the "China/Avant-Garde" exhibition held in February 1989 in the capital's National Art Gallery. On the day the show opened, like a strange foreshadowing of what was to come four months later in Tiananmen Square, the artist Xiao Lu fired pistol shots into her own neo-Realist creation of what appeared to be two occupied phone booths. She said afterward, "I did it because I did not want my work to look too finished." The exhibition was closed to stop

[3]Article by Joan Lebold Cohen, author on contemporary Chinese art. From *ARTnews* 91:104–107 F '92. Copyright © 1992 by the author. Reprinted with permission.

further neo-Dada happenings. Later it was permitted to reopen briefly, but those shots sounded the death knell for future public displays of such experimental art, at least for the time being. Subsequently, the art establishment conservatives denounced the exhibition as having been incomprehensible, ugly, and unserious.

Although Chinese avant-garde art suffered a setback, the closing of the exhibition could not completely reverse the changes that had occurred during the last decade. Enterprising Eastern seaboard artists can now function independently of the academies, finding patronage from the expatriate communities in Beijing and several other Eastern cities. Even academy artists must seek outside sales and commissions to supplement their much reduced state support, money that has been lessened by the government's economic reforms. It is also easier to arrange exhibitions, sales, and study abroad because of the larger international presence in China. To be sure, most Beijing artists still live in tiny spaces, but in contrast to ten years ago many now have comfortable furniture, color TVs, hi-fis, and electric fans bought with money earned from sales.

The 1980s, with their "open policy" and reforms, produced more than just an economic transformation. They connected this generation of artists to an international art community. This fact was reflected in the actions of many at the conservative Central Academy of Fine Arts in Beijing, who felt reinforced in opposing the Maoist line that art must serve politics. Defending themselves during the post-June 4 crackdown, they argued that art and politics are different.

Nonetheless, over the last two years there have been some adverse developments in China's art world as a result of the political situation. After the bloody massacre in Tiananmen Square, people go about their business as before, as if nothing happened. But one dejected student said of the symbol of the democracy movement, "The Goddess of Democracy has to hold her torch with two hands because democracy is so hard to support in China." Since 1989 many artists have filled their canvases with images of the bloodied students and workers. Meanwhile, Beijing's National Art Gallery has been closed for repairs, and the most progressive art journals, such as *Newspaper of Chinese Art* and Wuhan's *Wave of Art,* have ceased publication. So, apart from occasional exhibitions at other, smaller sites, it is difficult to see recent work unless one visits the art schools or the artists' digs.

Wang Yuping is a 1989 graduate of the Central Academy who was invited to join its faculty. He shares his grubby Academy studio with several other painters. Propped against all four walls are stacks of paintings, ten canvases deep. Wang shifts the stacks to show his visitor a picture from a series titled "Hell," which features a shadowy figure isolated on a large black canvas. He was invited to show in last year's exhibition at Beijing's History Museum in Tiananmen Square. One of his works there, *Running Away—Depression Is on the Way* (1991), is painted in fluent black and gray strokes. The ghoul-faced runner wearing an electric-pink jacket is fleeing a shadow, a small, black, barking dog, and a tiny open-mouthed figure who appears to be falling into an abyss. Does such an apparently downbeat theme express the artist's desire to escape from depression? Perhaps. Certainly, Wang's work radically departs from both the traditional Confucian mask that does not permit direct portrayal of feelings and the later Chinese Communist ideal of the healthy desirability of collectivism. In reaction, one critic at the Academy urged him to do work that was "more classical, not so unpleasant."

Paintings done in various realist styles, which, in the Chinese context, means using recognizable subject matter, are the kind most likely to be exhibited today. Sixteen young artists participated in the recent exhibition at the History Museum. Fang Lijun, a classmate of Wang's at the Central Academy who works in a surreal variation on Chinese realism, was not one. Visited in his damp, rented studio, he shows a giant-headed, screaming self-portrait. Fang was not invited to join the faculty of the Academy, and he talks of how he has fought to stay in Beijing since graduation: "I took a job so that I could get a residence permit." He later quit his job and now paints full time. His simplified style has a large-scale, Photorealist format, similar to that of Chuck Close's self-portraits.

That Fang was not invited to participate in the History Museum exhibition, nor indeed in any official Chinese exhibitions, is probably not due to his aggressive subject matter, which is no more "unpleasant" than that of Wang Yuping. The difference may be that he participated as a student in the now frowned-on 1989 "China/Avant-Garde" exhibition at the National Art Gallery.

Exceptions to the post–June 4 prohibition on avant-garde art appear to occur when traditional elements are invoked by artists because they can point to these images to defend their works against accusations of "bourgeois liberalization." One installation last year in Beijing that sparked hope for the future vitality of Chinese experimental art was Lu Shengzhong's *Calling the Souls* (1988–91), which took place at the gallery of the Central Academy's High School. Lu Shengzhong, an instructor at the Academy, used approximately a million traditional, red, cut paper silhouettes of the "soul" (which looks a bit like a paper-doll image of Steven Spielberg's creature E.T.) in an installation that spread over floor, ceiling, walls. Whereas many conservatives in the art world did not understand an installation of footprints that Lu made for the "China/Avant-Garde" exhibition, most visitors recognize that *Calling the Souls* draws from a Chinese folk-art source and therefore believe the image is old and nonpolitical.

In Lu's room at the Central Academy, he has hung red cut paper images of souls over the ceiling and walls. He recites the 1,200-year-old lines from the famous Tang-dynasty poet Du Fu concerning the host's reassurance to a traveler: "Warm water washes my feet/a paper cutout calls my soul." Then he explains: "The meaning is that the paper cut is the symbol of one's soul, and a person is set at ease by seeing it." Lu's success is attributable to his canny transformation of an ancient Chinese image. While he makes an installation—still an unconventional form in China—the "soul" allows him to ward off charges of spiritual pollution from the old-guard fanatics still active in modernizing China.

Economic development has lagged far behind in China's vast interior. The central Chinese city of Wuhan is on the Yangzi, hundreds of miles upriver from Shanghai. Wuhan hasn't attracted much foreign investment, and, with the exception of several new highrise hotels, the city looks unchanged. Moreover, despite recent, spectacular archeological finds, such as giant bronze bells from ca. 300–400 B.C., the city hasn't attracted many tourists.

Interestingly, though, there is a core of sophisticated modernists in the Wuhan art community. In 1985 many young Wuhan artists were frontrunners in the avant-garde "'85" movement that experimented with new forms, happenings, and other Dada-like ideas—remarkable considering that Socialist Realism was the only style allowed less than a decade earlier. Some Wuhan artists also participated in the February 1989 "China/Avant-Garde" exhibition that so outraged the political and artistic leadership in Beijing. Just four months later, Shang Yang, who was vice president of the Wuhan Fine Arts College, exhibited a provocative, mixed-media series titled "State" at Beijing's National Art Gallery. His most powerful painting has a huge tear in the tautly stretched, gray-white surface made of six pieces of cloth sewn together. The gaping mouthlike hole resembles a wound.

During the 1989 democracy movement demonstrations in Wuhan, Shang Yang and many of his colleagues and students marched to show their support for reforms. During the ensuing crackdown, the Communist Party called for reprisals. Shang was criticized in a public meeting by his colleagues and students, and others gave secret testimony against him. Later the artist said to a friend: "I am a painter who has never had much interest in politics or in high government positions, but when I was put in such a spot, I could not bear to see people cheated by the government." Forced to step down from the vice-presidency, he was barred from teaching for two years, his Communist Party membership was suspended, and he was deprived of his studio and art supplies.

The students who demonstrated neither graduated nor got jobs. Yet, compared to what happened during the Cultural Revolution—when artists were persecuted, locked up, or sent to the countryside for years of "reeducation"—their fate was not so bleak. Shang retains his professorial rank and his friends have rallied to help him with space and supplies.

Several well-known artists from northeastern China who showed in the "China/Avant-Garde" exhibition were attracted to Wuhan in the late 1980s because of the receptive artistic climate, good jobs, and the fact that there was no problem getting residency permits despite the lack of opportunities to actually sell art. Wang Guangyi took a job at Hubei Light Industry University, where he lives with his wife and daughter in two tiny rooms containing only a cot and a chair crammed in among scores of canvases. He talks about participating in international exhibitions in Paris and Australia and shows his visitor some bold, political Pop works. For example, he pokes fun at Mao's former population encouragement policy in his series "The Holy Family Produced in Batches," from 1989–90. Nine identical babies reduced to computer-graphic images are being born in a geometric grid against a brightly colored ground. And in his "Great Criticism" series, from 1990–91, he pictures oversize, Kodak yellow, Socialist Realist heroes holding giant pens high, set against a Communist-red ground, parodying gun-toting revolutionary soldiers. Each painting has one foreign product, such as Kodak, Casio, or Coca-Cola, enshrined in a black starburst beside its name in Chinese characters.

Why does the reactionary art leadership allow such scathing comments? Wang explains: "They leave me alone for three reasons: They fool the public into thinking that their policy is liberal; I have a big reputation; and the sale of my work earns foreign exchange for China."

Following the example of many of his seniors, who try to combine both the old and the new in a single work of art, the young Wuhan sculptor Fu Zhouwang made a bold "Tongue and Groove" sculpture series during 1990–91, using a traditional wood-joining technique. He uses this ancient woodworking system to create abstract compositions that dramatize the coming together of tongue and groove. His fanciful *Dragon,* for instance, which was drawn from the Chinese mythological creature, writhes on eight posts.

Since 1980, hundreds of Chinese artists have left China for America and Europe. Many have stayed in the West, including 11 of the 12 artists represented in an excellent exhibition titled "Chinese Art Meets West" at San Diego State University last June, the best of several recent exhibitions of Chinese art in California. Liberated from the artistic constraints imposed in China, this sophisticated international group nevertheless continues to feel strong connections to the motherland. And at home and abroad Chinese artists are still haunted by the Tiananmen massacre. Chen Danqing, for example, showed a scene from June 4 in San Diego. In his *Expression* (1991), he appropriates images from photographs, going beyond the Socialist Realism of his training into the realm of Photorealism. Chen says, "My generation and I are all children of the Chinese Communist Party. We grew up on its milk. Now I have lived in America for ten years, but I still have the Chinese Red Guard inside me." The canvas is divided vertically through the center: one half, in color, shows Chinese students dragging their wounded to safety; the other shows overblown, lewd and leering Spanish flamenco dancers in black and white. The artist comments on the two worlds he has painted here: "I looked for points to compare two views. I am, at once, very emotional and very cold. I am both the reporter and the reader. I want to express my deep feelings and also I want to hide them." Chen is significant, too, because his was one of the pictures auctioned by Christie's last September in Hong Kong. This was the first major sale of contemporary Chinese oil painting, marking the debut on the international art market of a previously ignored art field. The auction brought just over $1 million.

For "Chinese Art Meets West" another San Diego contributor, Xu Bing, a giant of the Chinese avant-garde movement and a recent arrival in the U.S., created *A B C D E F G* . . . (1991), clay bricks like oversize printing blocks with Chinese characters that make the sounds of the English alphabet. For his meticulously produced series, he used Chinese words, such as "somber morning" for *A*, "falling thief" for *B*, in an amusing way. But the jokes have a bitter edge and betray the expatriate artist's difficult situation. He is in a strange land that has an incomprehensible language. He has left his culture and his fame behind and must begin anew.

The richness of the Chinese cultural identity is not a casual matter and America has not been an easy experience. Many who have come here were famous in China. Here they are unknown. Moreover, the transition from the economic security of a state-run Communist system to the need to support yourself in a free market is difficult.

The 1990s mark the beginning of a new era for Chinese art. Oil painting, which became part of Chinese art at the beginning of this century, was finally acknowledged in the art market last year and, despite the crackdown, internationalist ideas continue to inspire the Chinese in the field of art as well as of government. "No U-Turn" was the logo for the "China/Avant-Garde" exhibition in February 1989, and there is ample evidence that the suppression of the democracy movement and the hardening of the Communist Party line hasn't thrown this new generation of artists off its course.

THE NEW HEROIN CORRIDOR—DRUG TRAFFICKING IN CHINA[4]

Testimony of Robert C. Bonner, Drug Enforcement Administration Official

Chairman Biden and members of the Senate Judiciary Committee and the Senate Caucus on International Narcotics Control: I am pleased to appear before you today to give testimony regarding the drug trafficking situation in the People's Republic of China [PRC]. I look forward to continuing the productive relationship that the Drug Enforcement Administration [DEA] has had with the Committee.

The heroin threat is of deep concern to DEA. Worldwide opium production has doubled in the past few years. Southeast Asia accounts for seventy percent of opium production with the overwhelming majority cultivated in Burma. China continues to emerge as both a consumer and major transit route for heroin and opium emanating from Burma.

Historical Perspective

For nearly three decades, China had virtually eliminated drug use and trafficking within its borders due to strict policies which banned the cultivation of opium poppies, prohibited the importation and use of narcotics, and effectively severed the lines of distribution. Beginning in 1979, however, several events began a reversal of this "drug-free" China: First, China began a process of economic liberalization and opened its borders to increased trade. Then, in 1980, the three countries of the so-called Golden Triangle—Burma, Thailand and Laos—produced the first of a continuing series of bumper harvests of opium. As legitimate cross-border trade increased, so did the smuggling of opiates.

Burma, the world's largest opium producer, plays a crucial role in China's drug trade. Opium growing areas and refining

---

[4]Statement by Robert C. Bonner, Administrator, Drug Enforcement Administration, before the U.S. Senate Judiciary Committee, 102nd Congress, 2nd Session, May 19, 1992.

sites in Burma abut China's Yunnan Province. Close ethnic and cultural ties between tribal peoples who live on both sides of the border facilitate the smuggling into China. China's transport and communication systems are most attractive to drug traffickers who continually seek to develop alternative routes to move their deadly product to market.

China's emergence as a major transit route was the result of an evolutionary process. In the 1980s, intelligence indicated that Thai couriers were carrying heroin on flights from Thailand to Guangzhou, a gateway to Hong Kong, sometimes by way of Manila. From there the drugs were transported by rail or ferry to Hong Kong. Also, the Chinese press reported that narcotics were smuggled by land routes into Yunnan Province from the Golden Triangle and then by air or truck to Guangzhou. Because of these developments, and with the encouragement of Hong Kong authorities, the Chinese began training their customs agents in drug detection. The effectiveness of their drug interception program at airports resulted in the development of land routes across China to move heroin and opium to consuming centers as well as to Hong Kong.

In 1987, the Hong Kong Customs and Excise Service (HKCE) reported a notable rise in narcotics shipping through China. DEA's Hong Kong office received information that heroin was being shipped via containerized cargo from mainland China. Reports also indicated that multi-kilogram shipments of heroin were being moved by truck from Burma and northern Laos, through southern China, into Hong Kong.

The drug situation had further worsened in China by 1990. Not only were drugs transiting the southern areas of China, but they were also being moved to major Chinese cities in other areas which were not on the main southern route via Yunnan, Guangxi, and Guangdong. An official of the Ministry of Public Security (MPS) acknowledged publicly that China had become one of the major transit routes for opiates. He also stated that the area involved in trafficking had expanded to include not only Yunnan and Guangdong Provinces, but also Shanghai, Shaanxi, Gansu, Sichuan, and Guangxi. This was corroborated by seizures and rapid increases in the local addict populations.

The extent of the problem facing the PRC was clearly acknowledged in October 1991, when Communist Party Chief Jiang Zemin called eradication of the use and trafficking of drugs to be "a question of life and death." Last year, the PRC reported that 1,919 kilograms of heroin and 1,980 kilograms of opium were seized in China, one indication of the magnitude of the problem. While these are significant numbers, it must be noted that since 1986, only four heroin seizures totaling 73 kilograms can be documented by DEA as being linked to China and destined for the United States.

The movement of opiates through China has also spurred opiate consumption there. A recent Chinese report states there are 148,000 registered addicts, and that the addict population is expanding both in number and geographic disbursement. The number not coming forth for treatment is undoubtedly much higher and the recidivism rate at local rehabilitation centers remains high. Intravenous injection of heroin is a growing problem and has contributed to an increase in the number of AIDS cases, especially in Yunnan province. The Chinese also have acknowledged some opium cultivation. The product of this cultivation is believed to be consumed within China.

The government of the People's Republic of China has taken strong action to stem the drug trade within its borders since the problem emerged in the 1980s. Several laws were enacted during the 1980s which were directed against drug trafficking, including restrictions on precursor chemicals.

The first provincial-level law banning drugs went into effect in January, 1990, in Yunnan Province. It covered not only the cultivation of opium poppies and the production, use, and shipment of narcotics, but also the harboring of traffickers and abusers. While serious offenses would be subject to penalties provided by the PRC Criminal Law, the provincial regulations called for prison sentences of up to 15 days, fines, and detention at labor camps for minor offenders. Gansu Province followed this precedent in July 1990 with a similar law.

In December 1990, the 17th Session of the National People's Congress Standing Committee amended the PRC Criminal Code to consolidate existing legislation and to provide more severe penalties for drug trafficking, including the death sentence for serious offenders. This "Decision on Prohibiting Narcotics Drugs" made the imposition of the death penalty easier by allowing provincial courts to sentence traffickers—a prerogative previously restricted to the Supreme People's Court. This change in the statutes has led to a sharp increase in executions. Also, the specified amounts of drugs required to bring charges under the PRC Criminal Code were halved from 2 kilograms to 1 kilogram for opium and from 100 grams to 50 grams for heroin.

Since a national conference on narcotics in 1991, the PRC has instituted a policy which it refers to as "stressing the three bans simultaneously," meaning eliminating narcotics trafficking, use, and cultivation. The government's stated goal is to eliminate the drug problem within three years. Greater efforts are underway to educate the people about the dangers of narcotics use, to publicize anti-narcotics laws, and to demonstrate the government's determination to put an end to China's drug problem by enlisting the aid of all levels of society and government.

US/PRC Cooperation

DEA does not have an office in China. However, our office in Hong Kong maintains regular contact with our counterparts in the PRC. Also, on several occasions we have placed one of our Special Agents in Hong Kong on temporary duty at the American Embassy in Beijing to further the cooperation between our two countries in narcotics enforcement. Our relationship with China has begun to take root over the past several years.

Contacts between the United States and PRC drug authorities began in 1984 when the U.S. Customs Service (USCS) conducted narcotics detection training for Customs officers in Beijing, and when the Department of State's Bureau of International Narcotics Matters (INM) hosted a Ministry of Public Health delegation. The following year, delegations from INM, DEA, and the USCS visited Beijing. These meetings gave U.S. officials their first opportunities to assess Chinese capabilities and needs in drug enforcement. U.S. officials called for more direct contacts between our respective enforcement agencies and encouraged increased participation in multilateral forums. In 1986, at the first Bilateral Conference between DEA and PRC narcotics authorities, participants discussed the need for increased cooperation, including the exchange of narcotics intelligence and drug enforcement training. A second conference held in Washington, D.C. in 1987 concluded with the signing of a Memorandum of Understanding (MOU) expressing a continuing commitment to bilateral and multilateral drug control.

U.S. agencies have held a number of training seminars to better educate the Chinese in basic and advanced methods to combat drug trafficking. Between 1984 and 1987, PRC representatives participated in 11 U.S.-sponsored narcotics training classes. The first DEA Drug Enforcement School was held in

Beijing in 1987 and provided training to 61 police officers from various provinces throughout China. Due to the enthusiastic response of PRC officials, a second training course was held in Kunming in 1989. A third training session is scheduled for October, 1992, for approximately 60 police officials from every province in China.

U.S./PRC meetings held in the mid-1980s and the MOU signed in 1987 provided a channel for the exchange of narcotics intelligence and cooperation in investigations. In August 1986, information supplied by DEA in conjunction with the Thai police resulted in the seizure of 22.7 kilograms of heroin in Kunming, Yunnan Province. This was directly related to the simultaneous seizure of 15 kilograms of heroin in New York City by DEA. In March of 1988, Minister of Public Security officers seized 3.3 kilograms of heroin concealed in a shipment of goldfish (referred to as the "Goldfish Case") and proposed that DEA make a controlled delivery to San Francisco where the consignee of the parcel was located. As a result, three heroin traffickers were arrested in the United States and others were arrested in the PRC. Following the success of this case, PRC security officials cooperated with agents from DEA, the Royal Hong Kong Police, and the Royal Canadian Mounted Police in arranging another controlled delivery of 39 kilograms of heroin to New York via Toronto, Canada. As a result, two suspects were arrested in Hong Kong and four in New York.

Unfortunately, the momentum achieved by the outstanding cooperation in these cases stalled in February of 1990 due to developments in the "Goldfish Case." Wang Zhongxiao, a PRC defendant who agreed to testify in San Francisco, requested political asylum during his testimony. Although his application was denied, the appeal process has prevented the U.S. Government from returning him to China. From the Chinese point of view, U.S. authorities have reneged on their promise to return the witness. PRC officials take every opportunity to remind DEA and other U.S. law enforcement officials of the detrimental effects of this incident on U.S./PRC law enforcement cooperation. By allowing Wang to travel to the U.S., the PRC became one of the first countries in Asia to participate in such witness exchanges.

In January and February of 1991, PRC officials expressed their appreciation of the benefits derived from intelligence exchanges, and were enthusiastic about receiving information from the United States. However, they made no commitments that information requested by the U.S. on narcotics arrests in the PRC would be provided unless there was an immediately recognizable U.S. impact or connection. In November 1991, I met with the Chairman of the National Narcotics Control Commission, Mr. Yu Lei, and other PRC counternarcotics leaders in Beijing and discussed the worsening narcotics trafficking problem in both our countries and the resulting need to increase bilateral and multilateral cooperation to close trafficking routes, end production, and go after Asian-based organizations.

While the Chinese acknowledged the seriousness of the drug trafficking situation in their country and its international implications, they stated that a barrier to further U.S./PRC cooperation would continue to exist until Wang is returned. I explained that DEA and the State Department shared their desire to return Wang to the PRC, but could not interfere with the judicial process. I emphasized that the international drug problem is too critical and that counternarcotics cooperation could not wait for Wang's case to be resolved. Neither statement seemed to have any affect on the Chinese position. PRC officials did maintain that routine cooperation on investigative leads would not be affected by the Goldfish Case. Unfortunately the relatively small number of responses DEA has received to numerous requests for information and corroboration of intelligence contradicts this assertion. However, it has been and will continue to be DEA's policy to supply the PRC police with all intelligence we believe will assist them in their enforcement efforts. In recent meetings with PRC officials in March and April 1992, U.S. Ambassador Stapleton Roy and the DEA Special Agent on temporary duty in Beijing pointed to my recent court affidavit on the Wang asylum case as evidence of the Executive Branch's determination to resolve the matter as quickly as possible.

Relationship Between Hong Kong and the PRC

Hong Kong authorities have been providing training and intelligence on drug matters in the PRC since the mid-1980s. Despite these contacts, the PRC has effectively limited the amount of bilateral cooperation by insisting that all routine exchanges of information be conducted through central government authorities in Beijing. The introduction of a 24-hour hotline between Hong Kong and Guangdong Province officials, however, may increase local cooperation.

For years, cooperation between the United States and Hong Kong law enforcement agencies has been excellent. Extradition of traffickers from Hong Kong to the United States has taken place under the U.S./UK extradition treaty and has been carried out in an exemplary fashion. During the past four years, more than 50 major drug traffickers have been extradited to the United States.

While extradition requests continue to be process and effected, a new extradition treaty will be negotiated between the United States and Hong Kong before the transfer of sovereignty in 1997 since no such treaty now exists between the PRC and the United States. China has indicated a willingness to allow Hong Kong to enter into extradition agreements with other countries even though no treaties exist between those nations and the PRC. We are hopeful that current negotiations with Hong Kong under the auspices of the Sino/UK Joint Liaison Group will produce an effective replacement to the current treaty.

A U.S./Hong Kong designation agreement went into effect in January of 1991, allowing Hong Kong courts to honor forfeiture orders from the U.S., Canada, and Australia, and seize drug assets under Hong Kong's Recovery of Proceeds Ordinance. Under the agreement, any U.S. law enforcement agency conducting a drug investigation in the United States, having identified narcotics-derived assets in Hong Kong, can provide Hong Kong authorities a court order based on evidence of the drug trafficking for asset forfeiture. Through the end of September 1991, assets of over $45 million have been frozen in both Hong Kong and the United States under the agreement.

Conclusion

For the foreseeable future, we expect that Thailand will remain the primary conduit for Southeast Asian narcotics destined for the United States and Europe. It will remain more practical for traffickers to ship large quantities of heroin from Burma to northern Thailand and then on to Bangkok for further movement. The roads and communication facilities are superior along this route to those in China. Sino/Thai traffickers have been in business for years and their modus operandi functions well. They have contacts not only in Thailand and throughout Southeast Asia but also in the United States.

But we are most aware of the substantial threat that is posed by the transit route through China. The emergence of this route over the past several years causes us great concern. We know that the potential exists for increased use of a cross-China route. There is also a very real threat that Asian criminal organizations will take advantage of the period of change in Hong Kong to enhance their criminal activities. This is evidenced by the increasing incidence of bold and violent crime in Hong Kong.

There is every reason to believe that Chinese authorities will increase their drug control efforts after the return of Hong Kong to PRC control. While we do not know what the future holds for increased DEA/PRC cooperation on drug enforcement, we have every reason to be optimistic and are convinced that the Chinese, perhaps more than any other people, know the human and social costs of opiate abuse. We are therefore confident that mutual cooperation will continue to develop, and we are putting forth a considerable effort to encourage it. We have been seeking to extend cooperation in the form of training, intelligence sharing and joint enforcement activities. Our efforts have been well received by PRC and Hong Kong authorities.

We fully expect that coordinated anti-drug efforts between our two countries will not only continue but will also increase in effectiveness. Such cooperation is certainly in the best interests of both our countries. We welcome the Congress's support.

BIBLIOGRAPHY

An asterisk (*) preceding a reference indicates an excerpt from the work has been reprinted in this compilation.

BOOKS AND PAMPHLETS

Baum, Richard, ed. Reform and reaction in post-Mao China: the road to Tiananmen. Routledge. '91.

Black, George. Black hands of Beijing: lives of defiance in China's democracy movement. Wiley. '93.

Byrd, William. Market mechanism and economic reforms in China. M. E. Sharpe. '91.

Clark, Paul. Chinese cinema: culture and politics since 1949. Cambridge University Press. '88.

Continuing religious repression in China. Human Rights Watch. '93.

Edwards, R. Randle; Henkel, Louis; & Nathan, Andrew. Human rights in contemporary China. Columbia University Press. '86.

Hamrin, Carol Lee. China and the challenge of the future. Westview. '90.

Harding, Harry. A fragile relationship: the United States and China since 1972. Brookings Institution. '92.

Hicks, George, ed. Broken mirror: China after Tiananmen. St. James. '90.

Joseph, William A., ed. China briefing. Westview. '92.

Leeming, Frank. The changing geography of China. Oxford. '93.

Lin, Jing. Education in post-Mao China. Praeger. '93.

Macchiarola, Frank J. & Oxnam, Robert B., eds. The China challenge: American policies in East Asia. Academy of Political Science. '91.

Mosher, Steven W. Mother's ordeal: one woman's fight against China's one-child policy. Harcourt Brace Jovanovich. '93.

Overholt, William H. The rise of China: how economic reform is creating a new superpower. W. W. Norton. '93.

Pye, Lucian W. Chinese negotiating style: commercial approaches and cultural principles. Quorum. '92.

Rittenberg, Sidney. The man who stayed behind. Simon & Schuster. '93.

Saich, Tony, ed. Chinese people's movement: perspectives on Spring 1989. M. E. Sharpe. '90.

Schell, Orville. Discos and democracy: China in the throes of reform. Pantheon. '88.

Segal, Gerald. Fate of Hong Kong: the coming of 1997 and what lies beyond. St. Martin. '93.

Selden, Mark. Political economy of Chinese development. M. E. Sharpe. '93.

Shih, Chih-yu. China's just world: the morality of Chinese foreign policy. Lynne Rienner. '93.

Terrill, Ross. China in our time: the epic saga of the People's Republic from the Communist victory to Tiananmen Square and beyond. Simon & Schuster. '92.

Thurston, Anne F. Chinese odyssey: the life and times of a Chinese dissident. Scribner's. '91.

United States/Congress/Joint Economic Committee. China's economic dilemmas in the 1990s: the problems of reforms, modernization and interdependence. 102nd Congress, 1st Session. U.S. G.P.O. '91.

United States/Congress/Joint Economic Committee. China's economy looks toward the year 2000. U.S. G.P.O. '86.

United States/Congress/Senate/Committee on Energy and Natural Resources. Energy needs of the People's Republic of China. 103rd Congress, 1st Session. U.S. G.P.O. '93.

United States/Congress/Senate/Committee on Finance. Extending China's MFN status. 102nd Congress, 2nd Session. U.S. G.P.O. '93.

United States/Congress/House/Committee on Ways and Means. United States–China trade relations. 103rd Congress, 1st Session. U.S. G.P.O. '93.

Wang, James C. F. Contemporary Chinese politics: an introduction. Prentice-Hall. '91.

White, Gordon. Riding the tiger: the politics of economic reform in post-Mao China. Macmillan. '93.

Wu, Ningkun. A single tear: a family's persecution, love, and endurance in Communist China. Atlantic Monthly. '93.

ADDITIONAL PERIODICAL ARTICLES WITH ABSTRACTS

For those who wish to read more widely on the subject of China, this section contains abstracts of additional articles that bear on the topic. Readers who require a comprehensive list of materials are advised to consult the *Reader's Guide to Periodical Literature* and other Wilson indexes.

At the Eastern brink: the Church in China: an interview with Gino Belli. Thomas H. Stahel. *America* 166:88–94 F 8 '92

In an interview, Gino Belli, the pseudonym of a longtime Christian observer of China, discusses the state of Catholicism in China: The last official count of the Catholic population in China was made in 1949–50, when it was determined that the population numbered 3.3 million. Even though the number of Catholics in the country has undoubtedly grown, the Catholic minority is still very small. The Catholic Church is nonetheless influential in China, mainly because it is influential in the outside world. Government authorities listen when the pope speaks about China, and they try to present a good face with regard to religious liberty when dignitaries from Christian countries are around. The Chinese Catholic Church is healthy and has made a lot of progress with the little freedom that it has been granted by the government. Prospects for political change in China are discussed.

Tough and smart on China. Harry Harding. *Brookings Review* 11:46 Wint '93

While the Bush administration's China policy has begun achieving results after a seriously flawed beginning, many in Congress are not aware of this change in direction and are calling for a more confrontational stand with China. They want to make the country's most-favored-nation status contingent on improvements in Peking's human rights policies, foreign trade, and arms exports, and they also want to set up a new radio service to broadcast news and information to the Chinese people. Despite flaws in both proposals, Bill Clinton has endorsed them, which has caused Chinese leaders to view his election with suspicion. Though it would not mean military confrontation, a crisis between Peking and Washington would be an expensive distraction for the new administration. Clinton says that he does not want to coddle dictators in Peking, but he should be both smart and tough. The writer makes suggestions on forming a strategy for a China policy.

It's time to put the screws to China's gulag economy. Joyce Barnathan. *Business Week* 52–3 D 30 '91–Ja 6 '92

Allegations have been made recently about hand-in-glove relationships between U.S. companies and Chinese labor camps. For example, former employees of Hastings, Michigan-based E. W. Bliss told U.S. Customs that the machine press company made deals with a prison in China's Jiangsu province. The company denies the charges. A Stanford University researcher says that 30 percent of Chinese prison earnings are split between prison authorities and officials in Beijing, and a lawyer at the Library of Congress states that 50 percent of China's prison-made goods are exported. Unfortunately, the needs of prison authorities, under pressure from Beijing to earn hard currency, and of U.S. importers, strapped by stiff competition and a recession, are merging. In their search for cheap products, U.S. importers are swept into the murky world of deal making in Hong Kong, the hub of trade with China. There, middlemen get things done quickly and cheaply, no questions asked.

The best way to change China is from the inside. Amy Borrus. *Business Week* 69 My 17 '93

China, which Washington saw mostly as a counterweight to Moscow for 20 years, is enjoying an economic boom that will make it a power in its own right, so Americans must rethink their relationship with this emerging colossus. Attacking China for human rights and other abuses with heavy-handed conditions on renewal of its most-favored-nation (MFN) status would be a mistake. The goal of enhanced individual freedom there will be best served by broader political and economic engagement with China. Thanks to economic reform, China is more outward-looking than before, and through trade, it is encountering Western ideas from entrepreneurialism to religious tolerance. Engagement makes more sense than isolation because it allows the U.S. to make hardheaded trade-offs that have impact, such as swapping resumption of U.S. military contacts with China for release of more political prisoners.

China and America: the resilient relationship. Steven I. Levine. *Current History* 91:241–6 S '92

Part of an issue on China. U.S.-Chinese relations are in much better shape than anyone is willing to admit. Signs of the relationship's strength include flourishing cultural and economic exchanges and ongoing dialogues on difficult political, economic, human rights, and security issues. The United States must not interpret the end of the cold war and the concurrent downscaling of security concerns as the end of China's importance in an increasingly global political and economic climate. However, given that China has too strong a commitment to the United States to cut itself off from it, U.S. policymakers can act with confidence in pushing for human rights and other reforms there. The article discusses cultural and reform movements in China and chronicles the history of U.S.-Chinese relations.

The new relationship with the former Soviet Union. Guo-cang Huan. *Current History* 91:253–6 S '92

Part of an issue on China. Though relations between China and the former Soviet republics flourish economically, political and military tensions throughout the region present challenges. The collapse of communism and the creation of the Commonwealth of Independent States have mobilized Chinese dissidents against the government and created national instability. Furthermore, Soviet disintegration has encouraged ethnic minorities in the provinces of Tibet, Xinjiang, and Inner Mongolia to demand independence or autonomy. Security issues in these areas as well as in neighboring Russia, Kazakhstan, and Turkestan continue to jeopardize stability. Political and economic turmoil in the once Soviet republics threatens trade with China, and those republics' potential to officially recognize Taiwan remains a diplomatic sticking point with Beijing. A commitment on both sides to maintaining economic and political relations should preserve relative stability.

China on the ecological edge. Rebecca Weiner. *E: the Environmental Magazine* 3:20–3 S/O '92

Development has gone wrong in China. Lester Ross, the author of several texts on China's environmental law, says that the misguided policies of the 1950s have led to today's crisis, which is one of rampant pollution and shrinking natural resources. He Bochuan, author of China on the Edge: The Crisis of Ecology and Development, reports that the country is on the brink of ecological disaster. According to Zhang Jiqiang of the Rockefeller Foundation, international efforts to promote green policies in China have not been successful because they focus on technology instead of on social solutions. China's growing ecological awareness, the role of Western development agencies in the crisis, the many sound ecological practices of China's people, the importance of education, and the controversy surrounding the proposed Three Gorges Dam on the Yangtze River are discussed.

The lessons of teaching about Tiananmen Square. Henry Kiernan. *The Education Digest* 57:51–3 Ap '92

An article condensed from the October 1991 issue of Social Education. The student protest/massacre in China's Tiananmen Square is a valuable subject for social studies teachers to address. The events surrounding June 4, 1989, continue to shape East-West relations and to offer a historical and contemporary perspective on the interplay of Chinese political and socioeconomic conditions. Teaching this subject enables students to examine the history of student protest in shaping China's history, the meaning of democracy, and the future of U.S.-Chinese relations. The writer describes the methods he has used to teach students about Tiananmen Square.

This time it's for real. Andrew Tanzer. *Forbes* 152:58–61 Ag 2 '93

It is not inconceivable that China could become the world's biggest economy early in the next century. Fueled with money from second jobs, flouted taxes, and underground economic activity, the Chinese economy is expanding 9 percent a year. Officially, per capital income in China is less than $400 a year, but nearly every independent study puts adjusted incomes at $1,000 to $2,000. Because the remnants of socialism still provide urban workers with huge subsidies, most of their income gains can be considered disposable income. Moreover, China is opening up faster to foreign companies and allowing greater access to consumers than did other Asian countries at similar stages in their economic development, and television is having a profound influence on the unjaded Chinese, who value ads for their information. No doubt, however, the China that offers a hospitable market for foreign businesses will someday provide strong competition for world markets.

China and America: 1941–1991. Nancy Bernkopf Tucker. *Foreign Affairs* 70:75–92 Wint '91/'92

It is often said that China and the United States have a special relationship, but Americans actually consider China to be of secondary importance, significant only in the context of crises involving other countries. Over the past 50 years, Americans have repeatedly tried to use China, allowing China's needs and interests to be sacrificed to the realization of objectives deemed more valuable. Neither country has ever been able to meet the expectations of the other, and their political differences have been aggravated by cultural discord. The cold war temporarily eased Sino-American tensions, but that era's normalization of relations was based on opposition to a common enemy, not on mutual understanding. Once the cold war ended, the primary impetus behind cooperation and compromise ceased to exist. Nevertheless, the United States still needs China, which in turn benefits economically and technically from its U.S. connection.

Where capitalism thrives in China. Ford S. Worthy. *Fortune* 125:71–2+ Mr 9 '92

With an average real annual growth of about 15 percent over the past 12 years, the Pearl River Delta in China's Guangdong Province has the fastest growing economy in the world. In 1978, when Deng Xiaoping first loosened the economy's Marxist straitjacket, the delta was a subsistence-level agrarian society with a few unproductive state-owned factories. Today, its per capita annual income is about $600—about double that of China as a whole—and it produces a disproportionate share of the world's toys, shoes, clothing, and other industrial goods. Western companies are starting to see the region as a major gateway for business. Guangdong's relationship with neighboring Hong Kong, which accounts for over 80 percent of the area's foreign investment and trade, and the political implications of the province's economic success are discussed.

A boom year for China. Jennifer Reese. *Fortune* 127:11 Je 28 '93

China, the world's most populous country, is racing to become the world's biggest economy. The International Monetary Fund estimates that China, which says its GDP grew 12 percent in 1992, is the third-biggest economy, after the U.S. and Japan. U.S. companies want to get in on China's boom, and they breathed a bit easier after President Clinton renewed the country's most favored nation trade status for another year. Taking away this status would have imposed punitive duties on Chinese exports to the U.S. and done little to protect U.S. jobs. Other countries could have quickly filled the vacuum, while China would have shut its doors to U.S. exports.

Humanism in China. David Lawson. *The Humanist* 53:16–19 My/Je '93

The writer discusses China's ancient humanistic tradition and describes the ways in which it has interacted with such 20th-century Western influences as Marxism and pragmatism. He says that the inclusiveness of the Chinese system of logic, which tends to reach toward harmony and synthesis, has given rise to a potpourri of political and cultural attitudes in present-day China.

China: the south rising. Robert S. Elegant. *National Review* 44:26+ S 14 '92

Under Deng Xiaoping's economic policy, which the leader calls Socialism with Chinese characteristics, the economy in China's southeasternmost province, Guangdong, is booming and is attracting capital from Hong Kong. Guangdong now has the world's fastest growing economy. Last year, the gross domestic product increased 20 percent, and industrial production grew by 50 percent. With the growth, millions of destitute countryfolk are coming to cities such as Guangzhou in search of work. The economic boom has brought with it an increase in crime, drugs, and corruption, as well as a rebirth of China's secret societies. Conditions in Guangzhou and Shenzhen are described.

Traveling in the new China. Timothy Tung. *The New Leader* 75:10–12 N 30 '92

Reflecting on a visit to his native China, an American China specialist surveys the signs of modernization and economic reform that have swept across China's major cities: Some parts of China have been so transformed by Western-style reforms that they are nearly unrecognizable. Beijing's modern skyscrapers obscure the ancient charm of the city's original buildings, and a political cynicism seems to mask the legacy of the 1989 massacre in Tiananmen Square. In Shanghai, financial concerns and a population explosion have become the city's main features. Elsewhere, prosperity and corruption have created a new affluent elite, leading to feelings of resentment and servitude among the majority of the population. Several Chinese citizens reflect on their country, and the controversy surrounding student leader Shen Tong is discussed.

Tibet is Asia's Lithuania. Dalai Lama. *New Perspectives Quarterly* 9:28–9 Wint '92

Part of an issue on the emerging cultural conflict between Western liberalism and East Asian Confucianism. Tibet's spiritual and temporal leader, who heads the Tibetan government-in-exile in India, discusses new opportunities for a free Tibet. He asserts that Tibet's struggle to regain freedom after more than 40 years of oppression by the Chinese government should receive renewed attention, given the political changes in the former Soviet Union and Eastern Europe. He also states that since China invaded Tibet in 1949, 1.2 million Tibetans have died. The country has maintained its Buddhist values of nonviolence and compassion, he claims, but there is growing frustration among Tibetans, and violence could occur. He describes his plan to visit Tibet to convince China's leadership of the true feelings of Tibetans and to urge Tibetans not to abandon nonviolence.

The American at Mao's side. Russell Watson. *Newsweek* 121:36 Ap 19 '93

Sidney Rittenberg is unique in the world of American business: He is the only American ever to have been admitted into the Chinese Communist Party. Rittenberg, who is a 71-year-old consultant for American companies seeking to break into the booming Chinese market, details his experiences in his new book, The Man Who Stayed Behind, which was written with Amanda Bennett. Drafted by the U.S. Army in 1942, Rittenberg was assigned to China, where he decided to stay on and work his way into the inner circle of the party. During the Chinese civil war and the Cultural Revolution, Rittenberg served obediently under Zhou Enlai and Mao Zedong, fervently devoted to the party line. However, after being imprisoned in China twice, for a total of 16 years, Rittenberg saw the limitations of communism and returned to the U.S., where business and capitalism became his new gospel.

The trouble with China [Most Favored Nation status and human rights abuses]. Frank Gibney. *Newsweek* 121:46 My 17 '93

With billions of dollars in trade and investment at stake, U.S. businesses cannot afford to ignore human-rights abuses in China. Because of human-rights abuses, China could lose its most-favored-nation trade status, which entitles its imports to low U.S. tariffs. There have been many accounts of forced sterilization of women and child and convict labor in China, and conditions for many workers have gotten worse as China's economy has grown. State-owned Capital Steel in Beijing, for example, works its employees 365 days a year and fines them for taking a day off for illness. A growing number of American companies are adopting human-rights policies binding on their Chinese contractors. Roger Sullivan, the former president of the U.S.-China Business Council, believes that Washington should stand up for companies that raise human-rights concerns and face Chinese retaliation.

China slows growth. *Society* 30:2+ N/D '92

According to a new demographic study published by the Population Reference Bureau, China is engaged in the most comprehensive, determined, and successful effort ever made to regulate population in any modern nation. The report reviews the reasons for domestic and international misgivings about China's one-child-per-couple policy, including charges of coercive family planning and female infanticide. Although China has slowed its runaway population growth, the one-child ideal never became a reality throughout the country. The total population increases by about 20 million people every year. Before the end of the century, China's population will top 1.3 billion. Several population-related problems that China faces are discussed.

Rethinking human rights. Robert John Myers. *Society* 30:58–63 N/D '92

Part of a special section on the social sciences. In recent decades, the question of human rights has been the primary issue preventing more amicable relations between China and the United States. To achieve a true harmonization of international human rights standards, it must be recognized that in China traditional ideas of the rights and obligations of the citizen to the state, based on Confucian philosophy, mingle with the more recent Marx-Lenin-Maoist view on the same subject. China's vision of the future, derived from the Sinic worldview, fears that embracing ideas such as human rights will disrupt the course of centuries, creating chaos. Changes that are occurring in many regions of China, however, will show the Chinese that freedom and prosperity go hand in hand. Through this realization, the human rights problem as defined by both the East and West will be reconciled.

How not to break China. Strobe Talbott. *Time* 140:53 Ag 3 '92

The attempt to impose trade sanctions on China to punish it for its internal tyranny and irresponsible international behavior is destined to backfire, just as other such efforts have in the past. Congress has generated various bills that would attach political conditions to China's most-favored-nation trade status, and the Senate will almost certainly pass a bill to punish China by restricting its trade with the United States. The leaders of the People's Republic deserve sanctions, but the Chinese people do not. Sanctions will harm mainly those Chinese who are involved in export businesses. The commercial success of these entrepreneurs is part of the larger process of coaxing China to abandon communism.

China's Faustian bargain. Orville Schell. *Travel Holiday* 175:37–9 N '92

China's industrial boom is degrading the country's environment. In the first half of 1992, China's industrial output rose 18 percent, and its foreign trade soared by 20 percent. As Chinese cities cut corners on pollution controls to lure foreign investment, China's air, water, land, timber, and wildlife are being ravaged. Petrochemical wastes are spreading toxic emissions into rivers and the sea, and the air in several major cities is filled with smog from coal-burning factories, power plants, and automobiles without adequate emission controls. Ironically, just as China acquires the airlines, ports, and hotels it needs to accommodate more visitors, it is destroying the natural scenery that draws tourists in the first place.

Still on the march. Susan V. Lawrence. *U.S. News & World Report* 112:36–9 Mr 9 '92

At a time when countries in NATO and the defunct Warsaw Pact are cutting their military arsenals and scrapping high cost weapons development programs, China is bucking the disarmament trend. China's defense budget rose 12 percent in 1991, and drives are currently under way to modernize the Chinese air force and build a navy. The country's expensive and ambitious drive to upgrade its armed forces could make Asia and the rest of the world volatile. China's lack of funds and Western countries' refusal to revive military cooperation may limit the military modernization program, however. Discussed are China's past efforts at military modernization; its weapons dealings with such countries as Iran, the former Soviet Union, and Syria; and the potential for a Sino-Vietnamese dispute over the Spratly Islands in the South China Sea.

Two people, one land. Susan V. Lawrence. *U.S. News & World Report* 114:47–9 Je 7 '93

Attempts to make Tibet part of the capitalist world have only exacerbated tensions between Tibet and China. After the recent biggest protests in 4 years in the Tibetan capital of Lhasa, Tibetan advocacy groups claimed that the influx of Han Chinese is the root cause of Tibetans' discontent. The Han Chinese are opportunistic migrants seeking economic rewards in new frontiers such as Tibet. This opportunism coincides with Beijing's interest in promoting economic development to reduce political disaffection. The recent turmoil in Lhasa suggests that economic development cannot make the Tibetans forget the grievances that have accumulated since China invaded their land in 1950. Moreover, not only is attracting investment difficult in an area whose links with the outside world are grossly inadequate, it will also fail to economically benefit the Tibetans, most of whom are semiliterate and without technical training.

Chinese students get distorted view. *USA Today* [Periodical] 120:14 Ap '92

A study by Stanford University's Richard Gross shows that China's portrayal of the United States in the education of its children is often exaggerated, absurd, ill informed, or disturbing. Whereas Gross's research on official history, geography, and social science texts revealed that young children are given comparatively fair instruction, it revealed that high school students receive the message that the United States is morally bankrupt. Emphasis is placed on such criticisms as the presence of racism, while events such as the U.S. role in the defeat of China's enemy, Japan, in World War II are left out.

Economic growth in the People's Republic of China. Li Peng. *Vital Speeches of the Day* 59:390–5 Ap 15 '93

In an excerpt from a speech delivered at the First Session of the Eighth National Peoples Congress in Beijing, Premier of the State Council Li Peng provides an overview of China's economic and social progress. He notes that in the past 5 years the economy grew an average of 7.9 percent annually and that progress was made in advancing socialist culture and ideology. He says that major strides were made in reform and opening up to the outside world, that people's incomes rose, and that their standards of living improved. These things occurred, he says, because the country has followed the Communist Party's basic line, and it should continue to do so. He discusses the steps China should take to continue growth; the country's plans to reunite with Hong Kong, Macao, and Taiwan; its diplomatic relationships with its Asian neighbors and other countries; human rights; the need for a world order; and the influence of international cooperation on the economy and the environment.

Was China just bluffing? John W. Garver. *The Wilson Quarterly* 16:12–13 Spr '92

In The Chinese Threat in the Vietnam War, an article that appeared in the Spring 1992 issue of Parameters, John W. Garver argues that China made a serious effort during the mid 1960s to prepare itself for a major war with the United States. Critics believe that the United States' fear of Chinese intervention, which led the United States to adopt a losing strategy of gradually escalating the bombing of North Vietnam and confining ground operations to South Vietnam, was unwarranted. Garver contends that U.S. strategists during that period had to consider the very real possibility that China would enter the conflict on Hanoi's side if the United States carried the war too far.

The dragon stirs. Anne F. Thurston. *The Wilson Quarterly* 17:10–15+ Spr '93

With an economy that has been growing dramatically throughout a decade of economic liberalization, China is the only communist state that is thriving today. Inside the country, however, the putative economic miracle looks very different. The rich are getting richer while the poor are getting poorer, and the quest for prosperity is proceeding with no agreed-upon moral framework, set of rules, or sense of working together. Prostitution, crime, and black-market activities are on the rise, and the moral foundations of society have yet to recover from the legacy of the Cultural Revolution. The people are searching for an alternative value system in religion and secret societies. Optimists believe that such activities will promote the development of a civil society when the current leadership departs the scene, while pessimists believe that China will descend further into chaos after Deng Xiaoping dies. Instability is really the only certainty.

China's secret texts [Nushu language used by Chinese women]. Vivian Chiu. *World Press Review* 39:50 Je '92

An article excerpted from the South China Morning Post of Hong Kong. Nushu, a written language passed down among Chinese women through the ages and known only to them, is generally regarded among Chinese academics as the first language of women's liberation in China, criticizing as it did the inequities of society. Chinese women created the language, which uses a different set of characters from that of standard Han, in response to the stifled existence that they were forced to lead. Barred from school and dependent first on their families and then on their husbands, women were enabled by nushu to support one another by sharing their joys and sorrows through the recording of true events. Zhou Shuoyi, whose Collections of Women's Scripts will soon be published in Beijing and who is hoping to publish a 1,300-word nushu dictionary that he compiled, theorizes that the language originated in Jiangyong county.